D1564045

Sunshine Paradise

The Florida History and Culture Series

UNIVERSITY PRESS OF FLORIDA

Florida A&M University, Tallahassee

Florida Atlantic University, Boca Raton

Florida Gulf Coast University, Ft. Myers

Florida International University, Miami

Florida State University, Tallahassee

New College of Florida, Sarasota

University of Central Florida, Orlando

University of Florida, Gainesville

University of North Florida, Jacksonville

University of South Florida, Tampa

University of West Florida, Pensacola

UNIVERSITY PRESS OF FLORIDA

Gainesville · Tallahassee · Tampa · Boca Raton
Pensacola · Orlando · Miami · Jacksonville · Ft. Myers · Sarasota

Sunshine Paradise

A HISTORY OF FLORIDA TOURISM

Tracy J. Revels

Foreword by Raymond Arsenault
and Gary R. Mormino

Copyright 2011 by Tracy J. Revels

Printed in the United States of America. This book is printed
on Glatfelter Natures Book, a paper certified under the
standards of the Forestry Stewardship Council (FSC). It is a
recycled stock that contains 30 percent post-consumer waste
and is acid-free.

All rights reserved

16 15 14 13 12 11   6 5 4 3 2 1

Library of Congress Cataloging-in-Publication Data
Revels, Tracy J., 1963–
Sunshine paradise : a history of Florida tourism /
Tracy J. Revels ; foreword by Raymond Arsenault and
Gary R. Mormino.
p. cm.—(Florida history and culture series)
Includes bibliographical references and index.
ISBN 978-0-8130-3542-0 (alk. paper)
1. Tourism—Florida—History. I. Title.
G155.U6R434 2011
338.4′791759—dc22   2010040985

The University Press of Florida is the scholarly publishing
agency for the State University System of Florida, comprising
Florida A&M University, Florida Atlantic University, Florida
Gulf Coast University, Florida International University,
Florida State University, New College of Florida, University
of Central Florida, University of Florida, University of North
Florida, University of South Florida, and University of West
Florida.

University Press of Florida
15 Northwest 15th Street
Gainesville, FL 32611-2079
http://www.upf.com

For John

CONTENTS

FOREWORD

Sunshine Paradise: A History of Florida Tourism is the latest volume of a series devoted to the study of Florida history and culture. During the past half-century, the burgeoning population and increased national and international visibility of Florida have sparked a great deal of popular interest in the state's past, present, and future. As a favorite destination of countless tourists and as the new home for millions of retirees and transplants, modern Florida has become a demographic, political, and cultural bellwether. Florida has also emerged as a popular subject and setting for scholars and writers. The Florida History and Culture Series provides an attractive and accessible format for Florida-related books. From avenging hurricanes to disputed elections, from tales of the Everglades to profiles of Sunbelt cities, Florida is simply irresistible.

The University Press of Florida is committed to the creation of an eclectic but carefully crafted set of books that will provide the field of Florida studies with a new focus that will encourage Florida writers to consider the broader implications and context of their work. The series includes standard academic monographs as well as works of synthesis, memoirs, and anthologies. And, while the series features books of historical interest, authors researching Florida's environment, politics, literature, and popular or material culture are encouraged to submit their manuscripts as well. Each book offers a distinct personality and voice, but the ultimate goal of the series is to foster a broad sense of community and collaboration among Florida scholars.

In *Sunshine Paradise*, Tracy Revels takes readers on a nostalgic, even blissful journey that is as much entertaining and engaging as it is informative and cautionary. If a novelist had dared imagine a storyline combining such a zany cast of characters and plot twists, publishers would have brushed away the manuscript as "too fantastic" and "over-the-top." But in reality, the history of tourism in Florida has more dips and dives than Busch Gardens' SheiKra or Sea World's Kraken.

"Tourism in Florida began with Americanization," notes Revels. A professor of history at Wofford College, Revels casts a wide net in this ambitious new study of Florida. From the first travelers who sought restored health and Florida dreams in territorial-era St. Augustine to today's tourists who seek restored sanity and childhood dreams, the Sunshine State has served myriad roles as sanitarium and sanctuary, tropical paradise and dream factory. As Revels argues, tourism is as much a reflection of reality as an escape from it. Race, class, and ethnicity both mirror and distort Florida and tourist attractions.

Sunshine Paradise deftly balances narrative and analysis, making for a very readable text. Revels discusses the complexities and forces shaping tourism, but does not forget that the narrative text remains at the center of great history books. Readers, buckle up for a wild and bumpy ride!

Raymond Arsenault and Gary R. Mormino
Series editors

Sunshine Paradise

Introduction

Florida is tourism. Every modern image of the state evokes travel for pleasure. To most outsiders, Florida is one big theme park, not a state but a "magic kingdom" of dreams and fantasies, where real life, with its mundane cares, is effectively banished. Sunshine, water, and thrill rides await the tourist who arrives clad in the official Florida uniform of straw hat, shorts, and sandals. Once noted for its fierce Seminoles, fragrant orange groves, and cattle-herding Crackers, Florida has become the province of talking mice, fairy princesses, and jolly pirates. Everyone, it seems, has been there and has a T-shirt to prove it. There is little to no hope of reclaiming any other identity for Florida; America would never relinquish its favorite toy.

But tourism was not always Florida's trademark. Until just after World War II, Florida was known primarily for its agricultural products. Cotton, citrus, tobacco, and sugarcane shaped the landscape, and early motorists were cautious to share the road with wandering cows. Tourism was a notable industry, one that Floridians were eager to exploit, but it was not the primary economic engine of the state, because before the war relatively few Americans had the money or leisure time for a vacation in Florida.

Yet tourism has existed in Florida since its beginnings. Indian trails and mounds around Florida's springs hint that its earliest residents made occasional pilgrimages to sites bearing some special, now forever lost, significance. In the 1820s, visitors were arriving in St. Augustine, Pensacola, and Key West, where the climate and fresh air were reputed to bring relief from tuberculosis and other respiratory complaints. By the mid-nineteenth century, the state was attracting sportsmen; many of them fired their guns at alligators from the decks of St. Johns and Ocklawaha river steamboats. Tourists curious about the native flora or the opportunities for Reconstruction investment began arriving at Florida's spas and along the coast by the 1870s and 1880s. In their wake, two great industrialists, Henry Flagler and Henry Plant, took on second careers as land developers and hotel builders, carving out twin tourist empires in the Gilded Age. These friendly rivals turned Florida into the American Riviera, where robber barons migrated every winter in order to conspicuously consume the state's abundant sunshine.

Democratization of tourism began in the 1920s, with the land boom and the Model T, as "tin can tourists" took to the still inadequate highways and inspired new attractions, hotels, and facilities catering to ordinary Americans. The Great Depression damaged but did not kill the budding industry; tourism helped Florida recover from the crisis with remarkable speed. During World War II, Florida's tourism industry was drafted into uniform. The use of hotels for military training and tourist attractions for United Service Organizations (USO) shows exposed a new class of Americans to Florida's many delights.

Post–World War II prosperity brought Florida tourism to the forefront, creating the modern image of the state as the great American playground. Reveling in new cars, two-week vacations, and a wonderful invention called air-conditioning, middle-class Americans began pouring into the state in the summer, initiating the ideal of year-round fun in the sun. The baby boom created a craving for novel entertainment, which Floridians fed with roadside zoos, tropical gardens, amusement parks, western towns, water skiers, and mermaids. Though garish, cheesy, and of questionable authenticity, the memorable attractions of the age of whimsy from 1945 to 1971 are today firmly entrenched in the nostalgia of a graying population. These attractions set the stage for the ultimate fantasy to arise from the swamps of Central Florida. Walt Disney World, and the massive theme parks and entertainment complexes that followed, completed the image and established Florida as the tourism capital of the planet.

For most Floridians, tourism is a way of life. Over 80 percent of Florida jobs are in the service industry, which provides food, lodging, and entertainment to guests. Lacking an income tax, the state draws most of its revenues from sales and hotel taxes. Walt Disney World alone provides more sales-tax dollars than any other business in the state. Florida needs every visitor, and native Floridians are trained from birth to love and hate tourists in relatively equal measure.

The benefits of tourism seem obvious. Tourism taps into Florida's most basic natural resources, its climate and semitropical beauty. Tourist facilities, though often unattractive, require less infrastructure than other industries, and though pollution generated by tourism is unavoidable, with careful management it can be more strictly controlled. Virtually anything in Florida can be turned into a tourist attraction. Old tobacco sheds convert into antique markets, and decrepit fish shacks are reborn as beachfront theme restaurants. Growing interest in ecotourism and heritage tours opens new possibilities for overlooked communities. The family vacation is a birthright the baby boomers have passed along to their offspring; the rituals of spring break seem unlikely to fade as long as there are college students eager for suntans, beer, and casual sex; and foreigners intrigued by Americana consider Mickey Mouse to be more American than Mount Rushmore or the Washington Monument. These factors alone would seem to guarantee Florida's continued dependence on tourism.

But tourism is not always the best economic investment. Recessions take their toll, as do international crises and natural disasters. A terrorist attack, a year of multiple hurricanes, or a well-publicized string of horrific murders can lead to a sudden drop in receipts. If gas prices rise too steeply, or layoffs become too common, the Florida vacation can quickly go from an eagerly anticipated adventure to an irresponsible expense. Nor are service industry jobs the kind of employment on which a balanced economy is constructed. Low-skill and low-status, they are hardly likely to appeal to workers who could find better opportunities out of state. Being a Disney cast member or a Miami Beach lifeguard might be a novel summer job, but it is rarely a career.

If there are serious drawbacks to tourism as an economic bulwark, the cultural problems are more deeply entrenched yet less thoroughly considered. What exactly does it mean to be a Floridian? Are native Floridians also Southerners? Do they even exist, or are they merely faceless robots, standing by to change beds, take tickets, and serve fast food to people on the go? Books on the character of the South often omit Florida from consideration, considering it an aberration on the landscape. But if Florida is not "the South," then what is it? "Sunbelt" alone hardly explains the sense of cultural disconnect that many Floridians, especially those born and raised in the state, often experience. For nearly a century, Florida has been defined by what outsiders expect of the state, a constantly evolving land of fantasy and illusion. Floridians are often complicit in this, readily promoting the gaudy, the inauthentic, and the impermanent, hoping to "skin the alligator," as fleecing tourists was called at the turn of the twentieth century. But as a result, many Floridians have come to feel like strangers in their own land, confused by the distorted image of fun, sun, and eternal youth that is projected onto them. Some are even humiliated by it. A native of St. Petersburg confessed to me that as a young man he felt great shame in growing up in a town known as "wrinkle city" for its population of elderly retirees and tourists whom no one would want to see in their bathing suits.

My personal experience with this cultural disconnect inspired this project. I am a product of a Panhandle farm, a third-generation Floridian. When I took up residence outside the state I was constantly asked if I had grown up on a beach or in the shadow of Cinderella's castle. I am frustrated by people who insist that I cannot be from Florida because of my thick Southern accent, and argue that a visit to Orlando or Miami is sufficient for understanding Florida. In trying to impress upon others the vast variety and beauty of my native state, I became curious as to how Florida's image has become so inseparable from tourism. In many ways I am a tourist; I confess an almost childlike fascination with theme parks and attractions. I undertook this narrative of the social and cultural trends that led to Florida's dependence on tourism as a way of understanding both my state and myself.

Florida is a state rich in history, yet for so many residents and visitors alike, that history goes back no farther than the opening of Walt Disney World. To better understand our state, our image, and our distorted, illusionary culture, Floridians should consider the long history and the development of tourism, which this narrative traces.

ONE

Salubrious Air

For generations, Juan Ponce de Leon was portrayed as Florida's first tourist. Countless books and articles claimed that the restless, aged Spaniard sought a magical fountain of youth that would restore his vitality. Stumbling upon the Florida coast, he eagerly drank from every spring he could find, asking natives along the way to serve as guides, hopeful that the next crystal-clear pool would make him young again.[1] According to the legend, Florida's first tourist sought a vacation in paradise, the trip of a lifetime that would literally renew his life.

Unfortunately, history is rarely as entertaining as fable. There is no credible evidence that Ponce de Leon was seeking anything more than the usual land and treasure when he arrived on Florida's shores on April 2, 1513. His adventure ended in a rather prosaic manner when irate Calusa Indians sent him scurrying back to Puerto Rico with hardly any time to collect souvenirs.[2] Yet the more fanciful version of the tale of Ponce de Leon is an apt metaphor for Florida tourism. A mystic land lures the voyager with grand expectations of pleasure and rejuvenation, but the sojourn comes at a high cost, and finally the wanderer packs and departs. Meanwhile, the natives grumble that the visitor has soiled the landscape while contributing nothing to the community, and speculate that more pasty-skinned outsiders will storm the beaches next year.

Tourism is a powerful force that has shaped Florida almost since the peninsula's discovery by Europeans. Most Florida residents consider tourism a phenomenon of the twentieth century, a product of highways, station wagons, and the middle-class summer vacation. It is Silver Springs, Cypress Gardens, Walt Disney World. Floridians with deeper roots will concede that tourism began with the two Henrys, Flagler and Plant, the barons of Gilded Age railroads and hotels. Others might consider the Victorian sportsmen and hunters Florida's original tourists.

Tourism in Florida, however, began before there was a word or a concept to frame it. A tourist is an individual who travels in search of amusement and pleasure. A traveler is generally considered to be a person who journeys away from home with a more concrete purpose, such as to seek an education or a business opportunity.[3] But the terms are blurred, especially in modern usage. A professor who travels to Orlando to attend a history conference and takes a day to visit Disney World fits both definitions. The word "tourist" was first used sometime in the early 1800s, applied to young men on the traditional "Grand Tour" of Europe. Most antebellum visitors to Florida were known simply as strangers, with the term "tourist" becoming more prevalent after the Civil War.[4] The words "tourist" and "traveler" are used interchangeably throughout this text, as they have both been frequently applied in travel literature from the 1800s to the present.

There were relatively few tourists in colonial America. Most Americans were either poverty stricken or people of moderate means, and as such could not afford vacations. Even those who could afford them were often discouraged by societal mores and religious teachings. The Puritans considered leisure sinful, and less devout Christians (or non-Christians) found they had few opportunities to travel or play. Making a living, farming, fighting Indians, and winning a revolution took up an inordinate amount of time. While planters or mercantile elites could sometimes indulge in long journeys, most Americans were satisfied with a brief visit to relatives or a few days at an energetic camp meeting. The only ordinary people who traveled were those whose livelihood depended on it, or those looking for new homes or better health. People living in the French and Spanish colonies were likewise confined by the rawness of their frontiers and the simple necessities of making a daily living.[5]

Spanish colonial administrators saw the advantages of Florida's geography, if not its pristine beaches and crystalline springs. Florida rapidly became a strategic outpost on the fringes of the Spanish empire. In 1565, St. Augustine was founded on Florida's eastern coast, primarily to provide protection for the Spanish gold fleets against English and French pirates. Florida's original settlers arrived to search for gold, to conduct trade, to fight for the Crown, or to harvest Indian souls for the Catholic God. The lonesome Spanish sentry, slapping futilely at mosquitoes and sweating buckets in his iron helmet, probably never imagined that Florida would ever be considered a haven for pleasure-seekers.

Even before the founding of St. Augustine, Florida's earliest nonnative travelers had little interest in natural beauty. Conquistadors like Panfilo de Narvaez and Hernando de Soto had God, gold, and glory on the brain, though certainly not in that particular order. Other adventurers were literally washed up on Florida's shores, the ragged survivors of shipwrecks. In 1696, Jonathan Dickinson, a Quaker merchant, was stranded near Jupiter Inlet along with his family and a weary band of survivors. They found themselves "amongst a barbarous people such as were generally accounted man-eaters."[6] After a period of intimidating captivity, the party was finally delivered to the Spanish in St. Augustine. Dickinson and other hardy individuals who made it back to civilization penned blood-curdling accounts of their experiences. To Europeans of the sixteenth and seventeenth centuries, Florida was wild, dangerous, and savage, an anti-Eden where desperate survivors were stripped of their clothing and beaten by hostile natives. These were not characteristics that translated into guided tours.[7]

Florida passed like a tepid potato from Spain to England in 1763. During the American Revolution, Florida received a lonesome tourist and student of nature, the famous botanist William Bartram. Bartram lavished praise on Florida, describing it as a "delightful territory" brimming with "expansive savannas" and "glittering brooks." Later visitors who consulted Bartram's *Travels* before journeying to Florida accused him of exaggeration. John James Audubon, the famous naturalist and illustrator, complained that Florida was more of a wilderness than a garden. But Audubon allowed that Bartram was "to be forgiven; he was an enthusiastic botanist, and rare plants, in the eyes of such a man, convert a wilderness at once into a garden."[8] Bartram's writings were among the first images of Florida available to Americans, and though his work influenced Romantic-era writers, it had no impact on peace negotiations and political entanglements. Florida was returned to Spain in 1783 as a reward for Spain's alliance with the victorious United States. But the upstart Americans proved to be bad neighbors, just as Florida's indigenous peoples excelled at being troublesome subjects. Border disputes between these fractious tribes led to skirmishes, and cattle stealing evolved into throat cutting. In March 1818, General Andrew Jackson received orders to pacify the disputed region. Jackson's invasion of Florida provoked a nasty diplomatic incident, but Secretary of State John Quincy Adams cleverly used the hot-tempered general as an arm-twister on a reluctant Spain, implying that if Spain refused to sell the Florida territory, America could easily unleash Jackson again and seize Florida by force. Spain ceded Florida for approximately $5 million as part of the Adams-Onis Treaty in 1819. With ratification of the treaty and the official change of flags in 1821, America gained a strategic, underpopulated, and thoroughly mysterious property.[9]

Modern tourism in Florida began with Americanization. Some of the very first American residents noted Florida's potential as a land of sunshine and balmy breezes. But there were still obstacles to tourism's development, mainly the refusal of the natives to surrender quietly to new overlords. As late as 1857, visitors were warned of Indian raids along the St. Johns. With distinguished ferocity, the Seminoles and their allies held the Florida interior through the better part of three wars. Until the resistance was muted (for it was never completely quenched, and today Florida's Seminoles remain as a proud symbol of Indian defiance), the white population clung to the port towns, primarily Jacksonville, St. Augustine, Key West, and Pensacola.[10]

Florida was admitted to the Union in 1845, and the 1850s saw the opening of much of the Panhandle. It was a boom decade for the young state, which quickly took its place as a province of the slaveholding cotton kingdom. The population clustered in the arch of Middle Florida, roughly from Jackson to Alachua counties. The planter elite dominated politics, but Florida society was composed primarily of simple farmers, the ubiquitous Crackers. In this raw age of scattered settlement and inadequate transportation, the industry that would eventually define Florida was born.[11]

The residents of St. Augustine were the pioneers of Florida tourism and tourism promotion. Seeking a means to encourage settlement and economic development, early boosters hit upon a potential gold mine in the form of tuberculosis victims. The "graveyard cough" was an all too familiar sound in antebellum America, the hallmark of pulmonary tuberculosis—then commonly called consumption or phthisis—which was a leading cause of death in the nineteenth century. The symptoms of tuberculosis included weakness, pallor, and a persistent cough; sufferers experienced a slow decline that was romanticized by poets and artists, and was even considered fashionable in circles where "rude health" was frowned upon as unfeminine.[12] But generally its victims found little to celebrate and sought relief from their pains.

Medical wisdom of the early 1800s held that consumption was a hereditary disease, not a communicable one, an inherited weakness of the lungs that could not be cured by bleeding or purging. While some practitioners placed consumption in the "act of God" category and advised their patients to endure it with Christian fortitude, others recommended fresh air, vegetarian diets, and moderate exercise. A change in climate and a long period of rest in a location with salubrious air and sunshine were considered most helpful. Doctors stressed how travel and new scenery could lift the spirits and hopefully spark the patient's will to fight the disease.[13] The increasing emphasis on nature's curative powers coincided with an expanding economy and a new willingness of educated and wealthy Americans to leave home in search of both health and pleasure. "Taking the waters" was already common among European elites, and by the early nineteenth century Americans of means who sought both cures and conviviality visited the notable spas of Virginia, Pennsylvania, and Connecticut. Saratoga, New York, was the most famous American watering hole, attracting tourists for its reputed healthfulness and its glittering social season.[14]

Florida would, at first glance, seem an unlikely spot to attract health-minded travelers. The territory was virtually unknown to Americans, who, if they had any image of Florida, considered it to be a wild, savage jungle. Settlement across the territory was sparse. Citizens of St. Augustine were well aware of these factors and their town's further drawbacks. St. Augustine was isolated, difficult to access except by sea, and regularly threatened by food shortages. But residents of the town were also cognizant of the fact that winter chills were virtually nonexistent, and people plagued with bad lungs and persistent coughs seemed to fare better with exposure to ocean breezes. Colonial visitors to St. Augustine had consistently written of the

pleasant climate and the warm sea air. Eager for anything that would promote the economy and lure settlers, St. Augustine's leaders recognized that
small investments in hotels and publicity would lead to large returns. Their
schemes required only invalids with soggy chests and fat pocketbooks.
Promising cures they could not deliver, physicians and boosters conspired
with local entrepreneurs to initiate the first wave of Florida tourism. In the
process, they unwittingly began building Florida's reputation as a sunshine
paradise, a land of fantasies and dreams.[15]

Scattered testimonials to St. Augustine's warm winters and bracing salt
air appeared early in the nineteenth century. In his 1822 book, *Notices of
East Florida*, William Hayne Simmons, a poet, land speculator, and doctor, advised that once St. Augustine was "cleaned up" from its Spanish occupation, it would gain a reputation as a salubrious place to live. Ironically, the last generations of Spanish settlers had been relatively healthy,
but an 1821 outbreak of yellow fever, just after the town's handover, was
unfairly blamed on Spanish lack of hygiene.[16] One of the earliest American
settlers lured by promises of healthy living was Dr. Andrew Anderson, a
prominent Boston physician who hoped his consumptive wife would rally
in the warm climate. Though Mary Anderson died, Dr. Anderson's faith
in Florida remained unshakeable, and he became a national booster and
an influential resident of his adopted city, where he built a plantation and
married his children's governess. He published pamphlets promoting St.
Augustine as a health resort, and by the 1830s a small but steady stream of
consumptives was arriving to take a rest cure.[17]

Reaching St. Augustine was a nightmare. Travel was onerous throughout the South, and the age of railroads was still a generation in the future.
Visitors to St. Augustine generally came by sailing vessels or took one of
the small steamers that plied the St. Johns, disembarking at Picolata. Anyone forced to spend the night there was exceptionally unlucky. The hotel
for steamer passengers soon gained a reputation for filth; one memoirist
claimed no one ever willingly stopped there twice. More fortunate souls
boarded a stage to the city. One traveler penned a vivid account of the trip:
"Deep white sand obstructs the stage, and not so rarely as one wishes the
wheels strike a pine or palmetto root with a most unpleasant effect on the
passengers, especially if they are invalids. After 3 ½ hours of this torture,
the stage is checked by the Sebastian river, over which a miserable ferry

conveys the tourist who at length finds himself in St. Augustine." Faced with a choice between seasickness or rattled teeth, most travelers preferred the ocean passage.[18]

For over a decade, St. Augustine lacked proper guest facilities. The first true hotel did not open until 1835. Rooming houses were sometimes referred to as hotels, but rarely if ever deserved that title. If they were on a parallel with similar establishments in Tallahassee, the new capital, then they understood "nothing of comfort or cleanliness" and often lacked such amenities as fresh sheets and teapots. Some guests took up lodging in taverns, where rest was impossible because of the nightly drinking and carousing.[19] The preferred arrangement was to take a room in a private home, which required letters of introduction. Two of the town's most famous residents, Mary Martha Reid, a former First Lady of the territorial era, and Clarissa Anderson, the second spouse of Dr. Andrew Anderson, took in boarders to supplement their widow's incomes. In 1835, the *St. Augustine Examiner* claimed the city had rooms for 300 guests, though only 165 visitors had been in residence the previous winter. John James Audubon visited briefly in 1831 and had nothing good to say about the town, calling it the "poorest hole in Creation." He was, however, kind enough to place the Castillo de San Marcos in the background for his drawing of a greenshank.[20]

The Florida House, St. Augustine's first hotel, was opened in 1835. By 1842, a timetable trip from New York to Florida was a reality, and for just over $50 an individual could take a succession of trains, steamers, and stages to St. Augustine. Business picked up as the second Seminole War ended and the old city fort became more of a reminder of antiquity than a practical means of defense.[21] In 1842, Clarissa Anderson wrote that all the town required to take advantage of its new security was for a "enterprising Yankee" to open and manage a "first rate house."[22] Her prophecy came true in 1847, when Burroughs E. Carr, the town's leading merchant, opened the Magnolia House, with accommodations for forty guests. The stately hotel on St. George Street soon expanded to add more rooms and a dining hall. By 1853, it was an impressive edifice, two stories high with forty-five rooms and a veranda on its eastern and southern sides, plus shaded grounds.[23] To promote his investment, Carr published a small volume, *Sketches of St. Augustine*, by Rufus King Sewall. The 1848 work promised to "inform people living in the North of the regeneration influence which Florida's balmy winter climate could work for sufferers of respiratory ailments." The book was more imaginative than informative; its author misnamed landmarks and related gruesome and largely fabricated tales of the "dungeons" in the Castillo de San Marcos. These romantic legends lingered as part of St. Augustine's tourist experience, as anyone who has ventured onto a trolley ride or ghost walk will confirm. Carr's Magnolia House was later vastly overshadowed by Flagler's resort hotels and burned down in 1926.[24]

The first tourists in St. Augustine discovered a study in contrasts. The Castillo de San Marcos guarded the harbor like a fairy-tale fortress, and the homes and streets possessed an aura of European decay, while Spanish, English, and African cultures mingled in the natives' dress and speech. Traugott Bromme, a German professional traveler, was fascinated by the town's gardens and unique homes. Many visitors thought St. Augustine resembled a village in Spain or Italy more than any American hamlet; Audubon claimed it mimicked a collection of hovels in France. The "Old World charm" of St. Augustine provided the enchantment of a foreign vacation without the inconvenience or danger of an ocean voyage.[25]

An early consumptive visitor to St. Augustine was Ralph Waldo Emerson, who arrived in the city years before his national reputation was established. Stepping from the sloop *William*, which he had boarded in Charleston on January 10, 1827, the young philosopher feared that he would not survive the relocation. Emerson spent nearly three months in St. Augustine, enduring a sojourn filled with mixed emotions. He was often lonely and homesick, and complained of being frequently bored. Determined to improve his health, he sat in the sun, took strolls on the beach, and went sailing. He exercised his mind by attending court sessions and meetings of the Bible and temperance societies, as well as observing elections and slave auctions. Like many others, he was fascinated by the blending of folkways, and was fortunate, during his departure from St. Augustine, to meet and befriend one of Florida's living tourist attractions, Prince Achille Murat, a nephew of Napoleon and an all-around character. Emerson recorded Murat's vivid descriptions of his plantation home in Tallahassee with such great enthusiasm that later historians mistakenly believed Emerson had traveled to the interior of Florida. After ten weeks of playing the role of invalid tourist, Emerson abandoned the "little city of the deep" with the guarded optimism that he had felt "better lately."[26]

The quaintness of the city was inspirational to literary types, even those not afflicted with consumption. In April 1843, the famous poet and journalist William Cullen Bryant visited the town and witnessed the tradition of young men serenading residents on the evening before Easter. He recorded the songs, sung in an unusual Spanish dialect, along with his impressions of the streets paved with "artificial stone" of shells and mortar. He also marveled at the abundance of pomegranate, fig, and orange trees, as well as the hospitality of his hosts. Friends feared that Bryant's antislavery stance in the *Saturday Evening Post* would cause conflict, but the poet had no complaints against his Southern sojourn, and St. Augustine's residents surely appreciated national publicity for their city, which appeared in Bryant's letters to the *New York Evening Post* and in 1850 as part of *Letters of a Traveler: Or, Notes of Things Seen in Europe and America.*[27]

Not everyone was as lucky as Emerson and Bryant. While a change in climate could provide relief for people in early stages of consumption, there was no true cure for tuberculosis, despite city boosters' claims. Many health-seekers thought they had been hoodwinked. An unnamed consumptive complained in 1839 that St. Augustine was not the warm and wonderful sanitarium he had been promised. He needed a fire in April, was overcharged by the local doctors, and found the town "small and dull," with little in the way of amusements for the mobile invalid. In his opinion, the only advantage St. Augustine possessed over Key West was the more regular arrival of mail and the chance of indulging in Florida land speculation.[28] An 1852 author agreed with the earlier assessment, leveling sharp criticism at physicians who sent hopeless patients off to dreary St. Augustine to die. "St. Augustine is the oldest and least prosperous city in the Union," the visitor wrote, while speculating that Palatka, Lake Monroe, Orange Springs, Suwannee Springs, and Tampa would perhaps become great resorts in time.[29] A third naysayer warned of fog, haze, and unexpected chills. He acknowledged that St. Augustine had a national reputation as "a restorative for consumptive patients," but in "this respect its character is, I fear, better than it deserves."[30]

Despite such pointed criticism, tourism was the bedrock of the St. Augustine economy by 1850, when *Colton's Traveler and Tourist's Guide-Book* recommended—albeit with misspellings—the city of "San Augustine" as one "often resorted to by those suffering under pulmonic affections."[31] New hotels were being constructed, older ones were improved, and innovations such as bathing machines were touted as the latest novelty. But with a growth in tourism came the inevitable griping, especially from longtime residents who questioned whether the seasonal visitors enhanced the city's atmosphere as much as they enlarged its economy. A visitor described watching St. Augustine–bound consumptives arriving in Jacksonville: "We saw some of them in the last stage of the disease, dragging themselves along, like disconsolate ghosts on the banks of Styx."[32] Audubon recorded an encounter with a visiting botanist, "a man of most comely appearance but one who unfortunately is possessed of Pulmonic Constitution so hoarse and thin that I doubt if he will surpass the winter." One native complained that the "funereal cough" in all quarters made every public venue seem like a hospital. While Northern spas were known as centers of courtship, only "old women and ugly children" seemed to arrive in St. Augustine. Invalids were obnoxious to the healthy, and the healthy were frequently the bane of the indisposed. Pool halls, saloons, and gambling parlors operated in St. Augustine, catering to both the sick and the well, who blamed each other when such dens became a nuisance. Residents complained that the sudden wealth generated by good winter seasons made the hotel managers "sassy" and insufferable. For residents and visitors, there was rarely any middle ground; one either came to love the Oldest City or loathe it with a passion.[33]

The winter months brought sick Northerners, primarily from New York, but in the summer months it was not uncommon for wealthy Southerners, including inland Floridians, to take up temporary residence in St. Augustine. The Deep South was infamous for its heat, humidity, and seasonal outbreaks of malaria, typhoid, and yellow fever. It was held that sea air would counteract such dangers, and St. Augustine's publicists did their best to encourage year-round tourism as a way of stabilizing the delicate economy. Ironically, Clarissa Anderson, the city's most popular hostess, used the profits generated from winter boarders to finance her extended summer vacations with relatives in New York and Massachusetts.[34]

Though by far the best-known and most popular city in the state, St. Augustine was not the only Florida locale advertised as being a curative resort. Other port cities promoted their good air and year-round warmth as a way of generating tourists and, hopefully, settlers. In 1792, American wanderer John Pope reported a conversation with the Spanish governor at Pensacola, who bragged that during his eleven years of residency he had never once been sick, perhaps due to the good air and the many bubbling fountains offering clean water. He claimed that the entire population of the town was unusually healthy, except for his garrison. A traveling moralist, Pope blamed soldiers' illnesses on inordinate drinking, spicy foods, and "intercourse with lewd women."[35]

Visiting Pensacola with her famous husband for the official transfer of Florida to the United States in 1821, Rachel Jackson called Pensacola Bay the "most beautiful water prospect I ever saw" and praised the town's sea breezes and flowers while despairing of its constant rain showers. She claimed that many people were arriving for their health, but the town was slow to accommodate them in comfort. The Panic of 1837 obliterated hopes for a railroad connection to Columbus, Georgia, and in the same year a hurricane wiped out the bathing houses, a novelty constructed just a few years previously. Despite the hopes and dreams of town promoters, tourism in Pensacola seemed cursed, especially as yellow fever epidemics swept the Gulf Coast. Between hurricanes, disease, roving packs of dogs, and poor transportation, Pensacola was unable to conquer its bad publicity and lure significant numbers of tourists or invalids. Not even a booster's promise that Pensacola was brimming with "a good lot of the prettiest girls you have ever seen any where . . . ready to join, at all times, a picnic—fishing party—sailing party—dancing party—and all such as that" could bring in tourism dandies and their dollars.[36]

Key West had a small population of health-hunting visitors in the antebellum period. One invalid chronicled his search for a perfect climate in the 1839 treatise *A Winter in the West Indies and Florida*. He painted an intriguing picture of a tiny village that did not, in the opinion of its leaders, deserve its reputation for fevers and agues. The anonymous sufferer wrote of the hospitality of its people and the "fine turtle and fish" offerings that made up for the lack of beef, poultry, and most vegetables. With only one tavern and boardinghouse, the town lacked facilities, but residents were willing to take guests into their homes, and the fare generally ran from $7 to $10 a week. Amusement came in the form of a ninepins alley and two billiard tables. Most important, the town boasted two doctors "of good reputation, and their charges are not very high." While in residence, the author met fellow invalids from Pennsylvania and New York, sadly noting, "there was not a single case of entire recovery among the whole." Still, he championed Key West over any other city within the United States in terms of climate. He was especially harsh on St. Augustine, where he migrated after his vacation in the Keys, proclaiming, "It is not only absurd, but almost wicked, to send a *sick* man here for his health, when it is just as easy to send him to a better place."[37]

An 1860 traveler admired Key West, but tempered his praise with a blunt assessment of the town's shortcomings as a resort. He found the climate delightful, not as intensely hot as Cuba's and better moderated by breezes. "This would be a paradise for invalids, with its perpetual summer, its balmy, health-giving atmosphere, and its ever verdant foliage, were there a great variety of land scenery, more pleasant drives, and better hotel accommodations. But it is sadly deficient in all of these hygeian [*sic*] requisites."[38]

A number of spas sprang up around the state's freshwater springs. Some of these institutions endured from the antebellum period into the early twentieth century. Entrepreneurs took advantage of "mineral waters" to construct lodgings on site or close by, hoping to replicate the success of such premiere resorts as Saratoga Springs. Their success varied depending on location, investment, and amenities. The entrepreneurs who developed spring-based resorts were bold in their promises, claiming that Florida waters were "efficacious in all forms of consumption, scrofula, jaundice, and other bilious affectations, chronic dysentery and diarrhea, diseases of the uterus, chronic rheumatism and gout, dropsy, gravel, neuralgia, tremor, syphilis, erysipelas, tetter, ringworm and itch."[39]

The White Sulphur Springs community was established in 1843, on the upper Suwannee River, and by 1845 tourists were arriving at the tiny village by stage from the train depot at Wellborn, eight miles away. Most of the early visitors were Florida or Georgia residents, but by 1866 advertisements for the facilities at White Sulphur Springs were appearing in Tallahassee newspapers, and feature articles on the spa were staples in the guidebooks of the 1870s. The spring was touted as a special cure for rheumatism. After a brief decline during Reconstruction, the spa was revived in the mid-1880s, its fortunes improved by its proximity to the railroad running from Valdosta to Lake City, with links to service from Macon and

Palatka. Renamed White Springs, during its turn-of-the-century heyday the site featured a four-level pavilion encircling the spring, with a retaining wall and bathhouse. An advertisement in an 1885 guidebook boasted of new hotel furniture and accommodations for 200 guests, with rates at $35–40 a month, $10–12 a week, and $2 a day. By 1907, four hotels were operational, complete with bowling alleys and dance halls. White Springs was both a spa for invalids and a popular Sunday outing for crowds from Jacksonville. A 1911 fire was the beginning of the end for the resort, which limped along with ever-thinning attendance until it closed in 1950.[40]

Similar developments occurred at Suwannee Springs, some twelve miles south of White Sulphur Springs. Crude facilities for bathers were in place by 1845, and shortly afterward accommodations for 100 visitors were advertised in local papers. Though the spring itself was "unimproved," proprietors promised the "very best fare that can be obtained in this section of the country," and "beds will be properly attended to and kept clean and airy." The promise of good food was met. In 1851, Clement Claiborne Clay, son of a former Alabama governor, reported that the hotel served excellent "gopher gumbo."[41] Little known outside of Middle Florida and more difficult to reach than White Sulphur Springs, it was not until the 1880s that entrepreneurs began serious efforts to expand Suwannee Springs' facilities and attract tourists. By 1890, the spring was encircled by a heavy masonry wall. At the attraction's peak as a year-round resort, a trolley line ran from the railroad station to the spring, and a large hotel, rows of cottages, special bathing pools, and a bottling works were operational. The hotel burned just prior to World War I, but the cottages remained open up to the 1950s.[42]

Orange Springs, on the left bank of the Ocklawaha River, offered a boardinghouse in 1843 and was filled with "bronchial and consumptive" patients by 1851. News of the spa spread rapidly. An 1855 visitor found the hotel crowded as "the place has a great name as a safe winter's resort for invalids for all the physicians now send their patients in countless numbers to Florida." Northerners frequented the spa in winter while Floridians arrived in the summer, utilizing the facility as a rest stop on the way to Silver Springs. The Civil War crushed the resort's trade, and despite a brief renaissance in the 1880s, the Orange Springs spa lost out again as railroad travel surpassed steamboat voyages. People with arthritis, rather than those with consumption, came to Orange Springs at the turn of the century. The resort lasted until 1925. A much-shorter-lived antebellum resort was established at Newport Springs on the St. Marks River, some twenty miles south of Tallahassee. A summer rather than winter resort area, its two hotels offered lodgings and social activities to guests, who were primarily the elite of the capital city. The hotels were sacked during the Civil War, and the resort never fully revived despite some effort to maintain cottages and cater to adventurous sportsmen.[43]

Two notable postwar resorts were established at Green Cove Springs (1869) and Worthington Springs (1895). Green Cove Springs became a regular stop for St. Johns River steamers and offered ten hotels by the 1880s. Its origins were humble. The spring was initially undeveloped except for crude bathhouses, which men and women were allowed to use at different hours.[44] The only Florida inland spa to develop a truly national reputation, Green Cove Springs was eventually proclaimed the "Saratoga of the St. Johns" for its dances, concerts, and races during the winter season. "Think of bathing in open air in December," one guidebook urged, "and yet this is a common everyday enjoyment here."[45] The end of steamboat travel meant inevitable decline for the spa, which was passed over by the railroad. Far more isolated was Worthington Springs, on the north bank of the Santa Fe River. Familiar only to locals, Worthington Springs was developed as a party spot rather than a serious spa, though a pool was built in 1895 and three hotels quickly followed. Catering mainly to holiday crowds who made the brief trip by railroad from Gainesville and Jacksonville, Worthington Springs remained popular even through the Depression, but the fiery destruction of the last hotel in 1937 marked the end of Worthington Springs' vacation prominence.[46]

Two springs in the Panhandle made late attempts to flourish as spas, taking advantage of the 1890s emphasis on the atmosphere of interior Florida as well as its waters. With a good bit of license, a pamphlet for Alachua County argued that "the atmosphere of Florida is a medicine that has cured thousands of patients," while a 1905 promotion for Leon County boasted of its "vast forest of pine, breathing forth their balm 'til the whole atmosphere is fragrant with it, and if there is a possibility for relief for the unfortunate victim of consumption, this in conjunction with the genial sunshine and soft, bracing air, will affect it."[47] Northern investors purchased Smith Springs, thirty-five miles south of Tallahassee, gambling that a new rail line from Tallahassee to Carrabelle would make their sanctuary accessible. Renamed Panacea Springs, the spa opened in 1898 and soon included hotels, a bathing pool, and the added attraction of convenient boating and fishing on the Gulf. A 1924 fire destroyed the original facilities, but the 1920s boom enabled the owners to rebuild and expand with more hotels, a dance pavilion, and seasonal bungalows. The Depression killed the resort, which had become popular with the Tallahassee crowd, along with residents of South Georgia. Hampton Springs, located five miles in the woods outside of Perry, became the home of a hotel/hunting lodge in 1908. The spring routinely changed hands. Railroad interests purchased the property in 1915, and by the end of World War I Hampton Springs had a larger hotel and a golf course. Closed in the 1920s, it reopened briefly when a Chicago-based company took over in 1927, only to fail again during the Depression and be briefly revived after World War II. A fire completed its destruction in 1954.[48]

One Southwest Florida spring enjoyed a half-century vogue. Safety Harbor, on the western shore of Tampa Bay, consisted of four springs, each with a different quality of mineral water, within a twenty-five-foot radius. In the mid-1890s, a Tampa doctor erected a canvas shelter around the springs, creating a tent city sanitarium. By 1900, a new owner had constructed the usual complement of hotel, pavilion, and water bottling plant, plus a dock for the Tampa excursion boats that were Safety Harbor's only transportation. A fire destroyed the initial compound in 1915, and a new hotel was constructed in 1923. A change in management in the post–World War II period resulted in a luxury resort that drew patrons from New York, Boston, and Canada. Safety Harbor Spa is still operational, billing itself as a place where "healing waters flow."[49]

Florida's springs had the natural requirements for the development of successful spas: they were beautiful, exotic, and untainted, but unfortunately for the state they were also remote. Their inland locations made them much less attractive to the small number of nineteenth-century people who possessed money and leisure time for travel. It required a truly determined or desperate invalid to make the bone-jarring stage ride to White Sulphur Springs, or to risk bedbugs and fleas at Newport. Without major investors or promoters, Florida spas had little hope of attracting guests in the antebellum age, and while spas along rivers and railroad lines had a brief heyday in the late 1800s, they were soon made passé by changing ideas about the merits of long rest cures and hydrotherapy. The decline of steamboat and railroad transportation, paired with the increasing vitality of automotive travelers, who shunned spas as old fashioned, guaranteed that such antique institutions rotted away by the mid-twentieth century.[50]

Springs with facilities that appealed to locale clientele, for holiday pleasure trips, were more successful and enduring. Yet some of Florida's most appealing spots went undeveloped throughout the antebellum period. Though Tallahassee journalists constantly pointed out the merits and possibilities of the huge Wakulla Spring, just south of the city, it remained a spot frequented only by rustic picnickers until a lodge was constructed in the mid-1930s, long after changes in travel and ideas about vacations had shuttered Florida's historic spas. Perhaps Wakulla was hampered by Tallahassee's bad reputation. The capital city was little more than a frontier village throughout the antebellum period. Even the City Hotel was owned by a well-known gambler and drunkard who had barely escaped a murder conviction.[51]

Silver Springs, destined to become the state's most famous natural wonder, was difficult to savor in the antebellum period. To reach Silver Springs in the 1850s required a slow journey via pole barge through the vine-choked reaches of the Ocklawaha, or a tortuous, spine-jarring ride aboard the stage line that ran from Palatka to Tampa. In 1855, Lady Amelia Murray, a lady-in-waiting to Queen Victoria, recorded that the overland journey from Palatka to Silver Springs took fifteen hours, and that while the water was beautiful, the accommodations were shockingly primitive. The historian George Bancroft had a similar experience, sleeping on a hard mattress of moss at his Ocala hotel, where he was offered "a piece of squirrel" for breakfast. In 1856, Dr. Daniel G. Brinton wrote that Silver Springs gave the most "dramatic transition from darkness to light that a traveler can make anywhere on the continent." To view such a wonder took more than just fortitude for bad roads and dingy rooming houses. From 1855 to 1858, stages required military escorts due to Seminole uprisings in the area.[52]

By the mid-1800s, Florida was becoming increasingly familiar to Americans, especially the reading and touring public along the East Coast. But familiarity did not always imply honesty. Promoters promised more than they could deliver, including cures for incurable diseases. Despite Florida's failure to be a true Lourdes of America, many who traveled to the state were pleased with it. An 1869 memoir invoked a scene that was common at midcentury aboard a St. Johns River steamship. "The invalid and the tourist flock eagerly to the steamer's deck, to drink in this balmy air, and feast their eyes on the green foliage of the forest which flanks on either side of the water's edge. The drooping spirits of the passengers rise as the steamer advances up the broad and beautiful river which so delights all eyes and gives eloquence to every tongue."[53]

Eloquence about Florida came naturally. George Bancroft rhapsodized, "when the west wind from the gulf does blow, it has a tale to tell from Paradise itself." Tourists, residents, and promoters naturally agreed with the wind and began to produce a vast collection of memoirs and travel guides designed to lure both travelers and settlers to the state. One such volume argued that Florida was "the spot for the jilted lover to forget his idol, and the disconsolate lady her imaginary devotee; for those fretted by the rough edges of corroding care to retire and find a respite from their struggles." Florida was "the store-house of the fathomless deep, where we can contemplate that great image of eternity; 'the invisible, boundless, endless, and sublime.'"[54] In short, the state offered something unlike any other, a tropical wilderness where travelers might be both renewed and reinvented. It also, in the years following the Civil War, offered unparalleled opportunities for development. "Every third man you meet from the North is arranging to build a hotel," one amused traveler wrote.[55]

Tourism in Florida was primed to stop coughing and come to life.

TWO

Sportsman's Paradise

Two steamboats approached each other in the Ocklawaha River night, whistling in the darkness. As they drew closer, the vessels ignited pitch-pine fires in braziers. One boat bumped the shore like a buggy on a steep mountain road. Suddenly, the other stern-wheel steamer broke around a curve, and the boats passed so close crew members could exchange pleasantries. The crowds on the bows cheered their pilots' bold feat. Constance Fenimore Woolson, a passenger, recorded the rival boat's departure. "Then we watched the glare glide on down the river. First the whole forest lighted up, then a gleaming through the white trunks of the cypress, then the same high-up flickering light over the tree-tops, and finally nothing save darkness." It was a grand Florida adventure, one that was increasingly common in the second half of the nineteenth century.[1]

A significant shift in the nature of Florida tourism began in the decade following the Civil War. While the state was still primarily known for its reputed curative powers, more and more people were arriving with no interest in being cured of anything except boredom. Though still boasting of the state's salubrious air, promoters increasingly recognized the need to brag on the quality of the hunting, fishing, and sporting life in Florida. A cultural change in the perception of travel and tourism was taking place across America, and Florida was a natural beneficiary, as it offered even more to the active tourist than it did to the invalid.[2]

As early as the 1850s, the growing American middle class began to view travel and tourism not as a sinful waste of time, but as a natural complement to labor. While journeys taken strictly for pleasure remained suspect, the Puritan work ethic that held all recreation in disrepute was fading. A vacation designed to restore one spiritually, physically, and mentally was considered worthwhile and even advocated by evangelicals who preached a "muscular Christianity" that considered bodily fitness a virtue. In general, Protestant churches came to approve of vacations, so long as the travelers sought spiritual uplift and avoided suspect activities like playing billiards and cards. A vacation was also a mark of rising status, a token that a family had reached a new level of prosperity. These changing attitudes coincided with a revolution in transportation, which made tourist destinations accessible to those of more modest means. American railroads were beginning to imitate the innovation of Thomas Cook, the British founder of modern tourism, arranging package excursions to popular destinations.[3] Saratoga Springs, once the province of the elite, saw a bourgeoisie invasion by the 1850s. By the postwar period, the belief in travel as a positive experience, rather than irresponsible indulgence, had spread across the nation, and those who could take advantage of journeys in which they could improve mind and body frequently did. Though Florida was still out of reach of the average American family, more people, particularly those residing in northeastern cities, began to consider its possibilities, especially if they could afford a winter vacation. Florida's reputation began to slowly change from that of a Southern sanitarium to a tropical playground.[4]

Led by loyalty to other Southern states, though by no means unanimous in the sentiment, Floridians seceded from the Union in 1861 and cast their lot with the Confederacy. Florida tourism stalled during the Civil War. Even before hostilities erupted, Northern visitors were made to feel unwelcome in the Oldest City, where the *St. Augustine Examiner* advised that anyone professing Union sentiments be "hung high as Haman," and prominent citizens openly expressed their suspicions that tourists were really spies, eager to learn the extent of city defenses. Frances Kirby-Smith, the mother of future Confederate general Edmund Kirby-Smith, shared her paranoia with her son, warning that even the weakest invalid harbored thoughts of abolition and would gladly cut Southern throats. The disappearance of Yankee visitors, combined with the gloom of war, made the 1861–1862 winter season, in the words of resident Hannah Jenckes, "dull beyond belief."[5] Some residents were delighted by the town's handover to Federals in 1862, well aware that the city would be used as a site for rest and relaxation. Union soldiers bought curios, pulled pranks, dug for buried treasure in the fort, and flirted with attractive Rebel young women. "The quaint old town was in itself a never-ending font of enjoyment and interest," one Yankee soldier later recalled.[6] Northern newspaper reporters with the troops romanticized St. Augustine and its residents. The military tourists helped the town's economy survive and proved vocal advocates of Florida's charms when writing company memoirs. Some even returned to the city after Appomattox to build lives and careers.[7]

The woman whose fervid prose helped foment the Civil War became one of Florida's most vocal advocates and a promoter of tourism during the Reconstruction period. In 1867, Harriet Beecher Stowe chose to establish a winter home in Florida, purchasing a parcel of land and a cottage at Mandarin, on the east bank of the St. Johns River. She described moving to Florida as joining a "mass hegira" of Northerners who were eager to resume wintering in the balmy climate. Stowe was soon producing travel articles for the *Christian Union*, depicting her new home as a "calm isle of Patmos," a wondrous, exotic hideaway. Her work, which was published as *Palmetto Leaves* in 1873, blended poetic license about the state with practical advice for tourists, answering questions about land prices and hotel rates. In the words of one Stowe biographer, *Palmetto Leaves* "painted a picture of Florida as a tropical paradise which remained as the Northern impression until the railroads and the motor car opened up the state as a winter playground."[8]

Already a popular figure in the North thanks to her antislavery best seller, *Uncle Tom's Cabin*, Stowe was readily adopted by Floridians for her efforts in promoting the state and being diplomatically uncritical of its racial issues. Stereoscopic views of Stowe and her family on the lawn of their Mandarin residence were sold in the North, leading steamship captains to promise the real thing to their passengers. Pilots always pointed out her orange groves, and Hubbard L. Hart's line paid her to make well-timed appearances on her porch, or to sit and work in the open where she could be observed.[9] While her fame was a factor in Jacksonville's growth as a tourist destination in the 1870s, the notoriety was often obnoxious to her husband, Calvin. He once caught a trio of tourists wandering just beyond the veranda, breaking off orange branches filled with blossoms.[10]

The steamboats offering free views of America's most famous literary figure were the pioneering force in postwar tourism. Florida was wet, blessed with a multitude of navigable rivers and streams. Water transit was far easier, faster, and cheaper than overland travel. Hubbard Hart's stern-wheeler line opened the Ocklawaha to Silver Springs, and by 1886 there were seventy-four steamboats on the St. Johns. Steamers served sportsmen, taking them on memorable expeditions up the Caloosahatchee and Kissimmee rivers. Residents of Ft. Myers, who considered steamboats a great novelty in the prewar era, now regularly saw them lined up at the wharves. To accommodate passengers along the Indian River, new hotels sprang up at the small settlements of Titusville, Rockledge, and Eau Gallie. Honeymooners in Middle Florida could book passage aboard the *Belle of the Suwannee*, which was famous for its bridal suite.[11]

The slow southern progress of the steamers hinted that more of the Florida "terra incognita" could and should be opened. In 1865–1866, Republican politician and future lieutenant governor William Gleason, accompanied by George F. Thompson, a Freedman's Bureau agent, made an extensive tour of South Florida, issuing a public report that boasted of the region's natural abundance and warm weather.[12] In a book on his southern travels taken just after the war, journalist Whitelaw Reid opined that Florida would recover its trade when it "begins to be used again as a grand national sanitarium."[13] More reports followed, published in newspapers and magazines and often composed by railroad scouts, virtually all of them emphasizing the potential for both settlement and tourism farther into the peninsula. In 1868, the state established a Department of Immigration, charged with promoting Florida for settlement, tourism, and investment. J. Berrien Oliver, an old Florida newspaperman, did his part by moving north, where he began publishing the *Florida New Yorker*, a monthly magazine that touted Florida's climate and soil, urging weary war veterans and others to head south.[14]

The problem, as always, was accessibility. Overland travel was simply too harsh; only railroads would open the interior that visitors as early as

William Bartram had described as lush and desirable. The few lines that existed in Florida were short and varied in gauge, leading to long waits to change trains and making the consumption of regular meals nearly impossible.[15] A complex lawsuit prevented the Florida State Internal Improvement Fund from using millions of acres of public lands until the 1880s. Stymied by fights over ownership and property titles, railroad development lagged, and tourism remained focused on the northeastern corner of the peninsula. Residents farther south could only nod along with the author of *Notes from Sunland*, who pleaded "that if any person who knows how to run a hotel, will start one in Braidentown [*sic*], he will most assuredly put money in his purse and at the same time satisfy a great public want." Predicting that a 100-room resort would be filled with sportsmen for half the year, and readily supplied with fresh fish, oysters, and game, the writer asked the central question that plagued all Florida communities located far from the railroads—"Shall we have a hotel?"[16]

Another problem that made Florida less attractive to tourists was the unpredictable outbreaks of disease. An antebellum yellow fever epidemic in Tallahassee wiped out much of the city's elite. Coastal towns were especially endangered, as evidenced by the epidemic that hit St. Joseph in 1841, ending its brief promotion as a holiday resort. Among its victims, along with some 75 percent of the residents, was former Florida First Lady Nancy Hynes DuVal. Ironically, she had gone there to "take the waters" as a rest cure.[17] Pensacola was especially vulnerable to the disease. An early resident explained that filth, strangers, and a cargo of spoiled codfish from Havana brought on the city's 1822 outbreak. The city experienced further epidemics in 1867, 1873, 1874, 1876, and 1905. Key West was also prone to episodic outbreaks, as was Jacksonville, which reported 427 deaths from the disease in 1888. A wave of yellow fever swept St. Augustine in 1841, but anxious town promoters downplayed its severity. Not until the Spanish-American War and the experiments of Dr. Walter Reed did Floridians gain a better understanding of the disease and how to prevent it. Malaria was also a seasonal threat, its cause mysterious and misunderstood. One guidebook author assured readers that tales of malaria on the St. Johns were exaggerated and that it "rarely gives trouble except to those who are unusually careless in exposing themselves, or in drinking well instead of cistern water."[18]

Hurricanes also threatened the state on a regular, if highly unpredictable, basis. Official records were not kept until late in the nineteenth century, but newspaper accounts reveal that Florida was struck by numerous hurricanes in the 1800s, including especially violent storms in 1846, 1851, and 1856. In 1870, the U.S. Signal Corps was charged with responsibility for weather forecasting and reporting, but the fragile nature of telegraph lines made raising an evacuation alarm in time a rather chancy proposition. A series of hurricanes slowed railroad construction in the 1880s and 1890s. The Keys experienced hurricanes in 1906, 1909, and 1910. A 1909 storm took the greatest toll of human life up to that time, with some 130 people killed. In the days before radio, tourists who lingered into the wrong season might find themselves enduring an unpleasant Florida novelty.[19]

Despite the problems of transportation and the harshness of the natural environment, tourists and potential investors seeking information were bombarded with enthusiastic information about the state. While early writers, often the survivors of shipwrecks, had portrayed Florida as a wild and savage hell, authors of the Reconstruction period portrayed it as an untamed paradise. Testimonials and guidebooks joined with railway promotional literature. Along with Stowe's columns, one of the first true guidebooks was Ledyard Bill's *A Winter in Florida*. Another best seller was the *Guide to Florida* by "Rambler," which appeared in 1873, 1875, and 1876 editions as a project of the American News Company and was choked with advertising for railroads and hotels.[20]

Honesty was not always a quality readily found in guidebooks and railroad promotional material. If one believed the hype, Florida offered nothing but first-class hotels, gourmet meals, and exclusive winter resorts. "Rambler" claimed that sudden changes in climate were unknown, and that there was never "an instance where relief was not obtained" from congestive complaints while in St. Augustine.[21] Invalids were advised that Florida's climate could work miracles on everything from asthma to Bright's disease, measles, uterine disease, rheumatism, neuralgia, nervous prostration, and even old age.[22] In 1904, a guidebook scored the prize for the biggest falsehood by claiming there was no insect or reptile problem in Florida. Naturally the authors of guides, and the railroad owners and hotel bosses who paid them, wanted Florida to be as attractive as prose and images of pretty young women picking oranges could make it. "We have no prejudices to overcome, for we are cosmopolitan; we want immigration of kindred races, that we may be a homogeneous people; we are all immigrants or their descendants; we give immigration credit for all we are and hope to become," one guidebook gushed, in a tribute that managed to be both disingenuous and racist.[23]

One of the better guidebooks was published in 1875. Sidney Lanier, the great Southern poet, composed a "spiritual guidebook" to Florida that included some of the most memorable passages ever written about the state. Titled *Florida: Its Scenery, Climate and History*, it was commissioned by the Great Atlantic Coastline Railroad. Lanier viewed the labor as "hack work" and referred to himself derisively as the "Poet-in-Ordinary to a long line of railroad operations."[24] Limited to just over two months in the late spring, his Florida tour was hardly a comprehensive journey. Lanier made the obligatory entrance at Jacksonville and pilgrimage on the Ocklawaha, stopped in at St. Augustine, rode the railway to Cedar Key, went by boat to Key West, then looped back to take the train from Jacksonville to Tallahassee. Such spastic travel forced him to rely on the observations of others, but he considered himself a poet of nature so he did his homework on the geography and flora of the state, even pausing to consult the libraries of prominent residents. He painted a vivid word picture of Florida as thriving and healthy despite the upheavals of Reconstruction, emphasizing its benefits to the consumptive, the tourist, and the investor. The competent work generated little notice, though the Boston *Literary World* judged it "an uneasy and sometimes brilliant" guide.[25]

As usual, investment money went to where likely profits were the highest, and for the mid-nineteenth century that meant the northeastern corner of Florida. The St. Johns River was the portal for travel and investment, and economic growth was so evident by 1876 that one observer commented, "it is as if a magician's wand had been waved over it."[26] The boom city of the Reconstruction period was Jacksonville, the junction of water routes into Southeast Florida and the railroad link across the central and western portions of the state to Cedar Key and Tallahassee. It became the gateway city to Florida, both a terminal destination for some and a rest stop for others. By 1869, the city, which had seen multiple Federal invasions in the Civil War, had four quality hotels: the Price House, the Taylor House, the St. Johns House, and the St. James. Financing a Jacksonville hotel was as close as one could come to a sure thing, a far better bet than purchasing a decrepit plantation in the interior. One 1874 reporter estimated that approximately 250,000 tourists visited Fernandina and Jacksonville, while another 50,000 went up the St. Johns and Ocklawaha rivers to Silver Springs. By 1886, Jacksonville had sixteen hotels, with the addition of such distinguished hostelries as the Waverly House, the Everett House, and the Windsor.[27]

Jacksonville tourists of the 1880s were active and constantly in search of tropical novelties. On Bay Street, known as "Curio Row," they stocked up on souvenirs including palmetto hats, sea-bean buttons, heron plumes, mangrove canes, and coquina figurines. Alligator teeth were fashioned into whistles and watch fobs. So many alligator-inspired products were offered for sale that a visitor argued for renaming Jacksonville's main street "Alligator Avenue, because of the myriad ways that animal is offered as a sacrifice to the curiosity and thoughtlessness of the crowds."[28] For almost two decades the yearly tourist treat was the Florida Sub Tropical Exposition and State Fair, which ran from January to April and featured displays of Florida produce, Indian wares, and foreign novelties. Visitors could rent horses and buggies for excursions to local springs, or spend quiet hours in the Bay Street Library. For less erudite tourists, there were other options. Even past the turn of the century, Jacksonville retained its reputation for illicit pleasures, including saloons, brothels, opium dens, and discreet gambling clubs. Jacksonville's heyday as the state's primary tourist city ended by 1900, however, when Henry Flagler's hotels drew the elite and their watchers farther south, to St. Augustine and then to Palm Beach and Miami.[29]

The new vitality of Florida tourists was everywhere evident in the 1870s and 1880s. "Touring" in the new style meant that the traveler was rarely content to spend a vacation in one place, but moved about restlessly and engaged in many "improving" activities. "This is an age of progress," one South Florida resident wrote, "the world moves, and Florida, after her Rip Van Winkle sleep of three hundred years, is moving with it."[30] Guests in Jacksonville, Fernandina, and St. Augustine increasingly left the hotel verandas and went to the beaches, where they rode horses or mastered the new sport of cycling. Long walks, lawn tennis, and croquet were popular. Visiting historic sites was a must, and the sudden boom in hotel dance halls, bowling alleys, and arcades spoke to a new vibrancy among the guests. Sunbathing "a la alligator" was now acceptable, though of course rather confined by Victorian-era bathing attire, which covered far more skin than it revealed.[31]

Sportsmen of all stripes were increasingly drawn to Florida in the post-Reconstruction period. Books on Florida hunting and fishing were best sellers. "It is the paradise of the sportsman," one railroad guidebook proclaimed. "It is the exhaustless field of research for the student of nature," with a "wealth of natural beauty unsurpassed in the world." The guide reminded readers that Florida had a surface area more than a fourth larger than the state of New York's with a population only about a third of Boston's, making it a vast territory for bloody sports endeavors. And while many of Florida's native creatures were "queer and unnatural," a hunter faced few dangers except from "Eve's old enemies."[32]

Guiding sportsmen into the tropical wilderness became a cottage industry. "Old Salts" were easily located hanging around the docks, eager to provide advice or hire out oxen teams and ships.[33] New Smyrna, Sand Point, Port Orange, and Daytona were towns nationally known for their hunting-guide services. A boat and sailing master could be hired for $4–5 a day in Cedar Key, and upon returning the exhausted fisherman could dine on Roquefort cheese, French wine, and oysters at a restaurant kept by a Swiss immigrant. Local guides generally provided the basics in terms of tents and cooking utensils, but wealthy sports enthusiasts were advised to bring their own tents, camping equipment, and firearms. Some shipped their accoutrements, including boats, from their northern residences to Jacksonville, Cedar Key, and Manatee. While most writers praised Florida's hunting guides as knowledgeable and fearless, one writer confirmed that the "great trouble with many of the guides is their inordinate fondness for liquor."[34] Still, the opportunity to shoot and fish, with the guarantee of success, lured famous sportsmen to Florida, including Gilded Age presidents Ulysses S. Grant, Chester A. Arthur, and Grover Cleveland, who made hunting and fishing trips to Central Florida. Even Annie Oakley, the legendary markswoman, was photographed drawing a bead on an alligator from a tour boat on the Tomoka River.[35]

Hardship of travel was part of the thrill for Gilded Age adventurers who embraced the ideal of going native, "casting aside the restraints of the market place and the demands of fashionable drawing rooms." The truly adventurous sportsmen bunked with the locals, who were generally hospitable, if lacking in social graces. In 1867, during his famous walk from Fernandina to Cedar Key, naturalist John Muir encountered a group of loggers, whom he described as "wildest of all the white savages I have met." Despite their fearsome appearance, they gave Muir a portion of their pork and hominy without "hospitality or grudge."[36] Sportsmen crossed paths with cattle drivers in Manatee County by the 1870s. One hunter recalled a night spent with a Cracker family, sleeping on the floor atop ragged piles of clothes and washing up in tin pans. He was obliged to pass around the family's single teaspoon and tolerate the presence of one "flea-bitten hog," which "had been brought up just like the children."[37]

In reports from the field, Florida residents were described as sometimes dangerous, often as listless and sullen, or, at best, as quaint and childlike. Crackers were expected to be rough and "picturesque." African Americans were supposed to be humble and docile, willing to sing old plantation songs for the amusement of whites and lug heavy bags around without complaint.[38] Both black and white natives often failed to live up to Yankee expectations and imaginations. One 1875 visitor recorded that the region between Tallahassee and Jacksonville was "a country with the dry rot," its people—black and white—shiftless and lazy. John Muir claimed that Crackers were covered in the most "incurable dirt that I ever saw, evidently desperately chronic and hereditary."[39]

It is difficult to know what illiterate residents thought of the Yankee sportsmen in their fancy boots and store-bought tents, especially those who, in the words of a fellow traveler, came "equipped with more prejudices than their well-filled traveling-bags could contain." But for poverty-stricken Floridians, the racial and social slurs were probably familiar, and at least the fees and tips helped families stay afloat during lean seasons. Tourism jobs were frequently available, and despite the racial tensions of the age, individuals like African American steamboat pilots Spencer Campbell and Clifton Lane won fame and respect in their professions. The majority of nonofficer personnel aboard Florida steamers were black; visitors often recalled the encounters with cooks and stewardesses who had been former slaves. Dan McQueen, the pilot of the *Belle of the Suwannee*, earned a master's and pilot's license, plus over $40 a month for his services.[40] While

most black Floridians endured travelers' insults and ignorance with fortitude, poor white Floridians were less generous with Yankees. A passenger
on an Ocklawaha steamer noted that his party was warned not to shoot
at alligators, because the Crackers—Florida's other wild creatures—often
shot back.[41]

Reconstruction-era guides enticed Yankee marksmen to come south in
the wintertime, so that the carnage could be perpetual. "It is during the
cold season, when northern sportsmen are confined indoors, that the
game is most plentiful in Florida. Deer, bear, wild cat, raccoon, 'possum,
wild turkey, ducks, geese, snipe, woodcock, quails, partridge, and curlews
are plentiful, and offer fine hunting; while the rivers, bays, and lakes invite
the stranger to the pleasures of the rod, filled as they are with schools of
the finest fish." Hunting on horseback was a thrill along the Indian River,
where "swamp ponies dash through the palmetto scrub with extraordinary swiftness. Many deer are shot on the beach." Even the most inexpe-
rienced greenhorn was guaranteed to take home some antlers, and an accomplished hunter like A. J. Alexander of Kentucky could kill sixty deer in
a three-week spree. Florida pumas were deemed as large as royal Bengal
tigers, giving Florida a safari mystique that appealed to big game hunters.
Moonlit bear hunts could be conducted on the beaches when the large
animals emerged from hibernation, eager to scoop up turtle eggs from the
sands. Sportsmen in search of feathered prey found Florida a happy hunting ground. Guidebook author "Rambler" bragged of taking five species of
ducks with one shot along Mosquito Lagoon, where thousands of the birds
nested. The same writer advocated shooting pelicans, though admitted that
the roseate spoonbills were nearly exterminated. According to "Rambler,"
game in Florida was so plentiful that natives "scorn to waste their powder"
on such measly trophies as opossums, raccoons, and squirrels.[42]

The exotic Florida creature most hunters anticipated bagging was the
alligator. "Alligator hunting is a sport peculiar to these southern latitudes
and can be enjoyed to perfection along the rivers, lakes, and lagoons of
Florida," one guidebook assured its readers. Passengers often shot at the
reptiles from the decks of steamboats, though it required a good eye to
find them, as they resembled rotten logs in the river, submerged and still.
"Hunting parties for Lake Harney are made up at Enterprise, on the Upper St. Johns. The expense is not much and the amusement prodigious,"

the guide continued.[43] A day would be spent blasting into the lake, which roiled with froth and blood as dozens of the creatures were hit. One party killed 162 alligators in a single afternoon. Conservation was never an issue for Victorian sportsmen, who were incapable of imagining a time when alligators might be endangered. "The hand of every man is against them," one witness wrote, "and they are slain by the hundreds; but this havoc makes no perceptible inroad on their numbers."[44]

Florida fishing was the other major attraction for sporting types. Punta Gorda acquired a reputation for tarpon fishing. At Jupiter, according to the 1875 guidebook by "Rambler," fish choked the inlet, and schools of bluefish and pompano "lash its waters into a foam. The strongest tackle is in momentary danger of being carried away. Men absolutely tire of working the reel. Their arms swell with the continual strain and what is called sport becomes the hardest kind of work." On the Indian River, the channel bass was the great game fish. President Chester A. Arthur proved to be the "First Angler" by snagging five ten-pound bass in Reedy Creek, near Kissimmee.[45]

The waters around Key West were also hailed as a fisherman's paradise, where legendary catches became staples of barroom conversation. Well-heeled anglers generally avoided stopping at Key West for more than tackle, however, as the town offered only a few shabby hotels. Its eclectic ethnic, social, and racial mixture was also disturbing to sedate Northerners. A few prominent tourists did enjoy their southernmost city sojourns, including James Henshall, a famous author of sporting and camping books, and Winslow Homer, the great painter who drew inspiration from the waters during his visit in the 1880s. By the turn of the century, the Keys were crowded with private yachts, as wealthy sportsmen stalking tarpon and kingfish followed in the wake of Zane Grey, novelist and angler whose articles in *Field and Stream* promoted Florida's bounty. After 1912, sportsmen and travelers sometimes made Key West their final destination before boarding boats bound for Havana. The city acquired a reputation as a party town, but also as a place where anxious boosters would buttonhole tourists, demanding to know what they thought of the burg and its prospects for development. One Chicago traveler was plainspoken—find ways to keep people in port longer and build better hotels. Without acceptable facilities, only the most determined traveler would opt for a vacation in Key West.[46]

Not everyone was willing to bestow the ultimate title of sporting heaven on Florida. An English hunter wrote in 1875 that Florida was not truly a paradise for sportsmen and that the Bureau of Immigration was issuing pamphlets bound to disappoint future tourists and homesteaders because of the "unsparing liberality" with which they painted Florida as a land of milk and honey and game. Anyone planning to travel or settle in Florida needed to be aware of the hard work required to make either hunting or farming successful. Though Florida was not Eden, the writer allowed "the sport is still sufficiently good to please those who go in for sport and not for slaughter; though the fare is hard, and the drawbacks neither few nor insignificant, I know no time I ever enjoyed more, taken altogether, than the months of wild life I spent in the forests, prairies, swamps, and mangrove-clad keys of Florida."[47]

Sensitive visitors and residents disliked Florida's new reputation as a killing field. "Sportsmen should not come to this land of promise and performance unless they can control their instincts," one sportswriter warned, allowing that the excess of game took away something of the thrill of the hunt. Harriet Beecher Stowe was offended by the pastime of shooting alligators from steamers. "The decks of boats are crowded with men whose only feeling seems to be a wild desire to shoot something," she complained to the *Semi-Tropical* magazine. She respected the desires of real hunters, but "to shoot for the mere love of killing is perfect barbarism, unworthy of any civilized man." She warned that a "war of extermination" would be waged against Florida wildlife without stricter game laws and protection. And in a practical vein, she noted that the passengers of the steamboat were probably in more danger than the river reptiles when "a perfect fusillade" was released at the cry of "dar's a gator!"[48]

The sportsmen and the first waves of active, vigorous tourists learned that Florida was a wilderness in more than just its abundance of fish and game. Still largely a frontier, in the postwar period Florida had its share of roughness and lawlessness. A resident of Mineral Springs in Suwannee County held that the entire region had been settled by dishonest and crude people, and begged his uncle, "Don't stop anyone from coming out but a rogue or a drunkard, as there are plenty of them now."[49] Most towns had only been settled for a brief period and lacked basic public services. Streets were by turns dusty or muddy; buildings had been rapidly thrown together. Visitors to Palatka complained about nearly being trampled by horses running wild in the streets and kept awake all night by wailing prisoners in the makeshift jail. Even long- established communities rarely presented pleasant facades. In 1900, Pensacola was deemed unfit to be a tourist town, due to its unpaved streets and central square that served as a garbage dump. Buzzards were ever present in Florida communities, a necessary evil for disposing of waste. Cockroaches were the bane of hotels; one Lakeland visitor claimed with only slight exaggeration that he had watched a herd of the nasty bugs move his thirty-pound suitcase across his room.[50] Human predators were also endemic where tourists gathered. Jacksonville was notorious for its cardsharps, pickpockets, and con artists who romanced wealthy widows. Pensacola's brothels were its major attraction, and illegal salons and clandestine gambling dens posing as reputable clubs were a mere stroll away from every Jacksonville hotel. Even Carry Nation could not reform the women of Jacksonville's notorious LaVilla brothel district during a 1907 visit. Critics charged that Florida town fathers purposefully looked the other way and refused to enforce ordinances, arguing that tourists required amusements, no matter how sinful, and that to crack down on them would be bad for business. Profits outweighed community standards, and tourists who would be in residence for only a brief period had little motivation to support better law enforcement.[51]

Some tourists held it was only their due to be catered to in this way, a payback for the outrageous prices they were being charged in hotels and restaurants. Floridians in tourist areas quickly became masters at "skinning the Alligators"—fleecing tourists who in turn felt liberated from hometown strictures and standards.[52] One of the few positive rebuttals to this practice came from Tallahassee. Traveling journalist Julian Ralph noted bowls of flowers sent by the women of the town to the tourist women staying in a capital city hotel. The gifts proved "that for perhaps the first time in our lives we were domiciled in a pleasure resort wherein the people had not been demoralized by so strong a desire for gain that all kindlier human impulses were crowded out of their lives."[53]

Most Florida tourists came as couples or in travel parties of like-minded adventurers. Family travel was still rare, but one option for vacationing families came through the Chautauqua movement. Founded at Lake Chautauqua in New York by John Vincent, a Methodist minister, the original purpose of the summer camp was to train Sunday school teachers. But the movement soon expanded and began to draw on the traditions of the 1820s lyceum, which had offered edifying lectures to city residents as a form of continuing education. Chautauqua combined religious sermons, musical performances, patriotic orations, and general amusements. It was a family-friendly vaudeville. Held under tents or in camps, there were some thirty Chautauqua venues across the nation by the mid-1880s.[54]

Florida's Chautauqua was based in the Panhandle and operated during the winter. A vacation at the Chautauqua encampment at DeFuniak Springs, where gothic-style buildings were erected around a lake and campground, cost far less than a stay at a resort. Steamship lines and railroads offered special excursion rates to the camp. Room and board was $10 for a week, and five days of lectures could be purchased for $1.[55] Middle-class families, often mingling with schoolteachers, lived in tents and cabins for weeks while attending nightly lectures, concerts, and fireworks. The *Tallahassee Weekly Floridian* hailed the inaugural season of 1886: "A year or two ago the site of this Chautauqua was almost unknown. . . . Had anyone been bold enough to venture this prophecy, that within a few short months this wilderness in Western Florida would become the site of a tabernacle where the highest achievements of art, music, literature, philosophy and religious culture would be presented before a multitude of eager and upturned faces, such a prophecy would have seemed utterly absurd." Chautauqua camps lasted for thirty years, offering one of the few truly family-oriented pleasures in the age before roadside attractions and amusement parks.[56]

The premiere Florida tourist attraction of the late nineteenth century with appeal to all travelers, young and old, sick or healthy, was Silver Springs. For decades, it defined Florida to Northern visitors who made the exotic journey to gaze into its pristine depths. Forming the headwaters of the Silver River, which flows into the Ocklawaha, it was easily accessible by Florida's small river steamboats. It became a mythic place, the end of a journey that could seem truly dangerous and treacherous to the naive tourist.

By 1868, Palatka was growing as a tourist town thanks to its proximity to Silver Springs. One settler noted that "Palatka is full of northerners—invalids and tourists—sail boats and pleasure parties pass daily and they often call and visit us. There is plenty of life and stir on the river." In the early 1870s, several hotels sprang up to accommodate steamboat passengers. The Putnam House, the St. Johns House, the Eggleston House, and the Underwood House were usually full, and in the wintertime local residents could make pocket money by taking in boarders. Most of the population was transient; the town's resident population did not reach 1,000 until 1875. Despite some complaints of frontierlike conditions, Palatka received increasingly good notice in guidebooks. "Rambler" recounted a mouth-watering meal served in one of the hotels: "Delicious waffles, noble wild turkey (nobly served), tender lamb, adolescent chicken, light, sweet bread, potatoes, green peas, and other delicacies that ravished the heart and made glad the digestive apparatus."[57]

Departing from Jacksonville or Palatka on vessels operated by the Hubbard L. Hart line, tourists made the slow trip to Silver Springs. Part of the journey was often made at night, a harrowing and yet astonishing feat, as boats navigated by the lights of bonfires kindled in huge iron baskets atop the pilot-house or on the bow. Once at the springs tourists could board a novel kind of vessel, the glass-bottom boat. In 1878, a local named Hullam Jones applied a pane of glass to the flat bottom of a dugout canoe. He hoped to make it easier for workmen to locate and remove sunken logs from the river, but the unique vessel's potential for showing off nature was obvious. Young boys operated similar boats in the 1880s.[58] Touted by myriad journalists, the voyage to Silver Springs was often irresistible to tourists wintering in St. Augustine or Jacksonville. An 1875 guidebook described the fascination of gazing into the springs' depths. "For sixty feet downward we could look. . . . The bottom of this basin was silver sand, studded with pale emeralds, eccentric formations of lime-crystals—a bed of white coral in forms and colors that reminded us of the cunningly-wrought silver basins of Genoa." The attraction garnered praise from a wealth of celebrity visitors, including Ulysses S. Grant, William Tecumseh Sherman, Harriet Beecher Stowe, Thomas Edison, and Sidney Lanier. By the 1870s, it was receiving 50,000 tourists annually, making Silver Springs the true center of Florida's tourism industry.[59]

A sharp contrast was the former center of Florida tourism, St. Augustine. The Reconstruction period was generally a gloomy time for the Oldest City. Residents who sympathized with the Confederacy resented Northern visitors, and potential Yankee investors were wary of the questionable legitimacy of land sales. Some Confederate widows, like the "Madame Oliveras" patronized by journalist Whitelaw Reid, braided palmetto knickknacks such as "toy baskets, hats, napkin rings" to earn "greenbacks from the Yankees."[60] But the city's history was instructive, and St. Augustine was accustomed to changing hands, adapting to new regimes. A sign of renewed life for the tourism industry was the construction of the St. Augustine Hotel in 1869, on the block just north of the old market, the first such edifice erected since the 1840s. Citizens were annoyed by the growing tourist competition from Jacksonville and the towns along the St. Johns River. Boatmen on the St. Johns and innkeepers in Jacksonville were accused of lying to travelers, warning them away from St. Augustine with tales of overcrowding and high prices. Yet no further construction was undertaken, and the city's economy stagnated in the 1870s. In 1876, only 2,000 people lived in the town, which still lacked a reliable railroad connection to Jacksonville.[61]

A small trickle of winter visitors kept the city alive as residents worked to find some gimmick that would draw more tourists. A dusty museum, crammed with bones, battle-axes, stuffed birds, books, the jaw of a sperm whale, and the city's oldest piano was singularly unsuccessful.[62] From 1875 to 1886, a group of Kiowa, Comanche, and Arapahoe Indians imprisoned in Fort Marion were enlisted as a kind of convict circus, encouraged to put on dances and draw pictures in return for privileges within the town. A "buffalo hunt" was staged, starring an uncooperative steer. The two-week visit of former president Ulysses S. Grant in 1879 was trumpeted as a coup for the town, sparking balls and parties. Even with these efforts, there was little to enliven the "Naples of America." The town that had once been the tip of the tourist frontier was in serious danger of becoming a "stagnant backwater," avoided by the more active visitors plying the rivers and forests. Despite one guidebook's assertion that St. Augustine was the "point-de-mire" of Florida, and that to miss it "would be like traveling through Italy without entering the gates of Rome," more visitors agreed with Sidney

Lanier, who thought the best way to spend one's time at St. Augustine was to lie on the seawall and yawn.[63]

By the late nineteenth century, Florida was more familiar to the nation, perceived as a place of wild beauty where the deprivations of the Civil War had not been as severe as elsewhere in the South. But the practicalities of travel made it unattractive to less adventurous tourists, and especially to the elite, who were accustomed to luxurious sojourns in expensive resorts.

A tycoon's honeymoon would soon change everything.

THREE

A Winter Playground

Henry Morrison Flagler had a talent for making money. A partner of John D. Rockefeller, in 1885 Flagler was a newlywed on the cusp of retirement, an immensely wealthy individual who could have devoted the rest of his life to enjoying the rewards of his illustrious career. Yet he had a strange hankering to build a hotel in St. Augustine. Across the state, Henry Bradley Plant was the star of a parallel success story, a man who could make or break towns by where he placed his railroads. When he learned that Flagler was building a hotel, he decided to construct one, too. These occasional partners and friendly rivals launched the idea of Florida as a millionaire's playground, and in the process turned tourism into a potent force driving the state's economic development.

Born on January 2, 1830, in Hopewell, New York, Flagler was a flinty, often puritanical devotee to the Protestant work ethic. At age fourteen he took his first job with a grain company, and after a Civil War–era investment in a salt manufacturing company failed, he returned as a commission agent. He met fellow agent John D. Rockefeller, and the men became interested in the growing oil refinery business. Flagler helped Rockefeller secure loans and capital, serving as a cofounder of Standard Oil. Their business thrived. In just seven years, Flagler was ensconced in a Fifth Avenue mansion, though it was little consolation as his wife's health began to fail. In 1878, he took her to Jacksonville, in hopes of recovery. Flagler soon found Florida too indolent for his tastes, and the couple did not stay long.[1]

Mary Flagler died in 1881, and two years later Flagler married Ida Alice Shourds, who had served as his first wife's nurse. The couple began a delayed honeymoon in St. Augustine in December 1883. It was a nearly comatose town the couple chose for their wedding journey, difficult for even a captain of industry to reach. A traveler departed a St. Johns steamer at Tocoi and rode behind a miserable "cotton mill" engine on a tiny track. Otherwise, one arrived via ship or a bone-jarring journey on the Picolata stage. Still, the city was warm in the winter, secluded, and romantic.[2]

Flagler perhaps agreed with an 1869 assessment that if the South was a hundred years behind the North, then Florida and St. Augustine were even farther back in time.[3] Yet something in the Oldest City appealed to Flagler, capturing his imagination. Flagler was intrigued by St. Augustine's history and potential for development, if only railroad lines and fine hotels were constructed. The Flaglers returned to St. Augustine early in 1885, and by the end of March the tycoon had made up his mind. He was going to tap the Oldest City's potential; he was going to open it up to the world and make it the "Newport of the South." He would build a beautiful, ultramodern hotel in the heart of the town, a hotel named for Florida's legendary discoverer. The Hotel Ponce de Leon would be a wonder of America, a fabulous lodge designed to blend with the Old World feel of the town. The Ponce de Leon was the extent of Flagler's plans in 1885, but it proved to be merely the beginning of Flagler's influence as a major developer of Florida via its tourism industry.[4]

Flagler's true motivations for building the Hotel Ponce de Leon remain a subject of speculation and debate. Flagler claimed that everything he did in Florida was simply for his own pleasure and to help the people of the state. Historians rarely credit such altruism without some skepticism. Rockefeller overshadowed Flagler in the story of Standard Oil, and Flagler wanted to leave his own legacy and make a mark in the business world independent of his more famous colleague. As a millionaire, he might simply have been indulging expensive fancies; his friends certainly accused him of such behavior. At least one biographer believes that Flagler was driven by remorse over his first wife's death and his failure to spend more time in Florida with her.[5]

Whatever his true motivations, Flagler plunged into the project with typical Yankee vigor. He established a lifelong alliance with Dr. Andrew Anderson, a St. Augustine native and one of its most influential citizens. Anderson sold Flagler parcels of land and assisted in negotiating for more property. In May 1885, Flagler and Thomas Hastings, a young architect, drew up a rough sketch of the Ponce de Leon after an all-night session in Anderson's parlor at Markland, the plantation home where Clarissa Anderson had entertained Yankee occupiers during the Civil War. That summer saw a flurry of activity and an unusual amount of local co-operation, as the entire community and surrounding towns were eager to see what the tycoon would do for their economy. The project became both Flagler's favorite plaything and his philanthropy, as it put hundreds of locals to work. Flagler made numerous visits to oversee the construction, on occasion even blending in with the workers.[6]

The Hotel Ponce de Leon was finished in the late spring of 1887, but did not officially open until January 10, 1888. It was one of the first major poured concrete structures in America, and had cost $2.5 million to build and furnish. The verdict was that it was worth every penny. Covering most of a five-acre lot, the hotel was designed to reflect the glories of the Spanish Renaissance, with sunny courts, cool fountains, long verandas, and massive towers. Tiffany glass twinkled, enlivened by the novelty of electric lights. The sprawling grounds featured tropical gardens and orange groves, while a nautical motif ran through the hotel's decorations, with mermaids, shells, and dolphins springing to life from doorknobs and fountains. Galleries featured murals of St. Augustine's violent history. The hotel contained some 450 sleeping apartments, arranged into single rooms, suites, and bridal chambers. Residents traversing the two miles of hallways and corridors at last arrived at rooms whose furnishings were valued at $1,000 each. Obviously, the Ponce de Leon's guests would not be struggling invalids or sweat-grimed sportsmen, but the crème de la crème of American society. The hotel's most notable first-season patron was President Grover Cleveland.[7]

Before the Hotel Ponce de Leon was completed, Flagler recognized the need for a second hotel, one more moderately priced, to absorb the overflow of expected crowds.[8] Work on the Alcazar, across the street from the Ponce de Leon, was begun in early 1887. The hotels shared architects, workmen, and furnishings, but the Alcazar was designed with a Moorish flavor. It opened to guests in 1888 and was fully completed in 1889. Smaller than the Ponce de Leon, the Alcazar was four stories high and built around a courtyard. Arcades housing shops and restaurants opened onto this cool space. Gardens bloomed and fountains splashed at the entrance. To the rear were more active pleasures, including swimming pools for men and women, tennis courts, a croquet lawn, and an archery range. Though the two floors of rooms accommodated relatively few guests, many travelers favored the Alcazar, and not just for its lower prices. Most European tourists considered it more aesthetically pleasing than the Ponce de Leon, and Americans liked the convenience of its shopping and activities.[9]

The steady influx of tourists made Flagler expand his resort holdings. In 1888, he purchased the Casa Monica Hotel, which flanked the Alcazar and had been under construction for years. Renamed the Cordova, it completed a picturesque neighborhood of Spanish-themed resorts that would have been shocking to the actual Spanish founders of the city. Just as Flagler had envisioned, the Oldest City could easily serve as an alternative to Europe; why cross the water when equally quaint sites and even better hotels could be found in Florida?[10] In a move that predated Epcot's miniature villages by almost a century, Flagler created a make-believe realm that reflected what Americans imagined the Old World to be like.[11]

The Hotel Ponce de Leon and its rivals revitalized St. Augustine. The Oldest City woke from a half-century slumber, eager to welcome the rich and active, though the occasional invalid was unavoidable. New businesses sprang up to cater to winter visitors. Flagler's guests were eager to see and be seen. Virtually every leisure activity could be indulged on the hotel grounds, in the city, or along the shore. Horseback riding, strolling, picking oranges, fishing, sailing, playing tennis, swimming, shopping, dancing, and feasting, the St. Augustine tourist was inexhaustible. The long days of sitting on the veranda and coughing into a handkerchief were a thing of the past. Even the laziest tourist could take in a nightly concert, and people-watching was a sport with so many of America's richest families in town for the season. "I know of no place, public or private, where the power of wealth so impresses itself upon the mind as at this group of Florida hotels," journalist Julian Ralph reported.[12] Women displayed wardrobes of "infinite variety," changing clothes several times a day. Lavish balls and parties were often capped with fireworks launched from the roof of the Ponce de Leon, and the *Tatler*, a society paper published only during the winter season, detailed what everyone wore, even speculating on the size and number of Alice Flagler's pearls.[13]

Tellingly, the beauty of Flagler's hotels was in stark contrast to the wild, overgrown interior of Florida. They were complementary contradictions, creating a strange new world where one might enjoy the natural warmth and sunshine, but the real focus remained on the artificial, the inauthentic. Flagler's complex was "a melody or poem in gray and red and green," so much more amazing because it stood on the threshold of a wilderness. Ralph insisted that entering a Flagler hotel was like being invited into a royal palace, but how many readers of his book had ever entered a real castle, much less one constructed in a jungle? An Alhambra in the forest was a Gilded Age fantasy. The mythic spires of Flagler's resorts reflected an artist's conception of a Spanish Renaissance palace, not a precise reproduction.[14] The hotels were an attraction independent from the climate, a forerunner of magic kingdoms to come, offering dreams for sale and thematic delights for those who could afford them.[15]

While the typical Flagler guest was wealthy, not all visitors were robber barons or silver mine heiresses. The Alcazar and Cordova developed as overflow hotels designed to be more modestly priced, if still charging rates well above what the average American of the 1890s could afford. Though certainly not out of the range of the upper middle class, it was difficult for people actively pursuing careers to abandon their professions during the winter months, traditionally the busiest for many occupations. Age became a factor; older men were far more likely to have the time as well as the money for leisure. Men who had "made their pile" could afford a lengthy stay in St. Augustine, if not always a suite at the Ponce de Leon. They almost always traveled with spouses, and older couples frequently chaperoned younger relatives, especially marriageable-age women. The second-tier Flagler hotels specialized in people who liked to bask in the reflected glory of the rich, perhaps hoping that a pretty daughter, niece, or cousin might attract the eye of an industrial scion. Those who could afford only the bare necessities for a vacation were not completely shut out, as old-style boardinghouses of St. Augustine still did a brisk business, charging $8–10 per week.[16]

Some young women even dared to come without their families, though never without an official duenna. The Pennsylvania Railroad advertised a special excursion to Florida for unattached young women. The young women would be placed in the charge of a female railway employee. This paragon would minister "to the necessities in a most intelligent manner, as experience has thoroughly educated her in the intricacies of railway travel and usage." Both a "companion and guide," the "chaperon also stands to unescorted ladies in the exact relation that the title implies."[17] Romance was common despite elaborate precautions, and wedding trips to St. Augustine were also famous, enough that a German guest called the Ponce de Leon "the El Dorado for honeymooners."[18]

Flagler was generally viewed as a bountiful benefactor to his adopted city. Not only did he bring tourists, he built churches, such as the magnificent Memorial Presbyterian Church where his daughter was buried. Flagler also contributed substantially to a host of civic projects, including street paving, drainage systems, electric lighting, and the construction of a new city hall and a school for African American children. He provided funds for an improved railroad depot and built homes for his workmen.[19] But Flagler was not satisfied with the grand hotels and city beautification; it seemed that he could not be still. He was determined to bring "to life . . . a region hitherto unconscious of its destinies." And that could be accomplished only through the improvement of Florida railroads.[20]

Flagler had no experience as a railroad man, but as an accomplished entrepreneur he understood the importance of improving transportation networks. He began by purchasing a number of small northeastern Florida lines. The Jacksonville, St. Augustine and Halifax River Railroad entered his portfolio in 1885, as a way of improving service to St. Augustine. Railroads quickly became collectibles to him. In 1888, he bought two more short lines, and later that year he bought a logging road that ran from East Palatka to Daytona, laid standard-gauge tracks, and made the route from Jacksonville to Daytona the most modern in the South. Bridges naturally followed, and by January 20, 1890, an all-steel bridge across the

St. Johns River allowed a traveling tycoon to step into his private railroad car in New York and not emerge until he could taste the tangy sea air of St. Augustine.[21]

The Flagler railroad grew like a vine, sprouting hotels as fruit. Flagler purchased and renovated the Ormond Beach Hotel, adding to its appeal with a golf course. The hotel quickly gained a reputation for romance. "What a sanctuary for Cupid's victims is that white sand road to the ocean at Ormond," a visitor chuckled. In 1903, Flagler's guests enjoyed a new sport when a pair of hotel managers introduced automobile racing to the beach.[22]

Flagler could have halted at Ormond, as Daytona residents were unresponsive to his development overtures. South of Daytona, Florida was an authentic wilderness, where scattered settlers and citrus growers depended on sailboats to transport their crops to market. So far, Flagler had only purchased and improved existing lines, not undertaken the Herculean task of unfurling ribbons of steel through a jungle. But the lure of South Florida, the frost- proof land of perpetual summer, was strong. Flagler was certain the region would appeal to tourists of his class, and anyone else who could afford the fare. Plus, providing transportation for citrus growers would be instantly profitable. In 1892, Flagler obtained a state charter to build a railroad along the Indian River as far as Miami.[23]

By November 1892, the line reached New Smyrna. On February 6, 1893, a train puffed into Titusville, and on February 27 it was greeted in Cocoa. The tracks reached Eau Gallie on June 26 as some 1,500 men worked to build up rail beds and lay steel as close to the coast as possible. On January 29, 1894, the Flagler train arrived at Ft. Pierce, and on March 22 the line was complete as far as Lake Worth.[24]

Flagler made a number of visits by boat to the Palm Beach area in the early 1890s. Just as in St. Augustine, he saw the sleepy hamlet's potential. Wedged between beautiful Lake Worth and the Atlantic Ocean, it was the most splendid location imaginable for a hotel. But building a Gilded Age resort in the wilderness of South Florida was a far greater logistical problem that constructing one in the heart of St. Augustine. On May 1, 1893, work began on the Royal Poinciana. Flagler's materials were hauled to the site in every way possible: via ship, train, and even aboard old Mississippi River steamers Flagler purchased specially for the project. Black workers were initially housed in a tent and shanty city they called the "Styx." Eventually all workers were moved to West Palm Beach. Like Charon in the underworld, they rowed across Lake Worth every morning to take up their duties.[25]

The Royal Poinciana opened on February 11, 1894, less than a year after its groundbreaking. Its entrance overlooked Lake Worth, and the Atlantic was only a few hundred yards to its rear. A massive wooden structure, it contained 1,200 windows and 1,300 doors, 540 bedrooms, and a dining hall that could seat well over 1,000 guests. Verandas, a casino, lounges, and parlors completed the amenities. At the time, it was believed to be the largest hotel in the world. In its heyday, guests would pay up to $100 a night for rooms and meals, though less extravagant lodgings were also available.[26]

The Royal Poinciana season ran from December to April. Guests stayed active with tennis, motorboats, and bicycles. A trolley cart pulled by a donkey took children to the beach. Clad in long skirts and white blouses with leg-of-mutton sleeves, women took seaside teas, while their husbands and sons puttered on the golf course in knickers and stiff collars. Fourteen hundred attendants raced to fulfill every whim, and could often be spotted pushing invalids (or lazy people) around in wheelchairs. A beach censor made sure that female bathers kept their black stockings up, lest a tantalizing bit of skin be revealed. The social scene peaked every year with a Washington's Birthday Ball.[27]

Wealthy Americans were the prominent celebrities of the Gilded Age, and the national media regaled readers around the country with tales and images of their follies on the beach. Americans goggled at the photographs and stories of life in Flagler hotels, where leaders of society gathered in a strange show of both simplicity and elegance.[28] "What, indeed, could more conspicuously signify luxury to a January-chilled general public," architectural historian Susan Braden writes, "than visual images and society-column descriptions of vacationing Astors and Vanderbilts yachting or playing golf or amusing themselves at tea dances held under the swaying Florida palm trees?"[29]

The Royal Poinciana proved so popular that Flagler followed his St. Augustine plan and immediately began construction of a second hotel on the Atlantic Ocean across from the Royal Poinciana. Opened in 1896 as the Palm Beach Inn and renamed The Breakers in 1901, it contained 250 guest rooms, along with a swimming pool. It was located next to a 1,000-foot pier. The Breakers burned in 1903 and was rebuilt in 1904.[30]

Flagler assumed his railroad and his string of resorts would end at Palm Beach. To push farther south would be foolish. Miami in the late 1800s was a squalid settlement, with only a few residents clustered around the remains of Ft. Dallas. Earlier attempts to settle the region with coconut plantations had been miserable failures. The region's one true potential, however, was tourism. Travelers had previously noted the region's possibility as a haven for invalids. In 1875, guidebook author "Rambler" advised "no spot in Florida is more healthy," but the lack of reliable transportation and comfortable accommodations stymied development.[31] One woman, however, was determined to see this change.

Julia De Forest Sturtevant Tuttle, a Cleveland widow, inherited a tract of land on the north bank of the Miami River from her father. She dreamed of developing Miami into a resort community, with her property as the centerpiece of a hotel complex. She needed the railroad to reach Miami before any construction could begin; therefore she wrote to Flagler, offering him part of her holdings. She was ignored. The tycoon was swamped with similar offers and schemes, and could hardly be faulted for avoiding yet another fervent plea for assistance.[32]

Nature intervened. The winter of 1894–1895 saw a record-breaking freeze that destroyed orange groves in Central Florida. Citrus production dropped from 5,500,000 to 150,000 crates in one year. As Flagler's line also carried massive amounts of freight, Flagler sent agents out to investigate conditions and offer loans to orange growers devastated by the event. According to the traditional story, Tuttle caught up with Flagler's representatives and presented them with a box of undamaged orange blossoms from her neighborhood, telling them to take the box to their boss. Intrigued by this proof of Miami's superior climate, Flagler traveled down to meet Tuttle, who gave him a tour of the tiny settlement, including the spectacular foliage of Ralph Monroe's estate at Coconut Grove. Flagler was hooked, and the railroad, renamed the Florida East Coast Railway, came south. For her determination, Tuttle would become known as the "Mother of Miami."[33]

Unfortunately for Tuttle, Flagler's hotel, the Royal Palm, meant that her dreams of a resort on her own property would go unfulfilled in her lifetime. Flagler continued to build ahead of actual demand, though he warned his hostess that he could not envision Miami as anything more than a "fishing village" for his guests, just as he saw West Palm Beach as a residence for the "help" at the Royal Poinciana. Work on the Royal Palm began in February 1896, and the Beaux-Arts-style hotel opened on January 16, 1897. Situated on fifteen acres where the Miami River empties into Biscayne Bay, the Royal Palm stood five stories high, providing guests with a spectacular view of the ocean, the bay, the pine woodlands, and even the Everglades. Featuring 400 guest rooms, a grand ballroom, and a casino, and powered by its own electrical plant, the Royal Palm quickly became known as the winter home of the Astors, Armours, Goulds, and Rockefellers. The Miami resort developed a reputation as the place for "nice"—that is, more sedate—millionaires to spend a long winter season, while the younger and more restless elite chose Palm Beach.[34]

Flagler became a city builder by default, as the hundreds of laborers required for his projects had needs of their own, especially for housing, medical care, and other services. The temporary workers' camp across from Lake Worth was incorporated as West Palm Beach. Flagler invested in building permanent housing for his future staff of the Royal Poinciana and The Breakers. Likewise, Miami was the "city that Flagler built." He provided paved streets and electricity along with hotels and recreation, and constructed a terminal dock for his line of steamships, making Miami the birthplace of the Florida cruise industry.[35] Flagler's generosity extended to churches, hospitals, and schools. His ecumenical openhandedness was frequently applauded: he constructed sanctuaries for Catholic, Methodist, and Presbyterian congregations. Thanks to Flagler's ambitions, major metropolitan areas of Florida were born virtually mature.[36]

The construction of hotels and streets in Miami was a welcome distraction to Flagler. In 1897, Alice Flagler was permanently confined to an insane asylum; Flagler never saw her again. He changed his residency to Florida and used his influence to have the legislature pass an act legalizing insanity as grounds for divorce. His immediate divorce—and remarriage just days later in 1901—harmed his reputation, but Flagler's continued contributions to Florida institutions, including the University of Florida, bought him a measure of forgiveness. For his new bride, Mary Lily Kenan, Flagler built Whitehall, a cavernous $2.5 million marble palace at Palm Beach.[37]

Flagler's final act of Florida development was his most ambitious but ultimately his least successful. At seventy-five years old, Flagler had invested some $30 million in Florida, but he was not finished. One of the most far-fetched proposals of the nineteenth century was to run a railroad over the many small islands all the way to Key West. As early as 1831, a Key West newspaper sent a letter to Congress, begging for such an extension to aid the sea-bound city. In 1894, Jefferson B. Browne, collector of customs for the Port of Key West, published an article in *National Geographic* called "Across the Gulf by Rail." It was essentially an invitation for Flagler to take action. Key West was home to just under 20,000 people in 1895, and all of them were hopeful that the fantastic project would finally become a reality, making their town the "American Gibraltar" and providing an essential link in a vast overseas chain that would connect Florida to Central and South America. The building of the Panama Canal was perhaps the final inspiration for Flagler to act, as he could more easily envision Key West's potential for shipping and tourism once the vital passage between oceans was opened.[38]

Work on the overseas extension, better known as "Flagler's Folly," began in 1905 and continued for seven years. At the height of construction, some 4,000 men labored together in rugged isolation from the mainland. Workers were recruited from Philadelphia, Pittsburgh, and New York; black laborers were brought in from the Bahamas; and a host of Greeks, Cubans, and Italians joined the ethnic and linguistic mélange. A small number of "Conchs," natives of Key West, provided expert advice along with strong backs. Provisions, including fresh water, had to be hauled in from the mainland. Flagler's men battled heat, mosquitoes, and their Puritanical boss's ban on liquor, which was often dodged with the assistance of "booze boats" that smuggled contraband to the laborers.[39] Hurricanes slowed progress, but also subjected the engineering of the trestles to important tests. A small tourist boom was generated by the hundreds of sportsmen, curiosity seekers, and families of workmen who came to the tip of Florida during the building of the extension. The first train crossed to Key West on January 22, 1912, pulling Flagler's private car. Ten thousand people gathered to cheer and toss flowers at Flagler, and over the course of the day seven more trains arrived bearing Florida governor Albert W. Gilchrist, plus the assistant secretary of war and a host of foreign dignitaries.[40]

Flagler's hotels were only "qualified" financial successes, and his overseas railroad never made a profit.[41] The "Eighth Wonder of the World" was a $20 million engineering marvel, but it never enjoyed the expected surge in either produce shipping or the transportation of tourists. Key West failed to grow; in fact, its population declined. The Labor Day hurricane of 1935 smashed the extension, ripping apart tracks and washing away embankments. The Florida State Road Department acquired the mangled line, and in 1938 the overseas highway opened. Automobiles instead of trains reached the Keys over Flagler's viaducts and bridges.[42]

Flagler did not live to see his final achievement come crashing down amid tropical gales. Increasingly feeble after the completion of the extension, Flagler, like his railroad, had reached the end of the line. Trusted associates operated the Flagler System, which included the Florida East Coast Railway, the luxury hotels, and a vast web of businesses, from realty agencies to electric companies, steamship lines, and ferries. Flagler spent his final years at Whitehall, dying of "old age and sheer exhaustion" in 1913. His body was carried to St. Augustine, where it rested at the Hotel Ponce de Leon before the funeral and burial at the Memorial Presbyterian Church.[43]

The second pillar of Florida tourism and development in the Gilded Age was Henry Bradley Plant, Flagler's friendly rival. A tale—perhaps fanciful but not impossible—claims that when Plant's Tampa Bay Hotel debuted in 1891, Flagler responded to Plant's invitation to attend the festivities with a mocking question—"Where's Tampa?" Plant immediately wired back, "Follow the crowds." In 1894, the exchange was reversed, with Flagler gamely urging Plant to follow the crowds to the Royal Poinciana at Palm Beach.[44]

Born in 1819 in Branford, Connecticut, Plant had a long career in the transportation business, beginning with his service as a deckhand on a steamship. With his wife, Ellen Elizabeth Blackstone, Plant moved to Georgia in 1854. The couple spent years living in hotels, and Plant would forever be an eager traveler. With the coming of the Civil War, Plant organized the Southern Express Company, which carried mail, packages, medicine, and supplies for the Confederacy. Trusting in the South's eventual recovery, Plant expanded his company during Reconstruction, and by 1875 it had some 3,000 agencies in cities and small towns, as well as a home office in New York. Plant's interests embraced another important facet of post–Civil

War recovery, railroad improvement. Plant bought short lines that crossed Georgia and Florida, and with a dozen partners (among them Henry Flagler) formed the Plant Investment Company in 1882, proposing further railroad development in the interior of Florida. The company purchased and constructed multiple rail lines, providing passenger and freight service to areas of Florida that had never before heard a train whistle. By the time his empire was complete, Plant owned 1.5 million acres of real estate and over 2,000 miles of railroad tracks. The most famous line of the Plant Investment Company was the Florida Southern Railroad, which stretched from Jacksonville to Tampa.[45]

In the 1880s, despite the threat of yellow fever, Plant decided to make Tampa his base of operations. This decision meant instant economic activity and prosperity for the port city, which triumphed over Cedar Key in the selection process. Plant built wharves, warehouses, and a small hotel called the Inn at Port Tampa. If "rails begat cities," Plant demonstrated that improved rail lines also revitalized existing communities, enabling them to grow to their full potential.[46]

In 1888, Plant began his masterwork, the Tampa Bay Hotel. His goal was to overshadow Flagler. Opened in 1891, the Tampa Bay Hotel soon became an attraction for a more international crowd, and was considered a wonder of the resort world.[47] Of Moorish design, two blocks long and four stories high, it contained 500 rooms and cost $3 million. Its furnishings, personally selected by Plant and his second wife, Margaret Josephine Loughman, during their tours of Europe, totaled $500,000 and required forty-one freight cars to transport. A "Gilded Age art museum where people could spend the night," the hotel's decor included chairs that had once belonged to Marie Antoinette, as well as a massive steam-driven music box.[48]

Guests of the Tampa Bay Hotel could enjoy a wealth of activities, including tennis, pitching horseshoes, golf, and billiards. The massive grounds provided attractive walks shaded by fruit trees and scented with flowers. Guides were available to take hunters and fishermen into the unspoiled landscape around Tampa. The dog-loving Plants even maintained a kennel on the property to provide canine companionship. A decade later, the grand hotel served as the headquarters of the U.S. Army during the staging operations of the Spanish-American War. Thousands of journalists, as well as celebrity warrior Teddy Roosevelt, made the Tampa Bay Hotel the "most famous hotel in the world." But despite its notoriety and novelty, the great hostelry, which had gone half a million dollars over budget, was never profitable. Plant claimed not to care; it was enough that he could sit in splendor and listen to his music box.[49]

In 1896, Plant began construction of another ambitious tourism project. The Hotel Belleview was the centerpiece of Belleair, a resort community overlooking Clearwater Harbor, just outside of Tampa. A planned community, it included one of Florida's first championship golf courses and a number of recreational and sports-themed buildings, among them a marvel of the age, an asphalt circular bicycle track capable of hosting international competitions. In sharp contrast to its predecessors' Spanish themes, the Belleview drew inspiration from airy Alpine chalets. Millionaires could park their private cars on separate tracks near the hotel. Set on a high bluff, the hotel provided its guests with a spectacular view of the Gulf of Mexico across Sand Key. It proved so popular that additional extensions were required into the 1920s.[50]

Plant, unlike Flagler, was a railroad man first. He came to the hotel business as an afterthought, but saw hotels as important and enjoyed both building new ones and revitalizing old ones. He scooped up existing hotels along his lines, most of them named for their home cities: the Hotel Kissimmee, the Ocala House, the Hotel Punta Gorda, and the Ft. Myers Hotel. He also added the Seminole Hotel in Winter Park to his vast collection.[51]

Plant's railways and investment brought people and activity to an underpopulated part of the state. Just as the state's east coast owed much to Flagler, the southwest corner of Florida saw Plant as a driving force, an integrator of transportation and travel industries, if not exactly a philanthropic benefactor. Plant lacked Flagler's passion for community development and do-gooding. Unlike Flagler, he did not have to build cities from scratch, only to bring development to sleepy towns. He encouraged tourism as merely another business proposition, not as a whim, and failed to develop any consistent theme or organization for his hotels. Plant died in 1899, and his widow successfully challenged and broke his will in 1902. She sold off his hotel empire. The Tampa Bay Hotel suspended operations in 1929, and in 1933 became home to the University of Tampa.[52]

Though of different design, Flagler's and Plant's hotels had much in common. All were designed to appeal to the wealthy traveler, not the ordinary citizen. All conveyed and signified glamour and modernity at the turn of the century. Theatrical, they were the castles of their time, and included the highest standards of technology and amenities.[53]

The Flagler and Plant hotels were also exclusive, and not only in terms of wealth. African Americans and Jews were generally not admitted. Staffing at the hotels reflected Gilded Age prejudices. Hotel employees were often stashed in barracklike dormitories or forced to reside in basements and attics. A strict hierarchy operated behind the scenes, designating service entrances and elevators for menials.[54]

African American workers in Florida's hotels were assigned the hardest jobs at the lowest pay. Black women were laundresses, a miserable, backbreaking profession in any era. African Americans who interacted with whites were forced to assume demeaning, childlike roles. The cakewalk, an entertainment in which elegantly dressed black couples promenaded or danced to win prizes from white guests, was a regular ritual in Florida hotels. Black waiters sang gospel songs, danced, and played baseball for their patrons' amusement. Though many workers surely found these expectations degrading, some African American individuals were successful in carving out tourism-related careers on their own terms. In Palm Beach, Haley Mickens managed the wheelchair concession, while in Miami Florence Gaskins operated a specialized cleaning service, keeping the resort wear of Royal Palm guests pristine.[55]

Rapid development and the constant shifting of focus from hotel to hotel, while exciting to the wealthy tourist, came with a price for certain regions of Florida. For the Oldest City, the southward march of railroad and the construction of ever-finer hotels meant that the elegant age of St. Augustine tourism was a brief one. The elite followed Flagler, who rarely returned after he opened his Palm Beach resort. A depression in 1893 and deep freezes in 1894–1895 further damaged the city's reputation. With the richest vacationers now in Palm Beach and Miami, St. Augustine became a turnstile city, catering to those just passing through. By the 1920s, St. Augustine had entered the "Alcazar era," where the B-list elite dominated the city and ordinary guests indulged in watching the semifashionable promenade. The great hotels declined in quality as Flagler's heirs failed as innkeepers. The Alcazar and the Cordova closed after the 1932 season, and the Ponce de Leon grew ever more shabby, having "long since lost any shred of its former chic," until it was abandoned as a hotel in 1967. Like its rival in Tampa, it now houses an educational institution, Flagler College. Otto Lightner purchased the Alcazar in 1947; it now shelters a museum of his Victorian art, as well as several businesses. After a stint as the St. Johns County Courthouse, the Cordova is again operating as the Casa Monica hotel.[56]

Flagler and Plant opened South Florida. In the words of a Miami city biographer, "Flagler's winter palaces civilized what until then had been a real jungle complete with Indians and crocodiles—one of the first instances where a pleasure industry, rather than farming, mining, or lumbering, did the pioneering."[57] What was opened for tourists naturally grew as people were needed to build homes and hotels, patrol the streets, clean rooms, and grow food. Together, Flagler and Plant brought enormous changes to Florida's economy. Their railroads connected aspiring towns with major cities, and the promotional literature they generated to advertise their hotels helped create a national image of Florida as a "comfortable, pleasurable, even utopian destination," luring tourists and settlers to the state. It was a synergistic relationship in every way between the railroads and the resorts, and the resorts and the people. Elite guests were pioneers; Crackers and millionaires could claim similar status as founders of Florida. Inevitably, by opening Florida to the elite, Flagler and Plant opened it to everyone. Florida would have developed without the tycoons' white-coated tourists, but at a much slower pace, with far less glamour.[58]

Though many Americans enjoyed living vicariously through the winter seasons of the fashionable, the wealthy tourists were not without their critics. One author described Palm Beach as "at best, as this country's social back door—at worst, as a kind of Buffet Society Babylon which some socially ill-advised soul unfortunately carved out of the wilds of a state which never should have been admitted to the Union, much let alone society, in the first place."[59] And by the late 1800s, the image of the tourist began to assume some of the negative stereotypes it bears to this day. Writers and cultural critics parodied the "gentle adventurers" in their long skirts and pith helmets, who ventured into the "wilds" of the Everglades (in reality, only a few miles from the their hotel) to pose with painted Seminoles, stuffed alligators, and grossly oversize, obviously artificial fish. Certainly these early travelers invited mockery, but the more serious observers pointed to how the growing influx of tourists led to demands for more facilities and infrastructure. In meeting tourists' basic needs for shelter, food, and amusement, the very attraction they came to view—Florida in its pristine wildness—was being destroyed.[60]

Even if their clients were mocked, the image that Flagler and Plant created of Florida was indelible and potent. "Partly as a result of this picturesque publicity, with its emphasis on Spanish and Moorish styles, the whole state of Florida came to be viewed as exotic, tantalizing, and fantasy-evoking," Susan Braden observes. Florida was, for roughly three decades, a state of imagination in terms of its atmosphere and its visitors, a paradise drenched in sunshine, Spanish towers, and tycoons' gilded dreams.[61]

But very soon, those dreams would be shared, and almost everyone would be encouraged to come and vacation in the new Eden.

Florida's oldest city and its first tourist destination, St. Augustine attracted guests who hoped the town's sea air and warm climate would cure tuberculosis and other respiratory complaints. Visitors often commented on the "Old World" aura of the city. The town's age and poverty are romanticized in this nineteenth-century print. While some guests found the city unique and charming, others complained about the poor facilities and lack of activities. Courtesy of Florida Photographic Archives.

Silver Springs was the principal Florida tourist attraction of the nineteenth century. After the Civil War, visitors reached Silver Springs aboard small river steamboats. This photograph from the 1880s shows the steamer *Okeehumkee* docked at the spring basin. Along with the well-dressed passengers are several African American crewmen whose knowledge of the river and its wildlife made for memorable voyages. Courtesy of Florida Photographic Archives.

SHOOTING ALLIGATORS.

Shooting at alligators from the deck of a steamboat was a popular pastime in the late 1800s. While sensitive residents and some sportsmen disliked the practice, it was irresistible to many travelers who could never imagine the big reptiles would ever be in short supply. This 1874 sketch of a scene on Lake Ocklawaha agrees with Harriet Beecher Stowe's assertion that steamboat passengers were often more endangered than the wild creatures whenever someone raised a cry of "dar's a gator!" Courtesy of Florida Photographic Archives.

In the nineteenth and early twentieth centuries, Florida's springs were utilized as spas, promising both relaxation and miracle cures. Entrepreneurs established hotels, water bottling plants, and swimming pools at most of Florida's major springs. Some resorts catered to out-of-state tourists, while others attracted mainly local clientele. White Springs, in Hamilton County, had a four-story bathhouse, where swimmers posed in this 1914 photograph. These resorts declined by the 1920s, as travel patterns changed and fewer people believed in the merits of spring water therapy. Courtesy of Florida Photographic Archives.

Henry Flagler's magnificent Hotel Ponce de Leon opened in St. Augustine in 1888. The opulent structure proclaimed a new era in Florida tourism, welcoming guests that included presidents, millionaires, and celebrities. Flagler established two more hotels in St. Augustine and went on to build the Florida East Coast Railway and a collection of ever more expensive resorts, including the Royal Poinciana in Palm Beach and the Royal Palm in Miami. Eventually Flagler's railroad stretched to Key West. Flagler's work helped make Florida tourism attractive to America's upper classes. Courtesy of Florida Photographic Archives.

Like his friendly rival Henry Flagler, Gilded Age tycoon Henry Plant established a grand hotel for the traveling elite. His Tampa Bay Hotel was a wonder of the world, and he soon built and purchased a chain of inns along his railroads, luring tourists to Florida's west coast. This 1896 advertisement highlights his hotels and their luxurious amenities, including ballrooms and swimming pools. The publicity generated by Flagler and Plant for their tourism ventures helped Americans develop an image of Florida as a winter playground for the rich. Courtesy of Florida Photographic Archives.

FOUR

Tin Can Heaven

"In time, this will be a real winter playground for New England and the Middle States; and here is the real wealth of Florida." In 1918, the author of *The Sunny South and Its People* was not always impressed by Florida, but he was willing to give it some worldly advice. "Good and sufficient hotels with reasonable rates, fair treatment of the tourists, and good highways connecting the many small towns throughout the State, will induce hundreds of thousands to visit it then who do not now; and thus the natives will have consumers for the fruits and the table foods they can produce. In this lies the future prosperity of the State."[1] Across Florida, entrepreneurs and civic boosters eagerly agreed with his assessment, and they began implementing a grand new age of tourism.

In the opening decades of the twentieth century, Floridians awakened to the possibility of tourism around the state and across class lines. Florida's cities learned a basic lesson from Flagler and Plant: winter tourists meant easy money. So what if guests were not Vanderbilts or Astors? As long as they stayed for a few weeks and spent money on food, goods, and entertainment, they could tide a community over the long summer doldrums. Why not build hotels, make some pictures, dream up some slogans, and see who would come?

New attitudes toward travel, conditions of prosperity, and advancing technology in the form of the automobile made the changes possible. The media played their role as well. This was the great age of promoters, publicity stunts, garish pictures, and lovely lies. Florida gained an international reputation as America's leisure paradise, and began moving away from its designation as a "Southern" state in terms of culture. Florida had been an asylum for the ill, a haven for the sportsman, and a playground for the rich. From 1900 to the end of World War II, Floridians flung open their doors and their palms, eager to harvest a new crop of on-the-move, on-the-make tourists. In the process, a sparsely populated state entered the mainstream of American life.

As always, a shift in American thinking about the merits of travel was an important factor in the rise of tourism among the middle and working classes. People had more leisure time than ever before; even industrial workers were beginning to receive regular vacations. As hours declined, wages rose, and by the 1920s the nation was experiencing an unprecedented wave of prosperity. The average American's income was approximately twice what he or she needed to meet the basic necessities of life. Thrift suddenly seemed old-fashioned; consumers were urged to buy on credit, to have the best of everything now and pay for it a month at a time. Traveling and watching motion pictures were the preferred recreational activities of the masses. People wanted to have fun, and things that had once been frowned upon—from makeup on girls' faces to weekends at the beach, sans bathing stockings—were now considered merely daring. America had finally escaped from its Puritan heritage, and few tourists considered social or moral uplift necessary to justify a few weeks away from home.[2]

Amusement parks were favorite vacation sites, with nearly 2,000 of the entertainment venues thriving around the country by 1919.[3] Jacksonville offered the tawdry allure of the amusement park in abundance. Though the city had lost its reputation as a primary tourist center, it offered a variety of entertainment complexes for both tourists and locals in search of cheap pleasures. The Ostrich Farm, Jacksonville's first amusement park, opened in the winter of 1898. Visitors enjoyed the novelty of watching ostrich races and riding in ostrich-drawn carts. The most adventurous tourist could even try saddling one of the big birds for a jaunt destined to end in humiliation. By 1907, the farm became a zoo and amusement park combined. The addition of animals (alligators, leopards, and sloths) along with shows (balloon ascents, dancing stallions, high-wire acts) and rides (merry-go-rounds and roller coasters) made the Ostrich Farm a local favorite, especially for young people who concluded their evenings with ice cream and courtship in the dance hall, all at a cost of a quarter. That same year the Dixieland Amusement Park opened in South Jacksonville. Billed as "the Coney Island of the South," the thirty-acre park along the river featured band concerts, a huge slide called the Dixie Drewdrop, a carousel, circle swings, a laughing gallery, and a "House of Troubles." It also offered river and pool swimming and a baseball diamond. Animal exhibits and souvenir stands completed the package, which lasted only a few years until fire destroyed the site. In 1916, the Southland Amusement Park was built on its remains, and the Ostrich Farm moved nearby. To the west of the city, the Jacksonville Electric Company operated Lincoln Park, an amusement park for African Americans. Equipped with a dance pavilion, roller coaster, food concessions, and a vaudeville stage, it was smaller than the parks open to whites. These corny, dangerous, and sometimes risqué amusements helped break the "rigidity" of the Victorian age, and offered enticement to almost everyone in Florida's gateway city.[4]

Along with providing cheap diversions, resort cities in Florida experienced a surge of hotel building in the early decades of the twentieth century. Many of the new hotels reflected the Plant and Flagler style, fantastic fantasies that played on Spanish, Moorish, or Victorian archetypes but rented rooms at more reasonable prices. Opened in 1910, Pensacola's San Carlos Hotel was built in the Spanish style with iron balconies, ivory embellishments, Louis XV tapestries, mosaic tiles, and large chandeliers. Described as "the culmination of an expression of progress by the citizenship of Pensacola," it was constructed partially on $100 subscriptions by locals, who had finally begun to see the wisdom of encouraging tourism as a way to attract further settlement and investment. The Vinoy Park Hotel, on St. Petersburg's waterfront, was a strange mix of Moorish arches and Georgian-style ballrooms. It promised "the blue sea and the sapphire sky and the same profusion of vivid flowers as greeted the earliest Spanish explorers on Florida's shores." Just as Flagler and Plant had drawn the moneyed elite, the Vinoy Park collected celebrity guests from the world of politics and sports, including Calvin Coolidge and Babe Ruth.[5]

St. Petersburg experienced a boom at the turn of the century, making it representative of the new style of Florida tourism. The opening of the Orange Belt railroad in the 1880s made the town more readily accessible, and as early as 1889 the railway was pitching tours of the "exotic and healthful" burg. A downtown pier offered swimming, fishing, and a toboggan slide, but these were not enough to bring in long-term visitors. While old-timers complained that attracting tourists would mean an end to simple pleasures, like hunting without a license or swimming naked in the bay, city fathers pressed on with plans. In 1897, newspaper headlines bragged that "No Place in Florida Offers Greater Attraction for the Tourist. . . . Broad Avenues, Fine Bicycle Roads, Elegant Hotel Accommodations." With the merger of the Plant System and the Atlantic Coast line in 1905, railroad promotion of St. Petersburg grew more fervent, and Northern travel agents organized Pullman car expeditions to the city. The first load of New Yorkers arrived in 1909, followed by tribes of midwesterners in 1913. To further promote the city, St. Petersburg resident Bill "Alligator Man" Carpenter took his show, which featured a six-foot-long specimen named "Trouble," all the way to Seattle, inviting people to spend the winter where real troubles were few.[6]

The massive publicity and coordination of transportation worked. Before World War I, St. Petersburg established a reputation as a town where the midwestern upper middle class, rather than eastern societal elites, came for long vacations. Most important, these tourists came back year after year, demonstrating astounding loyalty to the city. Beginning with the Illinois Society in 1902, guests formed "tourist clubs" based on home state identification. These institutions helped fellow travelers find lodgings and necessary services. They also served as tremendous community boosters.[7]

St. Petersburg voters elected Al Lang as their mayor in 1916, a choice that reflected the town's dependence on tourism. A sports promoter who had helped bring professional baseball's spring training to St. Petersburg, Lang sought new means of publicity for his town and sponsored a cleaning project that installed the famous green benches. Lang was also the driving force behind the Festival of States. Instituted in 1917 as a way of attracting guests and competing with other Southern cities' Mardi Gras celebrations, the four-day profusion of costume balls, parades, and concerts drew much of its participation from the tourist societies. Though severely shaken by World War I, the town continued to court tourists as a principal industry. In the 1920s, St. Petersburg was so deferential to winter visitors that it soundly defeated an attempt to levy tuition charges on the tourist offspring swelling public schools' rolls. Of course, not everyone was happy with the changes or was convinced that an economic dependence on tourism was healthy. One critic charged that St. Petersburg had "set out with malice aforethought to make itself a winter resort city par excellence and so it has no one to blame for what has happened."[8]

Most long-term tourists who lounged on the benches and marched in the parades arrived in St. Petersburg via the train, but by the 1920s a new form of locomotion had a great appeal to Florida's more restless travelers. In 1921, a guidebook of the Southern states eagerly encouraged tourists to plunge into the heart of the Everglades "where canal, railroads and highways have made possible what, only a few years ago, was thought of as a foolhardy venture." The author went on to praise the quality of Florida's hunting and fishing, urging his middle-class readers to enjoy tropical sports pleasures that, a generation earlier, were reserved for the elite.[9] If in 1900 the typical Florida tourist was a robber baron with a private rail car, by 1920 he or she was increasingly a citizen of moderate means who needed only a Tin Lizzie, a tent, and a can of beans to bask in sunlit splendor.

Much of the roar of the Roaring Twenties came from the internal combustion engine. Automobile ownership was increasingly common in America. Henry Ford's dream of a mechanized vehicle cheap and sturdy enough for all average workers to possess was now almost a reality. With the automobile came a sense of wanderlust, as thousands of people who had never before traveled abruptly took to the road. Auto camping quickly emerged as a new favorite pastime, appealing to the American credo of independence and trailblazing. A driver was freed of stuffy, class-conscious conventions on railroads and in hotels, and could whirl along at a blistering pace of thirty to forty miles per hour. Relieved of the necessity of staying in a downtown hotel, close to a railroad station, a family in a car could avoid inconvenient timetables and the outstretched, tip-hungry hands of bellhops and waiters. A few basics for cooking and sleeping allowed American families to go wherever they pleased, as any open field or clearing in a forest would serve as a campsite in an age before regulations or environmental concerns.[10] Florida's vast, unsettled spaces and warm climate made it a natural magnet for open-air adventurers.

Travel by auto depended on the availability of roads. Florida's lawmakers were finally making the much-needed internal improvements. In 1911, the first highway connecting Jacksonville and Miami opened. The Florida State Road Department was established in 1915. The Federal Road Act of 1916 and the Federal Highway Act of 1921 enabled the creation of major highways. Many of Florida's most famous roads were built in the early decades of the twentieth century, including vast stretches of U.S. 1, 4, 90, and 27. Opened in 1923, the stretch of U.S. 90 between Jacksonville and Lake City was the state's first concrete highway. The Tamiami Trail, linking Ft. Myers and Miami, was completed in 1928, allowing tourists to see the Everglades and make a relatively quick journey from one coast to the other. The Orange Blossom Trail took drivers on a scenic tour of Central Florida groves. Famous highways tied Florida to the rest of the nation. The Dixie Highway, opened in 1915, connected Florida to thousands of potential tourists in Chicago. By 1925, some 2.5 million tourists were arriving in Florida yearly, primarily by automobile, forming—in the words of a *Florida Highways* author—"a somewhat nomadic tribe." Once inside Florida they could, by 1930, travel 3,800 miles of roads surfaced with clay, grouted brick, macadam, concrete, or asphalt.[11]

Getting around in Florida via automobile had its dangers, and not just from getting stuck in a ditch and being overcharged by locals to be pulled free. It could be hard to find gas stations or repair shops. Collisions with wildlife and livestock were embarrassingly common. A 1926 travel book warned, "The principal motoring hazards in Florida arise not from dangerous grades but from roving razorbacks and range cattle and the fact that anybody may drive a car, no driving license being required."[12] One Polk County resident recalled seeing numerous cars simply abandoned on lonely Florida lanes. But travel on the rails, for those not blessed with private Pullman cars or first-class tickets, held pitfalls as well. A 1916 visitor described the dullness of the landscape, especially the "miles of palmettos, with leaves glittering like racks of bared cutlasses in the sunshine, the miles of dark swamp, the miles of live oaks strung with their sad tattered curtains of Spanish moss, the miles of sandy waste." Worst of all was the unceasing, choking dust that covered everyone in the cars with a flour-like layer of grime. It was enough to "make you wish that you were in the North again."[13] At least with one's own set of wheels, a traveler could set a course for whatever Florida adventure and landscape was most pleasing.

Intrepid and independent, the early motorists were known as "tin can tourists." The exact origin of the name is debated; some sources claim it derives from the Tin Lizzies (Model Ts) driven by tourists, while others hold that the sobriquet initially referred to the tin cans from which travelers ate, or the containers for water and gas that dangled from their modest metal or wooden trailers.[14] In 1919, the name was formally adopted by the Tin Can Tourists of the World, an auto club formed at DeSoto Park, south of Tampa. Gatherings of these wanderers, who displayed their memberships by welding tin cans to their car radiators, were held yearly until the club disbanded in 1977.[15] Most tin can tourists were solidly bourgeoisie, and though they enjoyed pretending to be wandering gypsies or free spirits, an encampment of motor travelers often had the air of Main Street, USA. No matter how diverse the people in terms of states of origin, all shared the American spirit of adventure, tempered by the basic values of thrift and community assistance that had sent their ancestors off in covered wagons.[16] In 1929, a German visitor wrote that Florida would one day be a winter garden where even the lowliest laborer would vacation; his prediction was perhaps based on the combination of automobiles and ordinary Americans he saw along the roads.[17]

One camper couple found almost more adventure than they could handle. The Bedells made a journey across America, beginning with Florida, where they picked oranges and photographed Seminoles. "We were somewhat annoyed by the pigs coming around our camp, nosing around to see what they could find to eat," Mary Bedell recalled. Her husband dove into a swamp only to hear "a noise like the honking of an automobile." He spotted "a dark body like a submarine scooting away in the water. He had been anxious to see an alligator, but had not bargained to have one share his morning dip with him."[18]

The rising number of automotive tourists inspired Florida entrepreneurs to begin catering to their needs. Mom-and-pop businesses, including restaurants, gas stations, and private camps, sprang up along the highways. By 1925, there were an estimated 210 auto camps in Florida. Some of the camps offered not only parking spaces but also washroom facilities, along with dining and dancing halls. Florida experienced a true hotel and motel boom, as foresighted developers recognized that weary travelers would eventually tire of outdoor adventures and long for such amenities as clean towels and firm mattresses. The number of rooms in lodging places more than quintupled in the 1920s, with the largest growth seen in Miami-Dade, Pinellas, Hillsborough, and Duval counties.[19] Along with development came jobs. One economic historian estimates that overall employment in Florida increased by more than 55 percent from 1920 to 1930, compared to the national average of 17 percent, and that the number of jobs in the Florida tourist industry more than doubled.[20]

The less affluent visitors were not always so eagerly courted by city fathers. In 1920, St. Petersburg, which relied almost completely on its winter clientele, debated the wisdom of its free tent city for vehicular tourists. Sensitive about unfavorable comparisons to East Coast rivals, some residents worried that an influx of budget-minded visitors would cause further damage to the town's reputation. Leaders feared that such visitors would contribute little to the town's economy or ambience. A popular saying, "the St. Pete tourist arrived with one shirt and a twenty dollar bill and never changed either all winter," was not the image the town hoped to project. The city abolished its free auto park in 1921, forcing campers to look for private accommodations.[21] Many Florida locations feared an influx of "riff-raff." It was a complex debate, whether a town should be hospitable to these tourists, whom the American Automobile Association (AAA) estimated would collectively spend over a billion dollars in Florida, or run the risk that the wrong crowd would show up and cause community disorder.[22]

The surging number of tourists and property speculators during the height of the Florida land boom highlighted the need for better infrastructure. Roads were improved. Signs bragged about mileage and expenditures: "346 miles of highways costing $3,000,000 for your enjoyment," one billboard in Polk County proclaimed.[23] Pensacola finally constructed a bridge across Pensacola Bay, making the development of beachfront tourism more likely for the city. West Palm Beach, considered by a previous generation to be merely the home base for Flagler's cooks and maids, became a tourist city in its own right. From 1915 to 1925, a record number of middle-class visitors came to the other side of Lake Worth, where they created tourist clubs and complained strenuously about the profiteering tactics of hotel owners.[24]

To lure guests Florida press agents tapped into the ballyhoo that marked the age, making Florida promotion an art form and creating the indelible images that would be recycled many times in the decades to follow. Miami's Carl Fisher scored a sizable coup when he virtually kidnapped president-elect Warren G. Harding for a January weekend at the newly opened Flamingo Hotel. The affable politician was photographed playing golf attended by an elephant caddy.[25] Everest G. Sewell, president of the Greater Miami Chamber of Commerce and later mayor of the city, was notorious for the "cheesecake" motion pictures of bathing beauties he distributed, often over the protests of religious groups. In winter, Sewell cleverly placed an advertisement on the electric sign at New York City's Forty-second Street and Broadway, reminding frostbitten Yankees that it was "June in Miami."[26] John Lodwick, a former sportswriter from Cleveland and press agent for St. Petersburg, established a number of effective gimmicks. Playing off the city's new reputation as a sports center, he staged impromptu "world championships" in competitions like shuffleboard and horseshoe tossing. These meaningless events drew crowds on the scene and national press attention. Realizing that word of mouth and local media were a potent force, Lodwick snapped pictures of tourists posing beside oversize fish or leering cartoon alligators, afterward sending copies to the travelers' hometown newspapers. He also distributed so many postcards of bathing beauties that a gullible Yankee might be excused for believing that Florida was populated solely by suntanned nymphs.[27]

Promotion and prosperity blended with the Florida land boom. Florida was no longer just the southernmost state, but a region of increasing attraction and accessibility. The rich had always come to Florida, and were arriving in ever-larger numbers in the 1920s, as World War I had ruined many of their European destinations. The middle classes were coming as well, watching and often mimicking the behaviors they observed. New racetracks, golf courses, and casinos bloomed and were soon bulging with celebrities. Changing social mores made Florida irresistible to vacationing members of F. Scott Fitzgerald's "flaming youth." Florida was also one of the "leakiest spots" in the nation, much to the delight of famous boozehounds like John Barrymore, who vacationed in Key West. Enforcing Prohibition laws would hinder tourism. Miami hotels served drinks openly, and one visitor noticed "two proper old-fashioned saloons" located just a stroll away from a police station.[28] Bathing suits revealed ever more skin, often shocking the sedate, traditional breed of tourists. Al Capone chose

Miami as his home, and other gangsters followed. Pensacola's notorious red light district flourished, though one madam latter complained that the "amateurs" were running the pros out of business. A German tourist in the early 1920s condemned Jacksonville, Tampa, and even St. Augustine as cities of "depravity" in an exposé of prostitution. Florida in the 1920s sported an aura of sun-baked decadence.[29]

Gambling became a large part of the Florida scene in the Roaring Twenties, especially in Miami. Discreet gaming rooms had always been part of the Flagler hotels. St. Augustine had the Bacchus Club, Palm Beach its Beach Club, and Miami the Seminole Club. Open to elite tourists only, they reflected an era of Gilded Age smoke and gentlemanly wagers.[30] But gambling for the less elite grew out of back rooms and bars, and by the 1920s the speakeasies and clubs attached to Miami hotels were welcoming a more diverse, if still rather swanky crowd. Though promoters like Carl Fisher often publicly disapproved of commercialized gambling, for fear of attracting the "wrong element," illegal nightlife was very much a part of the great boom. One of Fisher's homes, "The Shadows," was purchased by gamblers and reopened as the "Beach and Tennis Club." It was a club where nobody donned a bathing suit or swung a racket. Instead, the establishment contained seating for only ninety guests, who could dance to the sounds of an excellent orchestra, pay for overpriced dinners, and indulge in discreet wagering. Hotel nightclubs spotlighted premiere entertainers. There was little urge to shut the nightclubs down, no matter what illicit practices they engaged in. Especially after the land boom collapsed, hotel owners and promoters were grateful for any attraction to keep the tourists coming. One resident recalled that in the 1930s, Miami swarmed with "the theatrical, gangster, middle-class New York–Chicago people. . . . They made the hotels and they created an atmosphere . . . which certainly was quite different from any other town in Florida." Miami in the 1920s and 1930s was in a Monte Carlo mode, as glittering entertainment was financed largely by the profits from gambling rooms.[31]

Florida's pleasures, legal and otherwise, were not equally shared. Ordinary citizens and workers would have found a brief vacation problematic, and minorities were generally forbidden to enjoy the state's amenities, even if they possessed the cash to pay for them. In the 1920s, America experienced a backlash against the ideals of Progressivism. Racism, nativism, and prejudice were rampant, as demonstrated by the power of the re-vived Ku Klux Klan. As a part of the Deep South, Florida shared the social biases of the former Confederacy. African Americans were not permitted in hotels except as cooks, maids, and bellboys. Admittance to beaches and parks was either completely forbidden or restricted to particular days. Though Florida's Jim Crow laws were not as extreme as in some states, op-pressive social custom more than made up for statutes. For many years Af-rican Americans were forbidden to drive in Miami; only complaints from rich tourists that this custom hindered their chauffeurs got the practice changed.[32]

Simply taking to Southern roadways could be dangerous for African Americans. A traveler could never be certain about local customs and seg-regation "etiquette," especially in small towns. Reporting in a 1929 issue of the *Crisis*, the official magazine of the National Association for the Ad-vancement of Colored People (NAACP), a black motorist journeying in Florida noted a "For Whites Trade Only" sign on a gas station between Jacksonville and Daytona. "These Crackers persist in being fools," his com-panion chuckled, pointing out the station's complete lack of customers of any hue.[33] Black tourists were encouraged to consult *The Negro Motorist Green Book*, a special 1936 guide listing the few hotels, gas stations, and restaurants that would serve people of color. In 1939, the U.S. Travel Bu-reau, a branch of the Department of Labor, published the *Directory of Ne-gro Hotels and Guests Houses in the United Sates*. It was primarily a list of Young Men's Christian Associations (YMCAs) and private residences called "tourist homes" that would accommodate black travelers. Robbed of the pleasures of spontaneity, forced to always plan where and when they would stop, African American tourists were few in number. Those brave enough to make the trip depended on informal networks of lodgings ar-ranged by churches, or simply slept in their cars while touring Florida.[34]

Segregation was a strange curse, for while it kept African Americans from the social mainstream, it also guaranteed that certain areas of Flor-ida would flourish with black-owned businesses, including those geared to tourism. Locals and travelers enjoyed nightclubs famous for jazz and blues. St. Petersburg had the Manhattan Casino, Orlando the Ever Ready Club, and Jacksonville the Two Spot and Club Harlem.[35] From 1890 to 1938, Manhattan Beach, near Mayport, was a black Coney Island complete with dance pavilions and carnival rides. Acquired by a number of Flagler's railroad workers, the property attracted mostly local people, who arrived on trains, often as part of church excursions. In 1938, the last pavilion was destroyed by fire, an act that some residents blamed on whites jealous of their resorts' success and uncomfortable with its proximity to growing white neighborhoods. Bulter's Beach, on Anastasia Island some ten miles south of St. Augustine, was a recreational haven for blacks in the late 1920s.[36]

The most prominent African American resort community was American Beach, on Amelia Island. Developed on land purchased by the Afro-American Insurance Company, American Beach was a vibrant community and an example of black entrepreneurship. Visitors in the 1930s stayed in private homes, a custom that continued even after hotels were constructed. Lee's Ocean-Vu-Inn, American Beach's first hotel, opened in 1945 with a restaurant, ballroom, and accommodations for forty-five patrons. The hotel's guest books recorded visitors from as far away as Chicago, St. Louis, and San Francisco. Many black tourists were drawn by American Beach's reputation for jazz, gambling, and great food, making it a principal tourist center for African Americans up to the early 1970s. American Beach attracted a galaxy of celebrity tourists, including Zora Neale Hurston, Billie Daniels, Cab Calloway, Joe Louis, Henry Aaron, Ray Charles, and Ozzie Davis.[37]

Jews were also stigmatized and denied entrance to Florida's clubs and hotels. In the early twentieth century, signs reading "Christians Only," "Gentiles Only," or "Limited Clientele" were common in Florida. In St. Petersburg, the Vinoy Park, Soreno, and Don CeSar hotels barred Jewish guests. Older urban areas such as Pensacola, which had a long heritage of ethnic, racial, and religious diversity, somewhat muted the overt hostility, but invisible lines were still in place. The message was clear: Florida's preferred tourist was a white person with ready cash and sedate Christian beliefs.[38]

The rise of tourism affected another Florida minority in a very different way, presenting them with both the dangers and opportunities of cultural exploitation. The Florida Seminoles were a curiosity to the outside world, as they had lived in virtual seclusion in the Everglades and on the South Florida coast since the mid-1800s.[39] The completion of the Tamiami Trail forced many Seminoles to leave their homesteads, and the later founding of the Everglades National Park, with its ban on hunting, would strip even more natives of their traditional resources and folkways. Yet at the same time, curiosity about Native Americans and, to some extent, sympathy for them were on the rise. As early as 1895, Warren Frazee, who took the nickname "Alligator Joe," made a living showing off alligators in Palm Beach and later in Ft. Lauderdale. He established an alligator farm in Miami in 1910, and was probably the first professional alligator wrestler. With exaggeration that reflected pride in a local entrepreneur, the *Miami Herald* claimed "more visitors see Joe's performance in Florida each winter than go to any other single attraction."[40]

By 1915, an aggressive campaign to lure more tourists to Miami inspired new promotion of Seminoles as tourist attractions. In 1917, the owners of Coppinger's Tropical Gardens, a Miami tourist attraction, encouraged a small band of Seminoles to set up camp and receive visits from tour buses. Suffering from the effects of a recent freeze, the Seminoles accepted the offer, and the next year the family of Jack Tiger Tail agreed to camp for the entire winter season in return for money, rations, and clothing.[41]

The popularity of this venture made competition inevitable. Willie Willie, a Seminole, decided that his people could capitalize on white curiosity in a more thorough manner. He leased a part of Musa Isle from Coppinger rival John Roop and established the Musa Isle Village and Trading Post. Visitors could watch Seminoles in native dress performing traditional tasks, including making dinner, or attend a staged Indian wedding.[42] The trading post was active, drawing both Seminole and Cracker hunters, whom the tourists probably found equally exotic. A decade later, a Seminole village was also a featured attraction at Silver Springs. Both Coppinger and Willie put on alligator wrestling shows; a handsome young man risking life and limb to rub a gator's belly soon became a hallmark of the Florida tourist experience.[43]

In early 1929, another omen of tourism trends opened near Lake Wales. Edward W. Bok was an immigrant success story, a Pulitzer Prize–winning journalist and the editor of the *Ladies Home Journal*. Grateful for his prosperity, he commissioned the "Mountain Lake Sanctuary" on a 294-foot-high hill called Iron Mountain. The park, with its masterfully landscaped gardens designed by Frederick Law Olmstead Jr., reflecting pool, and carillon "Singing Tower" of pink Georgia marble and Florida coquina, was an exquisite addition to the sleepy environs. Bok claimed his goal was "to simply create symbols of pure beauty" and express his "appreciation and gratitude to the American people for their kindness and generosity." The Bok Tower was the first major attraction created to be a novelty. Bearing no direct relationship to the climate, history, native peoples, or natural wonders of Florida, it was built purely to be a landmark and lure visitors. Future attractions would follow its example, if not its aesthetic qualities.[44]

The great Florida land boom of the 1920s was, in large degree, an outgrowth of tourism. Writers such as Kenneth Lewis Roberts, who produced a number of essays about travel in Florida for the *Saturday Evening Post*, painted the state as "an accessible paradise," a democracy of tourists and new settlers where everyone, no matter how pale and poor, could grow tanned and rich.[45] Promoters and developers like Miami's Carl Fisher were not interested in hotels strictly for profiting from tourism. Instead, hotels were thrown up rapidly to accommodate crowds that could be lured into making purchases of home lots before departing for the North. Fisher envisioned Miami Beach as a village of winter homes, and was willing to use tourism as the bait. The guest books of hotels were carefully scrutinized, with tickets for polo matches and yacht excursions handed out to visitors who sounded like potential investors. Fisher claimed to have wined and dined one man on the assumption that he was a copper magnate, only to learn that he was a simple haberdasher. Tourists who accepted the invitations to play like kings often found land agents' cards waiting at the front desk when they returned. The hard sell came in March and April, when winter visitors who had fallen in love with South Florida were more responsive to the argument that if they did not buy their acre in the sun now, it would be sold when they returned for the next winter season. The boom that began in the early 1920s hit its peak from 1924 to 1926, when ordinary Americans who had scratched together enough cash for a Miami jaunt, via train or Tin Lizzie, became Florida property owners and land speculators.[46]

Like a vacation, the Florida boom was exciting, memorable, and short-lived. Sales had already begun to slump in the spring of 1926. Then on the morning of September 18, 1926, the most ferocious hurricane in Weather Bureau history roared across Miami with winds between 123 and 132 miles per hour and a storm surge of up to fifteen feet. Boats were wrecked, hotels flooded, homes destroyed. Most residents had never experienced a hurricane, and when the eye settled over the town, many rushed out and jumped into cars, eager to check on beachfront property, unaware that the danger was now even greater. The "second storm" was more intense, and hundreds of people were killed. Nothing in Miami was spared. Buildings associated with tourism, the hotels and casinos, were battered or washed away. "Hardee's and Smith's casinos might as well have been under a barrage of cannon for days," one survivor recalled. Damage was estimated at $112 million, and moralists held that the storm was God's punishment on South Florida for its wickedness. The disaster ended the land boom and dealt a severe setback to Miami tourism. Apparently unconcerned about divine retribution, one Miami resident observed that the only thing that kept the tourist season of 1927–1928 from being "a complete flop" was "the supply of good whiskey."[47]

Two years later, headlines across the nation screamed "Florida Destroyed! Florida Destroyed!" On September 16, 1928, another hurricane crashed into the state at West Palm Beach. A Category 4 storm packing 150-mile-per-hour winds, it brought nearly twenty inches of rain, causing massive flooding around the banks of Lake Okeechobee. Americans were horrified by accounts of entire families being stranded on rooftops or washed away by the murky waters, all within a short distance of one of the country's most famous resorts. For weeks afterward, decomposing bodies were collected, a repulsive task in the Florida late summer heat. An accurate death count was impossible, but perhaps as many as 3,500 people never returned from the storm. The image of bloated bodies piled like cordwood was a sharp contrast, and a bitter finale, to the scenes of beachfront idylls and freewheeling speculation that had defined Florida in the 1920s.[48]

The great national spree of the 1920s came to its conclusion with the stock market crash of 1929. With the bursting of the land market bubble and the impact of two brutal storms, Florida was already deeply mired in the Great Depression before the Great Depression officially started. By the late 1920s, the days of the happy-go-lucky tin can tourist, as well as the carefree snowbird aristocrat, were over. People living in cars were now more likely to be migrant workers or foreclosed families, destitute and desperate. For the first three winters of the Depression the state police went to the extreme of turning back travelers at Florida's borders if they lacked "provable means of support," an insult unimaginable in the boom years of the Jazz Age.[49]

Tourism's decline since 1926 made Floridians aware of the pitfalls of such an economy. However, the tourist crop was still the easiest to renew, a resource that could be revived with strategic planning and promotion. It was perhaps inevitable that Florida's leaders would stress the resumption of tourism as a source of recovery, and that the two great crises to follow—the Great Depression and World War II—would bring unexpected benefits to the state and encourage an even great dependence on tourism.

FIVE

Blitzkrieg of Joy

"Cancel your coal bills—and your cold bills—by substituting the glorious climate of Sunny Sarasota for those bleak winter months!" Civic boosters in "Florida's most attractive city" argued that it was actually cheaper to live through the winter in a Sarasota hotel than a Chicago apartment, an argument that seemed fanciful at best and desperate at worst. Such was the mood of Floridians in the early years of the Great Depression.[1] With traditional industries collapsing and markets floundering, Floridians turned to the one thing guaranteed to remain intact no matter how many stocks fizzled: Florida's warm weather and beautiful beaches. Tourism, which had been seen by so many as a luxury, now became Florida's lifeline, and was key to rescuing the state from the throes of the national economic crisis. If Florida entered the Depression early, it escaped early, with tourists leading the way.

Floridians in the resort areas fought a psychological war against the Great Depression. Tourist materials stressed Florida as a land of escapism and fantasy. In St. Petersburg, master promoter John Lodwick urged visitors to wait out the Depression in the city where "Sunshine Babies"—a group of Florida toddlers born during an eighteen-month period of exceptional weather—symbolized life without problems. St. Petersburg journalists insisted that residents banish the word "depression" from their vocabulary, especially if they were conversing with tourists. There was logic behind the semantics. Rich people would take vacations no matter how bleak the economy, and Floridians were willing to go to extremes to meet their every desire, if they would only come for the winter. On the other end of the economic spectrum, the New Deal enforced policies that granted paid vacations to industrial laborers, opening the possibility of a previously untapped market of travelers. Floridians were encouraged to treat all tourists, no matter their status, like royalty. State officials dispatched elaborate displays to the major fairs of the 1930s, including the Century of Progress (Chicago, 1933–1934), the Great Lakes Exhibition (Cleveland, 1936–1937), and the New York World's Fair (1939–1940), emphasizing the pleasures of tourism as recreation, and assuring visitors that it was not necessary to be wealthy to enjoy a vacation in Florida.[2] But despite these efforts, hotel construction halted, most rooms went unfilled, and the few tourists who did make the annual pilgrimage were suddenly frustratingly thrifty. If tourism comprised a crop, from 1929 to 1934 the Florida harvest was severely blighted.

In 1931, the state legislature made a dramatic decision. Desperate for revenue, it legalized pari-mutuel betting at racetracks. One of the principal advocates for this shift in policy was Joseph E. Widener, the owner of the Hialeah racetrack. He staged a grand opening of his course in January 1932, ushering in a host of celebrities and icons of wealth, including a number of Whitneys and Vanderbilts. With an entrance that resembled an opera house facade and landscaped in massive botanical gardens, Hialeah quickly became more than just a place to bet on the ponies. It served as a symbol of Florida's continued power to draw in elite visitors. It was also the first track to have photo-finish equipment installed, earning Hialeah a reputation for honesty. Tropical Park and Gulfstream soon followed, all vying for the best racing days.[3]

Also legalized in 1931, dog racing and jai alai appealed to different segments of the local and tourist population. Both sports had been in existence since the 1920s, but grew in popularity with the advent of sanctioned wagering. Dog racing lacked the cachet of horse racing, attracting a lower-middle-class crowd, which owners catered to by introducing night racing and low minimum wagers. Jai alai, a form of handball developed in the Basque regions of Spain, brought a complex betting system and a new language, making it difficult for all but the most sophisticated of world travelers to understand. Its grace and excitement easily translated, however, making it a spectacle tourists flocked to, even if they rarely signaled to place a bet. Legalized gambling was essential to the growth and recovery of South Florida, especially Miami.[4]

The New Deal brought change to Florida, and in many ways helped to lay the foundation for an even deeper dependence on tourism. The Works Progress Administration (WPA) and Civilian Conservation Corps (CCC) labored to build parks, roads, airports, and campgrounds, establishing and improving facilities for future visitors. An especially beautiful WPA/city-backed project was Sarasota's Lido Beach Casino, known as the "quarter million dollar casino" for its cost. It featured three dining areas, a ballroom, two lounges, two pools, a bathhouse, and thirty-nine cabanas.[5] While all infrastructure construction in Florida indirectly benefited population growth and tourism, one project's sole aim was to create a tourist mecca. In a unique and visionary experiment, Julius F. Stone Jr., the Federal Emergency Relief Administration (FERA) director for Florida, used federal funds to reinvent Key West.

Salt manufacturing, commercial fishing, salvage work, and sponging, the bedrock of the island's traditional economy, all collapsed at the end of the 1920s. Nearly two-thirds of its residents fled. Tourism had never been a potent force in Key West; like the few other hotels on the island, the one luxury venue, the Casa Marina, closed. Poor sanitation and wretched, neglected buildings made the old port an eyesore. Faced with the choice of providing relief while evacuating the remaining citizens or developing some new way for the community to survive, Stone proposed that if the locals would volunteer to do the work of cleaning the town and prepping it for the coming tourist season, FERA would provide relief and money for better infrastructure. His goal was the creation of a quiet tropical retreat, an antidote to the glitz and artificial glamour of Miami, a place where the "tired businessman, invalid or artist could go."[6]

In July 1934, FERA began implementing Stone's vision. His short-term goal was simply to get the city operational and attractive for the winter of 1934–1935, in the hopes that a sudden influx of tourists would pay for expansion of the town's public utilities, including water, sewage, and electrical plants, in the following year. Over 4,000 volunteers signed on, working to clean the streets, build parks, construct affordable tourist housing, and establish recreational activities. Outhouses disappeared while bungalows were spruced up. Parks and playgrounds sprouted. Key West received national publicity. Air travel subsidies and reduced ferry rates, plus a general improvement in the economy, brought a sudden wave of tourists crashing on the shores. Approximately 8,000 guests registered at Key West hotels during the 1934–1935 season.[7] Despite the horrific Labor Day hurricane in 1935 that knocked out the railroad connection to the mainland, the renewal of a tourist season allowed for longer-range projects to begin in 1936, with residents back at work and off the relief dole. Key West soon gained a reputation as an easy-going, nonconformist paradise.[8]

Naturally, this development did not please everyone, especially locals who disapproved of the "artsy" types. Earlier creative immigrants, like John Don Passos and Ernest Hemingway, were appalled by the influx of people they saw as pretenders, including the artists Stone brought in to conjure idyllic images for national publicity campaigns. Locals fiercely resisted Stone's attempts to make them more picturesque, including his insistence that they don Bermuda shorts and tennis skirts, which they considered indecent underwear. Katy Don Passos warned a friend, "The New Dealers are here—they are called New Dealers but what they really are is Old Bohemians, and Key West is now a Greenwich Village Nightmare—They have stirred up all the old art trash and phony uplifters . . . and they're painting murals on the café walls, and weaving baskets, and cutting down plants and trees, and renting all the houses." While Hemingway cruised to Cuba to avoid the bourgeoisie throngs eager to see his home, other residents eventually learned either to get along with the tourists or avoid them all together. Tourism might eventually ruin the island's rustic charm, but, as one reporter noted in 1935, "You cannot ask people to starve for the sake of being quaint." However uncomfortable the initial fit, the Key West community could credit its continued existence to this new, tourism-focused image.[9]

Miami was one of the first cities in the nation to recover from the Depression, and after 1935 could boast of increasing prosperity, much of it built on the town's growing reputation as the entertainment center of the tropics, oozing glitter and seductive vice. The annual tide of winter visitors was greater than the resident population, and the Depression did little to dull Miami's glitzy reputation for naughtiness. "You can be as wicked as you like, or as good, in Miami," a British travel writer assured his audience. Horse racing, dog racing, dice, roulette, slot machines, and nightclubs were all tropical temptations. But sin was hardly limited to games of chance. "Miami lives on its legs," the writer also revealed, going on to refer to the city as one great "girly show."[10] Ironically, with the growing emphasis on betting and nightclubs as the backbone of Miami's tourism industry, the new arrivals were not as active as city fathers had hoped. Though sunbathing was eternally popular, true sportsmen were harder to find. Carl Fisher had imagined a Miami filled with swimmers, boaters, golfers, fishermen, and polo players. Instead, Florida tourists were increasingly passive, expecting to be entertained on arrival rather than to seek out their own pastimes.[11]

By the end of the 1930s, Florida tourism had largely recovered from the fallout of the land boom and the Depression. The comeback was evident as early as 1934, and in 1935 some two million tourists visited Florida, leaving over $6 million behind. The *Tampa Tribune* proclaimed tourism "our richest crop" for good reason. New Deal agencies improved Florida roads, parks, and airports, and the WPA *Guide to Florida* was a masterpiece. Tourism expansion of the 1920s was soon matched in the 1930s, despite the few hard years of the early Depression. Another significant change was the increasingly diverse composition of tourists as a whole. Florida was no longer limited to the wealthy, or to the adventurous. Along with the tin can tourists resuming their wanderings came nouveau riche nightclubbers to Miami and elderly persons scouting retirement home possibilities in St. Petersburg. Families visited Silver Springs and toured the collection of canals and greenery at the newly opened Cypress Gardens. Intellectuals, writers, and free spirits went to Key West.[12] In 1934, with a foresight rare in his profession, historian Frederick W. Dau projected that Florida's tourism "will ever be the most important crop."[13]

An intriguing snapshot of Florida tourism on the eve of World War II is glimpsed through a pair of guidebooks. *Cue's Guide to What to See and Do in Florida* warned potential visitors not to expect a miraculous tropical landscape to appear upon crossing the Florida border, and chided those who thought that a single visit to Palm Beach qualified them to speak of truly knowing Florida. The author assured readers that Florida summers were not as bad as reported, but that the cows roaming the highways were still a very real danger. "If you see feeding cows, slow down."[14] The *Florida Hotel and Travel Guide* estimated that the average visitor stayed in Florida for two weeks and spent $8 a day, a healthy sum by midcentury standards. The author noted that while winter remained the "high season," ever more visitors were choosing to board air-conditioned trains and take advantage of the hotels that were now staying open, with reduced rates, in the summer. The *Guide* advocated loafing, sunbathing, and golfing as the principal Florida activities. Its advice on clothing, however, seems to best reveal the differences between tourism in the glamorous prewar period and today. Assuring readers that full formal attire was rarely expected, the *Guide* warned, "only a sloppy man will go into a dining room sans coat and cravat." Women were urged to choose "a few outfits of inherent quality and impeccable taste."[15] Another sign of the times was the "restricted clientele" listing on the vast majority of resorts advertised in the *Guide*. Even Miami, which had been one of the more open resort areas and claimed a growing Jewish population, experienced a backlash of anti-Semitism in the 1930s, with many hotels and motor courts pasting "Gentiles Only" signs in their windows. One North Beach hotel sneered, "Always a view, never a Jew."[16]

While guidebooks and the press portrayed Florida as a land of swag and sin, local boosters liked to direct attention to record crowds of tourists in the churches, or the staid midwestern visitors playing shuffleboard at their tourist clubs. The biggest problem was that both the wealthy and the only moderately well-off tended to go home in March, leaving the estimated 60 percent of the Florida population that was dependent upon tourist revenues holding their collective breath for the health of the next season.[17]

The impending international crises fueled the record tourist seasons of the late 1930s. Money rolled in from European rearmament, and the threat of another world war made a good excuse for living in the moment, enjoying ever bigger and better vacations. With Europe in turmoil, leisured Americans looked more readily to a domestic version of paradise. One traveler confided to *Reader's Digest* in 1937, "I wanted a tropical foreign country, but I wanted this foreign country to be inhabited exclusively by Americans and run along American lines. I wanted . . . French Riviera's gay summer all year round but with none of its dirt and petty cheating on the part of the tradespeople. In Florida I found what I wanted." Businessmen mingled with titled European refugees in South Florida's clubs and casinos. The Hialeah racetrack reported record-breaking wagers of $43 million. The winter of 1941–1942 looked promising. Then on December 7, 1941—which happened to be the opening Sunday of tourist season—Japanese bombs fell on Pearl Harbor.[18]

The immediate mood was one of extreme pessimism. Cancellations poured in, the season was doomed. But before the war was a month old, Florida's tourism promoters rallied, finding ways both to justify and promote tourism in the face of a national crisis. It might seem inappropriate, but with such a large percentage of the Florida population dependent on tourism income, it was necessary. Disguised as "a contribution to civilian morale," Florida hoped for at least one more profitable season.

Miami press agents, demonstrating something less than sensitivity, proclaimed a "blitzkrieg of joy" that included sports tournaments, boat races, chowder parties, and festivals. War was the new tourist theme, as Kate Smith sang from an oceanfront suite, Lou Costello auctioned off a "victory suit," and Sabu paraded for war bonds. Tourists were urged to do their patriotic duty by staying fit with daily beach exercise. Star-spangled burlesque revues were staged in nightclubs. Tourists made significant donations to the Red Cross. Unimpressed by the hoopla, *Life* magazine summed up the atmosphere: "If all the state felt about the war as do its purveyors of amusement, Florida would be in a deplorable condition."[19]

Reality returned on the night of February 19, 1942, when the tanker *Pan Massachusetts* was torpedoed by a German submarine and went down some forty miles south of Cape Canaveral. U-boats stalked the Florida straits; Florida beaches were frequently littered with oil, debris, and bodies from lost ships. Some vessels burst into flame within sight of land. Since resort lights served as glowing backdrops that made merchant vessels easier to spot, the military ordered a blackout for the entire eastern coast. Rumors of German landings, along with gasoline rationing and limitations on public transportation, sent the last of the winter tourists scurrying home.[20] Florida's principal industry appeared to be an early war casualty. Many small attractions, especially botanical gardens, closed due to gas rationing and public disapproval of their "frivolous" nature.[21] Though a call went out for "fewer tuxedoes and more overalls," Florida was not an industrial state. Its lack of smokestacks guaranteed that it would see little benefit from military spending on armaments. The one thing it did have was an ideal climate for military training and, thanks to the tourism industry, plenty of beds, dining rooms, and places of amusement for the thousands of new recruits who would soon be shipped southward.[22]

Florida had seen a growth in military installations before the war. Naval air bases were constructed at Jacksonville, Miami, Key West, and Pensacola, with army bases located at Tampa, Orlando, and Camp Blanding (near Starke). There was also a gunnery school at Eglin Field, near Valparaiso. These bases buzzed with activity; they would be instrumental in training service personnel in everything from jungle warfare to coastal patrol to antisubmarine tactics. The year-round sunshine offered unceasing opportunities for instruction, as did the vast open spaces and variations in environments, many of which mirrored conditions that might be expected in the Pacific theater. Eventually, 172 different military installations operated in Florida during the war, but few were immediately available for the influx of recruits.[23]

Faced with this logistical nightmare, military officials turned to the tourism industry for a solution. The move was not without precedent, as troops had bunked in the Tampa Bay Hotel and Miami's Royal Palm during the Spanish-American War in 1898. Negotiations were opened with the Florida Hotel Commission for the armed forces to rent hotels, assuring their owners of an approximate 6 percent profit. Undersecretary of War Robert P. Patterson, who was credited with the scheme, had sharp words for skeptics who questioned putting raw recruits into luxury suites: "The best hotel room is none too good for the American soldier."[24]

Soldiers, sailors, airmen, and marines quickly filled the vacuum left by the fleeing tourists. On February 20, 1942, the first 400 enlisted men arrived in South Florida. The Army Air Corps announced that it would train its officers at Miami Beach and billet them in resort hotels. Within days, 500 candidates arrived to bunk at the Boulevard Hotel and drill at the Miami Beach Municipal Golf Course. Eventually 85 percent of Miami Beach hotels were converted into hospitals, barracks, and classrooms. By war's end, 20 percent of the Air Corps' nonflying enlisted men had received training on the Miami shores, and 25 percent of the corps' chair-bound officers were graduates of the Florida school.[25]

Taking over Miami Beach hotels had a number of both obvious and hidden advantages. Commandeering hotels for barracks saved the government time and money. The vast stretch of beaches made excellent stages not only for calisthenics but also for more advanced war games and sea rescue drills. The sudden influx of servicemen was good for town businesses, as family members traveled south to be with their loved ones on furloughs, jamming into motels, tourist courts, and apartments. Though far more conservative in their spending, they helped reinvigorate Florida's economy. Perhaps most important, service personnel found South Florida to be a dose of fantasy and beauty before the grim reality of war. "It was surreal, going to the mess hall early in the morning, with the colors of the sunrise on those white buildings," airman and poet Harry Shapiro later recalled.[26]

The military presence soon spread to Miami. Most of the hotels along Biscayne Boulevard housed service personnel, who could be seen drilling in Bayfront Park. The Coast Guard took over the Royal Palm Club, a former casino. Personnel from friendly nations, including Britain, France, Norway, Cuba, Chile, Uruguay, and eventually Russia also trained at the Submarine Chaser Academy, adding a colorful ethnic and linguistic babble to Miami's theaters, bars, and beaches. In historian Gary Mormino's memorable phrase, "Wartime Miami resembled a combination of Casablanca and Grand Central Station."[27]

The military invasion quickly spread to Ft. Lauderdale, Boca Raton, Pompano, and Coral Gables. The Tradewinds, the Boca Raton Hotel and Club, the Silver Thatch Inn, and the Miami Biltmore served as housing, schools, and even hospital wards. In the fall of 1942, the Coast Guard commandeered the now-creaky Hotel Ponce de Leon in St. Augustine; later, the SPARS, the women's division of the Coast Guard, arrived in town. Women in uniform were a common sight in Daytona, where they billeted in hotels and camped in Bethune Park. Like their male counterparts, they received basic training on the beaches.[28]

The state's west coast had been especially hard hit by the Depression, and people there were grateful to have military tourists to replace the tin can tourists. The Army Air Corps took over the Vinoy Park Hotel and eventually fifty-eight others, including the stately Don CeSar. Henry Plant's beautiful Belleview Biltmore Hotel in Clearwater often hosted 3,000 personnel at one time. Its practice range and two of its fairways were converted into drill fields, making a game of golf impossible until the military relinquished control in 1944. Even areas of Florida where tourism was a minor facet saw a military influx. Tiny Wakulla Springs Lodge in Wakulla County housed the families of servicemen and was the frequent site of USO dances. It even served as a location for a military film on amphibious fighting techniques.[29]

The influx of servicemen and service money was a welcome relief, especially to the resort communities. Despite free entertainment and cheap beer on bases, most military types preferred their fun in town. Retail sales rose, and restaurants and bars thrived. Illegal enterprises, such as gambling dens and brothels, found wartime business better than the tourist trade. It was estimated that the average Pensacola naval cadet spent most of his monthly $75 salary on "girls, games, goods, and drinks" in town. Flaunting restrictions, South Florida nightlife never dimmed. "Fort Miami Beach" operated nearly at full blast; one observer noted, "Black markets are rampaging. Everyone's having a wonderful time." Gambling hit new highs, with observers betting that wagers at the Florida tracks could have purchased three heavy cruisers. Appreciative of the troops' sacrifice, and their business, Floridians generally responded positively to the service personnel. Resorts offered golfing privileges, while communities organized free transportation to beaches. Individuals like Michael V. ("Mike") Chrest, a restaurant owner in Hollywood, became nationally famous for hot coffee and hospitality. Following the segregation practices of the time, black Floridians organized USO shows and outings for African American recruits.[30]

Tourist attractions in particular were rescued by the sudden influx of servicemen on weekend leaves. Officers were generous with passes to local curiosities.[31] St. Augustine thrilled to uniformed hordes of military guests from Jacksonville and Camp Blanding who swarmed the Castillo de San Marcos, the Fountain of Youth, and the Alligator Farm. Drew Field airmen were frequent tourists at St. Petersburg's Sunken Gardens, the Pier, and the Wood Parade. Cypress Gardens developed its legendary ski show when servicemen arrived and asked when it was to begin, having heard rumors of the aquatic feats performed by young daredevils. Never known to miss opportunities for publicity, Cypress Garden's impresarios also staged Women's Army Corps (WAC) beauty pageants amid the flowers. For many service personnel from landlocked states, just seeing bright beaches and blue water was a thrill.[32]

Though military needs had come to the rescue, the presence of large numbers of service personnel did cause problems, especially for smaller communities. Festivals and celebrations were postponed, and locals worried about moral corruption from the sudden influx of outsiders. Military exercises damaged golf courses and springs; hotels would have to be refurbished after their lengthy occupation. Cigarettes tossed by careless airmen set fires in the Everglades. Fortunately, major disasters were averted.[33]

The disaster Floridians could not tolerate was a year without a tourist season. Even with the military presence so strong, Floridians were unwilling to let the 1942–1943 winter season pass unnoticed. State and national leaders sought ways to encourage tourism within wartime restrictions. President Franklin Delano Roosevelt agreed with the Atlantic Coast Railroad's slogan, "Civilians need furloughs, too." Secretary of Commerce Harold Ickes urged vacation travel "as an aid in the promotion of national morale," claiming that long hours and exhausted workers equaled declining production.[34] Florida's spokesmen took similar stances, working to counter the prevailing opinion that tourism was wasteful. Governor Spessard Holland proudly dispatched a series of Florida tourism exhibits to major Northern cities. In-state tourism was encouraged with new vigor, with promoters hopeful that Florida's residents would venture into new areas of the state and indulge in some recreational spending. Comptroller J. M. Lee cut through the hype to the heart of the problem, stating, "In a state such as ours it (tourism) is necessary in order to meet the costs of government in the present war emergency."[35]

Practical efforts to create a successful tourist season included a national promotional campaign, special railroad rates, and the squelching of unpleasant rumors. The most prominent of these was the "I hear the army has taken over the state, and it's impossible to get a room" rumor, which the Florida State Chamber of Commerce debunked by publishing lists of available accommodations in resort areas. Some 328,934 vacancies were counted, despite the military build-up. New York Times correspondent Dora Byron assured readers that the Atlantic Ocean was not filled with Nazi mines and swimming was perfectly safe. More important for snowbird society, Florida would not be "dead" for the season, she predicted.[36]

Sports fans were told golf tournaments would be held on schedule, baseball spring training would commence, and horse racing would go on even if wood-burning locomotives had to be resurrected to get people to the track. Governor Holland secured two more trains for the Florida routes in order to ease an expected transportation crunch. The more practical Florida Highway Patrol reminded potential visitors that blackouts were in place and resorts crowded, but in small towns in Florida the sun was still shining, the fish were biting, and the grass was green on the fairway.[37]

Combined, these efforts made for stability if not profitability. Compromise seemed a theme, and the nervous hoopla of the previous year was gone. Horse racing was suspended before the end of the season, much to the disappointment of gamblers, and transportation remained a problem. Beach hotels bragged about being "a step to the ocean," while those that were not so splendidly located offered bicycles to their guests. Some tourists found the strong military presence agreeable. Watching a group of WACs swim at Daytona Beach, an elderly gentleman commented, "If this is war then I'm all for it." Between the military, service families, and a severely limited number of tourists, it was a slim but adequate season. Hotel owners agreed at its conclusion that it was "vastly better" than they had expected the previous autumn.[38]

The summer of 1943 brought a new stage in the war and a new threat to Florida tourism. Most of the permanent military installations were completed, and the servicemen were departing from hotels and resorts. The Army Air Corps abandoned 206 of the 434 hotels it had occupied, and the other branches followed. Florida hotel owners were frantic about how they would fill up their rooms, and began eagerly promoting the next season.[39]

The 1943–1944 season "broke early and big," according to *New Republic* observer Philip Wylie, who noted that in Miami, the standard khaki uniform was being replaced by more colorful civilian sportswear. The Office of Defense Transportation made no real attempt to force people to stay home, and the number of out-of-state license plates proved that gasoline could be purchased at affordable black market prices. Miami hotels were booked solid through the end of the season, as Florida experienced a 50 percent rise in visitors. The reopened Hialeah racetrack was taking in more than $600,000 a day while the dog tracks were back in the money with an average of $100,000 in wagers each night. The Orange Bowl was jammed with 28,000 spectators who watched Louisiana State University battle Texas A&M on New Year's Day. Nightclubs and casinos once again flourished, lacking big-name entertainers but not high spirits. Though the city of Miami was still technically under strict regulations, Wylie reported that "there are in practice more ways to get around gasoline rationing, liquor shortages and the OPA [Office of Price Administration] rent ceilings than there were ways to get into a speakeasy during prohibition."[40] South Florida also welcomed a host of celebrities, including Treasury Secretary Henry Morgenthau Jr., Chicago mayor Ed Kelly, the Joseph P. Kennedy family, Orson Welles, Chico Marx, Walter Winchell, and Cornelius Vanderbilt Jr., who grumbled over paying $4 for a brandy and $2.50 for a cocktail.[41]

The resurgence of tourism came at a cost in bad publicity. Seasonal rents skyrocketed, but the families of servicemen—unlike the society crowd—could not afford them. Desperate for the last chance to see their loved ones before they were deployed, wives and children began sleeping in cars. The sudden homelessness of their families generated in the servicemen an almost "maniacal fury" toward Miami landlords, who were kicking out average folks in order to rent rooms to wealthy tourists.[42] Other outrages included the disregard some hotel owners, by now immune to the sight of men in uniform, had for those serving their country. When the head doctor of a temporary hospital on Collins Avenue asked the manager of the hotel next door to impose a curfew on the hotel's noisy outdoor dance parties so the wounded could get some rest, the manager replied, "Nothing doing."[43] The greed of proprietors and selfish attitudes of wealthy tourists created a brief scandal and an air of national disgrace. Wylie concluded that only the ill and the war-connected had any right to be in Miami, but he refused to blame Floridians in general, recognizing the state's desperate need for a tourism industry. Instead, he criticized the poor planning of the War and Navy departments and the "wishful, witless self-indulgence" of the rich.[44]

Many Americans viewed the Florida tourists of 1943–1944 as deserters who got just what they deserved when a sudden energy crunch made it almost impossible for them to get home. Gas rationing had tightened over the winter, and railroad space was severely limited. There was a mad rush for the station, as over 15,000 people tried to travel north. The railroads estimated that it would take three months to evacuate the tourists without the addition of special trains. Some tourists became refugees, sleeping in parks and railroad stations when their money ran out, causing disturbances to other travelers. Though *Time* magazine opined that few except the tourists would be appalled if they had to crawl home on "their tanned hands and knees," the Office of Defense Transportation rescued the marooned travelers by authorizing both the Florida East Coast Railway and the Seaboard Railroad to operate one extra train, made up of old and borrowed coaches, per day. The great exodus began on March 1, 1944, when 300 passengers boarded in Miami, and 322 more loaded in Jacksonville, proceeding north with stops at Washington, D.C., Philadelphia, and New York. Many of the riders were swindled by con men who sold them $5–15 "reserved seat" tickets, only to learn upon boarding that there were no reserved spots on the day coaches. The nation laughed at the dingy cars and disheveled passengers on the "refugee specials," while critics seethed that the indulgent escapees deserved a worse punishment than being forced to return in old-fashioned cars.[45]

National critics blasted Florida for the debacle. Rhode Island's state senators, perhaps influenced by their governor, who had been forced to cancel a Florida jaunt, passed a resolution condemning the Sunshine State for withholding gas for return trips. Governor Holland disingenuously replied, "We greatly appreciate our tourists and want to do everything in our power to help them when they are right. . . . Unfortunately there are many who come to Florida in disregard of rationing regulations." Miami hotel owner Andrew G. O'Rourke placed the blame on a higher authority. "If the government doesn't want to have the tourists here," he asked, "why does it let them come south?"[46]

By the 1944–1945 winter season, the Allies' victories boosted morale while the vanquishing of gasoline shortages helped return life to something resembling normality. Railroads were back to regular schedules, and by the first week of December 1944 the Miami Chamber of Commerce was receiving up to 100 calls a day inquiring about accommodations. Prudently, the Miami Beach Serviceman's Housing Cooperative attempted to give service personnel and their families first priority by leasing apartments at lower rates and appealing to homeowners to open spare bedrooms. Those fortunate enough to find a place to stay could enjoy 120 days of horse racing as well as the Orange Bowl game and many other traditional events.[47]

V-E Day and V-J Day brought the war to its conclusion, but failed to soothe the always jumpy nerves of Florida's tourism boosters. Despite the industry's amazing ability to adapt to circumstances, and the determination of the rich and even the not-so-rich to winter in Florida, officials worried that a lack of planning would result in a postwar slump. As early as 1943, the Florida State Chamber of Commerce announced "detailed plans for post-war and even pre-post-war promotion of the tourist trade, and the development of manufacturing and industry, offers the only safe course in preventing Florida's becoming the first post-war casualty." The 1945 legislature voted an unprecedented $1 million for tourism promotion to prevent that unlikely (in hindsight) catastrophe.[48]

The 1945–1946 season was one of "new and bewildering prosperity." Even jaded casino owners were astonished at the number of people eager to gamble away wartime savings. Approximately 2.5 million tourists visited the state in 1945, nearly the number of the last prewar season. By 1950, that number had doubled.[49]

Florida's tourism development from the 1920s to the end of World War II resembled a clattering roller coaster ride, filled with peaks (like the land boom) and dips (the Depression, the wartime rationing). Throughout it all, tourism had continued to grow, becoming an ever more essential part of the Florida economy. By the 1940s, Florida tourism was no longer limited to invalids seeking health, sportsmen after game, or the wealthy craving self-indulgence. More ordinary Americans had come to Florida, often as "tourists on duty." The strength of tourism at midcentury was an essential component of Florida's phenomenal postwar growth; one historian dubbed it the "single most important cause" of the population surge in South Florida. The state's overall population rose from 1,897,414 residents in 1940 to 2,777,307 in 1950. Many of the newcomers were discharged servicemen and women, some of the 2,122,100 who trained and toured in the state. The wartime prophecy of a Miami Beach hotel owner that soldiers "will come back to us either as citizens or guests" was coming true with a vengeance.[50] Florida's beauty and its potential for economic development had a great appeal to the vigorous, mobile young people of the greatest generation.

Florida tourism had survived a series of economic trials, but its foundations were now deeply planted, acknowledged and supported by its government. A spectacular age of tourism was about to begin, as social, cultural, and economic factors launched a new breed of tourists and redefined the state as a great land of fantasy and amusement for all.

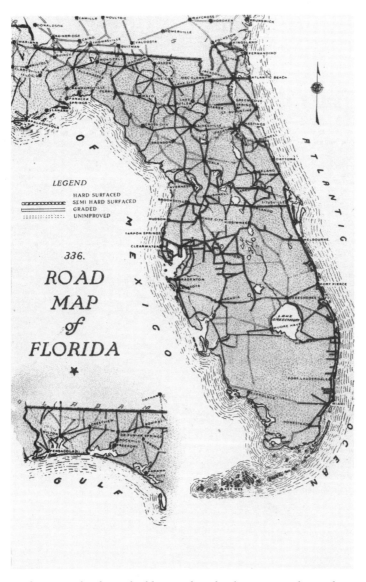

LEGEND

HARD SURFACED
SEMI HARD SURFACED
GRADED
UNIMPROVED

336.

ROAD
MAP
of
FLORIDA

By the 1920s, Florida was building roads and welcoming travelers in their Model Ts and other early automobiles. As this map illustrates, the quality of roads varied greatly across the state. A traveler would have to be prepared for almost any kind of surface. Tourists also had to dodge livestock. Florida was still an agricultural region, and free-ranging pigs and cattle were a very real danger to drivers in the first half of the twentieth century. Courtesy of Florida Photographic Archives.

Early automotive travelers in Florida were known as "tin can tourists." In the 1920s and 1930s, a traveler needed only the basics of a vehicle, a tent, and some cooking supplies to enjoy Florida's balmy climate. Though they celebrated their independence and wanderlust, tin can tourists enjoyed fellowship, often camping together in city or private parks. These visitors were snapped during Christmas festivities at De Soto Park, near Tampa, in 1920. Courtesy of Florida Photographic Archives.

During World War II, Florida's tourism industry met military needs. Thousands of service personnel lived and trained in Florida resorts. Hotels and casinos were converted into barracks and hospitals, and beaches became drill fields. In this startling wartime photograph, servicemen wearing gas masks exercise on Miami Beach. After the war, many men and women who had trained in Florida returned as tourists and new residents, and the image of Florida as a vacation destination for families began to dominate public perception of the Sunshine State. Courtesy of Florida Photographic Archives.

Florida's Seminoles were living tourist attractions to many visitors. Driven from their homes in the Everglades and denied access to traditional activities of hunting and fishing, many Seminoles turned to tourism, opening trading posts and villages. Alligator wrestling quickly became an emblem of the trade, as demonstrated in this twentieth-century postcard of a daring young man from the Musa Isle Indian Village in Miami. Courtesy of Florida Photographic Archives.

Famous for exotic flowers, Southern belles, and champion water skiers, Cypress Gardens was the premiere Florida tourism attraction between the end of World War II and the opening of Walt Disney World. Entrepreneur and owner Dick Pope Sr. masterfully promoted not only Cypress Gardens but also the entire Florida tourism industry. The diversity and charm of the midcentury attractions, as well as their increased promotion in all forms of media, shaped Florida into a family-vacation paradise years before the arrival of the major theme parks. Courtesy of Florida Photographic Archives.

Florida's 160 state parks offer a taste of the "real Florida" to visitors. A number of former tourist attractions, including Weeki Wachee Springs and Homosassa Springs, are now part of the state system. State parks provide a variety of activities and are leaders in ecotourism. In this 2009 photograph, youngsters take the daring plunge from the diving platform at Wakulla Springs. Though its water quality is endangered and its glass bottom boats rarely run, Wakulla Springs remains popular with locals and traveling nature lovers. Photo by the author.

SIX

State of
Imagination

In his 1962 presidential address to the Southern Historical Association, Rembert Patrick quoted a disgruntled Floridian who claimed to live "in the biggest, gaudiest sideshow on earth. . . . It's the nation's perpetual vaudeville show." The resident was disgusted with state and local officials who did nothing to discourage purveyors of questionable entertainment or to rectify historical inaccuracies presented to tourists as irrefutable "facts."[1] But the naysayer was swimming against a strong tide. Florida was becoming a state of imagination.

Between the end of World War II and the opening of Walt Disney World in 1971, without any coherent plan or structure, Floridians created a new image for their state. Governors Fuller Warren and Farris Bryant became nationally recognized spokesmen, regularly hamming it up for the cameras to promote tourism, and virtually every Florida chief executive made travel promotion a top priority.[2] Florida was abruptly family friendly and no longer Southern, except for a few spots in Cypress Gardens, where pretty young women in hoop skirts sat amid bowers of camellias. In the ever-growing quest to provide diverse entertainment and rake in tourist dollars, Florida became a land ruled by kitsch, an escape from wars both hot and cold and something unique in the South and the nation. Florida's modern reputation, as a place not quite as real as everywhere else, was firmly established in the decades that bridged the gap between the greatest generation and the advent of the almighty theme park.[3]

The postwar period was a boom time for Florida tourism. The end of rationing and the pent-up buying power wielded by Americans who had endured a decade of economic depression followed by long years of war-time self-denial made for an explosion of self-indulgent spending. Many of the servicemen who had trained on Florida's beaches were eager to return, some just to vacation but others to settle and begin new lives in a state they considered ripe with opportunity. In a Florida expression, they had "gotten sand in their shoes." Immediately after the war, many young people wanted to travel, and it was now socially acceptable for young women to travel together, unchaperoned by their seniors. The baby boom meant that newly affluent families were eager to vacation with their offspring, provid-ing youngsters with the kind of experiences they could only have dreamed of as children of the Great Depression.[4] A 1949 U.S. Department of Com-merce survey found that 62 percent of all American families planned to take vacations, and 23 million families had already traveled, spending some $7 million. Tourism would be an ever-larger slice of the American economic pie.[5]

A number of factors heralded Florida as an ideal destination for Amer-ica's increasing mobile population. The continuing construction of high-ways made Florida more accessible, and Governor Fuller Warren's 1950 "fence law," which forced the removal of livestock from roadways, proved Florida was committed to tourism above agriculture. Improved mosquito control made the state healthier. Florida advertising grew slicker and more overtly exotic and erotic. Television brought Florida into the nation's liv-ing rooms. Diving off a boat and swimming to the beach in front of the Kenilworth Hotel, Arthur Godfrey told his audience of fifty-four million, "Don't take my word for it. Come on down. Experience it for yourself." It was the greatest tourism advertisement of all time, and Miami Beach's ever-growing reputation as a place where the Rat Pack played, while Jayne Mansfield wowed the paparazzi in her bikini and James Bond spied on Goldfinger, made the Sunshine State chic, even as the booming postwar economy made it affordable.[6]

Perhaps most important, air-conditioning was becoming more common in public buildings and in motel and hotel accommodations. The principle behind air conditioning was discovered in the 1830s by a Florida physician, John Gorrie, who experimented with mechanized cooling devices at the U.S. Marine Hospital in Apalachicola. In 1851, he patented the first ice-making machine, but the larger use of compression to cool air would not come about until the early 1900s. Air conditioning in the South was at first restricted to industry, but by the 1920s it became popular in movie theaters. The 1930s saw the advent of cooled railroad cars, and in the postwar period the trend passed to buildings of all varieties. This blessing made it possible for families with children to enjoy a Florida vacation in the summer, when the kids were out of school and rates tended to be lower.[7]

Air travel was also an important factor in opening the state to a different breed of traveler. "Package air tours" that offered transportation, lodging, and various kinds of sight-seeing excursions, all for a single price, flooded the market in the 1950s. These discounted fares had great appeal to singles (especially young working women), who came with friends to enjoy holidays and flirtations. Novice travelers preferred package tours for the convenience of organized activities and a precise fare.[8] Air travel, once strictly limited to the wealthy, could now be enjoyed by anyone willing to undertake prudent savings for the trip. As a 1962 business-oriented guide to Florida announced, "you don't have to be a millionaire to acquire a Florida tan in February."[9] By 1964, more than 100,000 tourists a year were coming to Miami on package tours. There was no concern about lacking a place to stay; during the 1950s, Miami Beach had covered its sands with hotels of all stripes, allowing city boosters to brag that since World War II, they had constructed more hotels than the rest of the world combined. In 1961, the Florida Hotel Commission reported 1,374 hotels, 24,338 apartment houses, 5,765 motels, and 10,200 rooming houses in the state.[10]

The new breed of tourist also came with a changed attitude about what a family wanted to see and do. New expectations shaped the tourists and, at the same time, the state. Whereas earlier visitors arrived in Florida seeking health, sports, society, investments, or simply a place to avoid winter chills, the new tourist fit firmly into what sociologist Erik Cohen defines as the "recreational mode." The tourists of the postwar period had no strategy beyond passive amusements and pleasure. Recreational tourists were willing to accept make-believe and delude themselves into enjoying contrived situations. Increasingly for these visitors, long days on the beach were not enough. They sought novelty and whimsy, which Floridians were talented at providing.[11] Florida tourism was coming of age with the four basic conditions necessary for it to flourish: a population with adequate funds and time for travel, reliable transportation, comfortable and safe destinations, and a body of images and descriptions designed to excite the imagination and lure patrons. A 1959 survey found that approximately 11.3 million tourists visited the state each year, spending an impressive $1.77 billion. Eighty percent of them came by automobile. The bustling economy had provided people, leisure, and reliable transportation; Florida could easily fill in the rest.[12]

Florida largely discarded its Old South roots, at least in terms of tourism promotions. Few attractions played upon the image of plantations and slavery. The Lewis Plantation near Brooksville, which sought to romanticize slavery, was a short-lived experiment. The Stephen Foster Memorial, opened at White Springs in 1950, fostered an antebellum nostalgia for the composer of "Old Folks at Home" with dioramas depicting plantation scenes and a miniature steamboat ride, but Florida's Crackers were not commemorated. Town leaders were quick to realize, in the words of historian Lamar York, that "the tourist economy in Florida probably would not rise significantly from an enhancement of the state's regional character."[13]

Segregation was clearly holding the state back, however. While promoting itself as exotic and unique, and distinctly not Southern in anything but location, Florida still ascribed to Jim Crow. Florida's laws were not as harsh as the rest of the South's, but custom always seemed to prevail over legality.[14] Many attractions forbade nonwhite visitors, or shuttled them off to separate entrances and facilities. Silver Springs, still Florida's most famous attraction, was off-limits to people of color. African Americans were welcome only at nearby Paradise Park, where glass-bottom boats and a snake show mimicked the attractions upstream. The advertising for Paradise Park even featured an attractive African American woman in a bathing suit, just as most Silver Springs brochures included a cheesecake photo.[15] Beaches were also segregated. While Miami worked to present a sophisticated, cosmopolitan image, black recreation was confided to certain areas. Martin Luther King Jr. and his family, for example, vacationed at the "Colored Only" Virginia Key Beach.[16] Even blacks traveling in menial capacities to whites were pushed aside. A visitor from New Orleans wrote to the manager of the Wakulla Springs Lodge, inquiring about a room for his valet. He was told that the servant might find lodgings in the homes of Wakulla's cooking or cleaning staff.[17]

Though shunned as tourists, African Americans remained essential to the Florida tourism industry. They continued to make up a majority of cooks, waiters, maids, and bellhops in hotels. Many served as entertainers. At Silver Springs, Aunt Silla, an aged black woman, was the resident storyteller of the "legend of the bridal chamber" until her death in 1950. The boatmen of Wakulla Springs were famous for the knowledge of wildlife and their imaginative chants that supposedly summoned fish to perform for guests. African Americans drove carriages in St. Augustine and pedaled rickshaws at Palm Beach. Families, often multiple generations, worked together in resorts. Segregation made black Floridians simultaneously visible and invisible to most visitors.[18]

In the early 1960s, protests erupted against segregation, including the color lines in tourism. Florida's African Americans were able to use tourism to their advantage, especially at beaches, where they staged "wade-ins." In St. Augustine, black youths participated in a wade-in at white beaches and picketed the Tourist Information Center. Tourism was the city's "Achilles' heel," and civil rights demonstrations before visiting Northerners helped generate sympathy and awareness. Town leaders feared disruptions of tourism would threaten the community's livelihood; the 400th anniversary of the city's founding was tense and uneasy.[19] Economic pressure and threats of further boycotts slowly brought about changes in racial policies, if not always attitudes. The Civil Rights Act of 1964 forced desegregation in all public facilities, but throughout most of the period African Americans found themselves unwelcome and shabbily treated at hotels, parks, and attractions. Over time, as young black people tested the new laws and demanded the right to be tourists on par with whites, resorts like American Beach crumbled, a loss to black culture and the economy of already depressed African American communities.[20]

Florida's beaches were the first and foremost attraction of the 1960s. People had long enjoyed walking along the shore or delicately splashing in the surf, but the Gilded Age made water sports popular, and "sea bathing" (swimming) finally came to be accepted for both sexes. Swimsuits grew ever smaller, and a suntan—once the mark of common laborers—became a symbol of vigor, athleticism, and leisure in the 1920s. By the 1960s, beaches were no longer the provinces of the rich, or even adults. Spring break, the annual pilgrimage of college-age youth in search of sun and fun—whether defined by escape from classes or an orgy of sex and alcohol—had its origins in the 1930s, when students traveled to Ft. Lauderdale to participate in the Collegiate Aquatic Forum. Their numbers grew substantially in the 1950s. In 1960, the hit MGM movie *Where the Boys Are*, featuring young sex symbols George Hamilton, Jim Hutton, and Connie Francis frolicking in the Florida surf, made the rite sacred. In 1961, some 50,000 co-eds showed up in Ft. Lauderdale. Their number was a boom for businesses, but a headache for law enforcement and local residents who thought the spring break follies promoted a dissolute image of their city.[21] Over the years, the hot spots for spring break shifted; students came to prefer Daytona, and later the Gulf Coast cities. The ritual, however, remains an important pillar of Florida tourism and state identity, and wherever the college kids gather, communities face the same debate over how much debauchery is socially permissible.[22]

In this grand age of tourism, Florida's visitors listed the beach (whether in Miami, Daytona, Clearwater, or Panama City) as the number one destination, and swimming in the ocean as the activity they most eagerly anticipated. When co-eds went back to the books, families piled into hotels, motor courts, and campgrounds on both the Atlantic and Gulf shores. But there was only so much beachcombing a restless family could take, a factor that made the twenty-five-year period between World War II and the opening of Walt Disney World an ideal time for creative, unregulated, and haphazard amusements.[23]

It was the great era of roadside tourist attractions. Historian and cultural critic Daniel Boorstin cleverly defines a tourist attraction as any venue with "no purpose but to make the owner wealthy."[24] Florida already possessed legions of beautiful places for swimming, sunbathing, and exercising, but its residents were quick to grasp economic benefits of the changing nature of its visitors. Children—never previously a major factor in tourism—were now a growing proportion of the traveling population. To be successful, an attraction just needed a gimmick that would cause the kids to nag mom and dad to stop the car.[25] If the attraction could be sold to the parents as "educational," all the better. A series of 1962 advertisements distributed by the Florida Development Commission played to the expectations of young families. Entitled "Summer Fun," cartoon panels pictured children riding buggies in St. Augustine, taking archery lessons from Seminoles, and donning space helmets. "Bet I know more about missiles than any kid in school," the son exclaims, while the father breathes a sigh of relief that the vacation cost less than he thought it would. Florida's tourists initially came for the sun and sand, but the "good old summer budget vacation time" had something for everyone.[26]

Between 1946 and 1954, over thirty new major attractions opened in Florida, and countless minor ones sprang from local imaginations. In the words of writer John Margolies, a roadside attraction was "an essential part of the Florida tourist experience" but also "much ado about nothing." Anyone with a collection of American Indian artifacts, a large garden, or an exotic animal could put up a billboard and charge admission. Individuality was key; families or sole operators, not large corporations, ran most attractions. While this generated great diversity, and some of the most wondrous nonprofessional advertising ever produced, it also meant that many of these novelty sites lacked not only any claim to authenticity but humane animal care or sanitary facilities as well. To fight substandard ventures, the Florida Attractions Association (FAA) was formed in 1949, and created a code for site maintenance. The FAA provided unified advertising and publicity for its members, who were encouraged to display the FAA emblem. By 1954, Florida "Welcome Stations" marked the border at every major route. Famous for cups of free orange juice, the stations offered maps and brochures, encouraging visitors to look for the FAA emblem as a guarantee of safety and merit.[27]

To qualify as a "roadside attraction," a Florida tourist site needed to meet several qualifications. Built to attract tourists, it was located near a major highway, charged an admission fee, operated strictly for profit, utilized gaudy promotional materials, and played on some aspect of Florida's flora or fauna, though this characteristic was often the most tenuous. Attractions could generally be placed into five categories: botanical, aquatic, zoological, historic, or novelty. A majority of the attractions of the age were small, no more than five acres, and relatively cheap to enter, though their kitschy souvenirs, the proud talismans of a Florida vacation, were decidedly overpriced.[28]

Jungle-, garden-, and spring-themed attractions were among the first to emerge as major players in the postwar era, a natural enough fit for a state already famous for offering "the enchantment of the tropics, the unfamiliar vegetation, the exotic bird life."[29] Unsatisfied with nature's bounty, eager promoters found ways to make these attractions even more spectacular and unusual. Vero Beach entrepreneur Arthur McKee purchased an eighty-acre hammock, hired famous grounds designers, and imported plants and trees from other countries, opening McKee Jungle Gardens in 1932. After the war, McKee upped the jungle quotient, hiring beautiful young women to scamper around in Tarzan-inspired costumes and cavort with imported exotic animals. Across the state, St. Petersburg's Sunken Gardens, which opened in 1935, added flamingos, monkeys, and birds to compete.[30]

The most famous Florida garden attraction was located in Winter Haven. Cypress Gardens was the brainchild of Dick Pope, a promoter remarkable for his ability to survive any adversity. He developed the attraction in 1936, after reading that a similar botanical garden had turned a profit for its Charleston owner. When regular tourism disappeared during World War II, Pope's wife and children improvised water skiing feats to entertain visiting servicemen, accidentally initiating the shows that would make the attraction world famous. A 1940 freeze left unsightly holes in the foliage, but the Popes promptly rounded up local beauties, clad them in pastel hoop skirts, and stuck them in the gaps, thus creating the iconic image of the Florida garden belle, an ideal of romance that had nothing to do with the brutal realities of Florida's plantation heritage. For his determined efforts at promoting not only his own attraction but also other Florida venues, Pope was affectionately called "the man who invented Florida."[31]

Visitors seeking a true Florida botanical experience could venture to the Everglades National Park, which opened in 1947. The river of grass was Florida's most impressive and unique natural attraction. But it came with a human cost; hunting and fishing were the lifeblood of the Glades residents, including its large population of Seminoles. Residents were literally burned out; homes that had taken lifetimes to build were torched overnight. While some rangers demonstrated sensibility, and paid no attention to the Gladesmen who continued to hunt alligators, others were eager to remove the locals. "The villagers felt just like they'd been deliberately cut off from the world, just so tourists could sightsee in their homeland," one local recalled. "I often wonder who they think settled and looked after this place before they ever even saw it. One thing's for certain, it sure wasn't a tourist or a park ranger."[32]

Almost all of the attractions of the 1950s and 1960s would feature tropical denizens in some format, but several attractions based their appeal solely on feathers, fur, and scales. In 1959, Busch Gardens began offering free entertainment for visitors to its Tampa brewery, including a motley collection of birds, black angus cows, Clydesdales, and jungle animals. In Naples, Jungle Larry's Safari was a part of Florida's Caribbean Gardens. The popular safari theme extended in 1954 with Africa USA near Boca Raton. In 1967, Lion Country Safari billed itself as the first "cageless zoo," where visitors drove through open fields in their own cars while bored lions watched their inedible meals putter by. The idea was not really so original; in 1933, Miami's Monkey Garden was a place where "humans are caged and monkeys run wild."[33]

Aviaries and bird shows easily fit into the Florida mystique. Almost every tourist attraction featured a flock of flamingos or parrots. In 1936, Franz Scherr converted a former nudist colony into the Parrot Jungle, an attraction that remained family owned and operated for decades. The stars often flew away, but inevitably came back.[34] Sarasota Jungle Gardens concentrated on birds, as did Birds of Prey, an Ocala attraction featuring falcons, eagles, hawks, and vultures. Inevitably, animal attractions posed risks to the Florida environment, especially since escapees could do serious damage to indigenous wildlife. In 1961, several red-whiskered bulbuls (birds native to India) flew away from the Miami Rare Bird Farm and established a colony in south Florida, where they soon numbered in the hundreds. While not especially dangerous to local birds, they were blamed for helping spread nonindigenous plants, including the noxious Brazilian pepper.[35]

Porpoise shows, which were hugely popular in this period, all traced their ancestry to Marine Studio. Located between St. Augustine and Daytona, the aquarium was built to accommodate filmmakers and opened to the public as an attraction in 1938. It was turned over to the Coast Guard during World War II, and reopened as Marineland in 1946. The porpoise show, which featured tricks and astonishing leaps, debuted in 1951. Imitators quickly emerged under ever more imaginative names: the Miami Seaquarium, the Gulfarium in Fort Walton Beach, the Theater of the Sea in Islamorada, Neptune's Garden in Marathon, St. Peterburg's Aquatarium, the Sea-Ormama in Clearwater Beach, Ocean World in Ft. Lauderdale, and the rather blandly titled Key West Aquarium.[36]

Reptiles, especially snakes and alligators, fit the Florida tropical motif. Florida's Reptile Land in Lawtey advertised "over 100 animals from different parts of the world" but relied on alligators to sell trinkets. The oldest reptile attraction was the St. Augustine Alligator Farm, which dated to the 1890s. Alligator wrestling remained a featured attraction of Coppinger's Tropical Gardens in Miami. Gatorland in Kissimmee, which opened in 1949, became even more popular after it added a huge, open-mouthed stucco alligator entrance in 1962.[37] Gatorama opened in Palmdale in 1957, and the Snake-A-Torium at Panama City Beach distinguished itself from smaller reptile exhibits with its memorable billboards that stretched from the Alabama line to the forked tongue painted in the parking lot.[38]

A gentler take on Florida wildlife was Tommy Bartlett's International Deer Ranch, a petting zoo that shared a parking lot with Silver Springs. Operated by the star of CBS television's *Welcome Traveler*, the park was organized around a Christmas theme and featured tame deer and barnyard animals. In 1962, Bartlett's name was removed, and the park was incorporated into Silver Springs, along with the Ross Allen Reptile Institute, which was famous for its demonstrations of snake venom milking.[39]

Animal performers were featured everywhere, but only one Florida attraction had mythological creatures entertaining on an hourly schedule. Champion swimmer Newt Perry, a former manager of Wakulla Springs and a stunt coordinator for novelty films, partnered with Walton Hall Smith to purchase the Weeki Wachee Spring near Brooksville. They invested in a sunken seating area, and Perry trained generations of young women to swim as mermaids in the spring's depths. The mermaid shows combined synchronized swimming with feats of underwater bravado, including eating meals and making deep dives that gave the impression the mermaid had drowned. The shows grew ever more elaborate over the years, and depended as much on the beauty as the athleticism of the mostly female cast. A clever promoter, Perry never missed a chance to get his mermaids in the news, and his heirs continued the tradition. Publicity stunts at Weeki Wachee included movies made on site, underwater weddings, and visits by celebrities, among them an awe-struck Elvis Presley.[40]

A number of much smaller attractions grew out of private collections of novelties, authentic or otherwise. One determined exhibitor was Esmond Gerard Barnhill, a photographer who collected hand-colored postcards and American Indian artifacts. In 1953, he opened his Ancient America Museum near Boca Raton, on the site of a Calusa Indian mound. When his relics failed to draw large crowds, he bemoaned the typical tourist's obsession with "dog tracks and nightclubs," closed Ancient America, and relocated his collection to Palm Bay, where he opened his Indian Springs Museum. Still seeking the elusive tourists, he moved a third time to Kissimmee and opened Indian World Museum and Trading Post, which was described by one critic as "a hodgepodge of genuine artifacts, ordinary antiques, and personal keepsakes put together without regard for interpretation or authentication." Another bizarre museum was James Melton's Autorama in Hypoluxo. An opera star and host of TV's musical variety show *Ford Festival*, Melton assembled nearly 100 antique autos, plus collections of toys, music boxes, baby carriages, and a giant cyclorama called "America the Beautiful." Wood Parade, a St. Petersburg attraction operated by craftsman Earl Gresh, featured samples of forestry products from around the world, hand-carved tackle boxes, purses, and fishing lures, plus sixteen large wooden murals of the life of Christ. These attractions had very limited appeal and did not survive after the deaths of their owners.[41]

One small attraction based on an individual's quirky passion endured into the 1990s. The Cypress Knee Museum near Palmdale featured gnarled cypress roots that suggested faces, animals, and objects. Founded in 1934 by Tom Gaskins, the roadside attraction eventually included a museum, factory, souvenir stand, and catwalk through a cypress swamp. Gaskin's clever handmade signs and his amiable interactions with tourists, including personally led tours of his swamp, made the site nationally famous. His son assumed this role after Gaskins's death in 1998, but the Florida Turnpike and other major interstates had long since bypassed the museum. The quaint attraction became a relic of the past. Thefts and vandalism eventually shuttered the museum in 2000.[42]

While most tourist attractions combined different forms of entertainment, sometimes just a single ride was enough. Treasureland, near Tampa, was nothing more than an indoor "dark ride" that took patrons through "an exciting and rib-tickling adventure in piracy brought to life by electronic animation . . . through the refuge of the swamps and a rip-roaring battle at sea." A blatantly obvious plagiarism of Disneyland's "Pirates of the Caribbean," but with boats that moved along a dry floor and animation that had all the realism of department store mannequins, the attraction's lifespan was shorter than a pirate's carouse.[43]

Many attractions incorporated Florida flora and fauna, but only one tried to depict Florida history in dramatic form. In 1965, the "symphonic drama" *Cross and Sword* opened in an outdoor theater in St. Augustine. Written by Pulitzer Prize–winning author Paul Green, the play was commissioned in celebration of the city's 400th anniversary and was designated the official state play in 1973. Blending dance, pantomime, and poetic dialogue, *Cross and Sword* was a rare attempt at combining tourism and culture. It ran seasonally until 1996.[44]

St. Augustine remained proud of its status as the nation's oldest city, but one would hardly have recognized this distinction based on the proliferation of tacky attractions that had little relation to real history. Ripley's Believe It or Not Museum, Potter's Wax Museum, and the Old Jail traded on the bizarre and hideous, as did Buddy Hough's Tragedy in U.S. History Museum, which featured items owned by Lee Harvey Oswald, plus a number of infamous celebrity "death cars." All the museum's articles were of dubious authenticity and decidedly bad taste. The city tried to close the museum as soon as it opened, but Hough, a propane dealer, fought back and eventually won in the Florida Supreme Court. The museum remained a community embarrassment until Hough's widow sold off the collection two years after Hough's death in 1996.[45]

St. Augustine's most famous inauthentic attraction was the fabled Fountain of Youth, which traded on a host of conquistador legends crafted wholesale by imaginative promoters. It was not only the site of the magical water but contained a coquina pyramid where Ponce de Leon's armor was buried. Local historian Charles Reynolds had vigorously debunked these tales in 1937, revealing that the fountain was nothing more than an artesian well excavated from a previous home site. Tourists still swallowed the water, and the hokum, with glee.[46]

Across the state, the landmark of kitsch, Goofy Golf, opened in 1958 at Panama City Beach. Miniature golf had been a craze of the 1930s, but tourist maven Lee Koplin created a new kind of course that resembled a theme park, complete with oversize figures of a sphinx, chimp, and sea monster. Over the years, the original course grew into an even gaudier feast, complete with jungles and caves. Similar courses featuring dinosaurs and windmills sprang up across the state, providing cheap family fun for guests, though some residents considered the attractions permanent eyesores.[47]

By the early 1960s, Florida tourists were becoming savvier, requiring something beyond the old array of zoos, gardens, and springs. Movies and television had an impact in the family station wagon. The launches at Cape Canaveral drew thousands who were excited by both the reality of the space race and the popularity of science fiction serials. To compete with what tourists saw on TV, many older attractions added more rides and shows, becoming a kind of interactive vaudeville. Cape Coral Gardens near Ft. Myers was a typical victim of the push for more diverse attractions in one place. Its advertising promised "something for every member of the family, from thrilling action events to quiet, serene beauty, from memorable classical music to magnificent sculpture, from dramatic fountains to sleepy lagoons." It lasted less than half the decade.[48] Even attractions poorly suited for expansion tried to change with the times. Birds of Prey, for example, was renamed Florida Adventureland when it added rides and attractions. Along with the additions to older sites, new amusement parks that drew inspiration from television and movies were constructed as the competition for tourists began to boil.[49]

The western town was an obvious example of how mass media transformed Florida tourism. Florida as frontier was not incongruous. In its antebellum youth, Florida had been filled with fierce Indians, outlaws on the run, and whip-wielding Cracker cowboys. Tourism promoters, however, had no interest in tying their parks to genuine Florida history. Their frontier belonged to Matt Dillon, Maverick, Paladin, and other TV heroes. In the 1960s, the frontier town became a fixture of Florida tourism, with shootouts erupting in every corner of the state. Pioneer City was located near St. Augustine, and Brooksville was home to Ft. Dodge.[50] The most famous of the western-themed amusement parks was Six Gun Territory in Ocala. Opened in 1963, the property was the brainchild of R. B. Coburn, who had previously created North Carolina's Ghost Town in the Sky. The park resembled Ghost Town on a much larger scale, with 254 acres for stagecoaches, train trips, gunslinger duels, and Indian settlements. Can-can dancers and carnival rides completed the bill. A ski lift and a concrete mountain marked its entrance.[51]

The success of frontier towns led to bizarre competition between Panhandle tourism entrepreneurs. In Panama City, Goofy Golf legend Lee Koplin replaced older attractions around an existing miniature train ride to create Tombstone Territory. The park featured everything one would expect to see in the Wild West, including a jail, saloon, hotel, and trading post. Koplin's rivals, the Churchwell family, also operated a train ride on their Long Beach Resort property. They decided to add a western town and named it Petticoat Junction, in honor of the television show that starred Edgar Buchanan, a family friend. The show had nothing to do with the West, but that failed to stop the construction of a frontier theme park. The showdown between the sites led to a proliferation of giant concrete caves, totem poles, and longhorn cattle in an area that had once been as sleepy as a true ghost town. The long stretch of Gulf coastline known as the Miracle Strip had been dormant before the Depression, but in the 1950s it exploded not only with western towns and Goofy Golf courses but also with amusement parks, observation towers, and boardwalks.[52]

Perhaps more appropriate to Florida—though its theme was only a thin veneer—was Pirate's World, an eighty-seven-acre park in Dania, opened in 1966. What had been pirated were the rides, which were purchased secondhand from older, more famous American amusement parks. The Crow's Nest observation tower was in reality the Belgian Aerial Tower from the 1964–1965 World's Fair, and the Steeplechase ride, consisting of molded horses that traversed an undulating track, had arrived from Coney Island. Carnival-quality rides, a log flume, and rock concerts made Pirate's World appear to be an old-style amusement park straight out of a more disreputable, dangerous era.[53]

As new parks were created, a number of classic Florida attractions received facelifts. Though places like Silver Springs could claim a long and distinguished pedigree of tourism, age and reputation were not enough. A site had to modernize to keep up, and that often meant passing to new ownership with less classical ideas about what a Florida attraction should entail.

Silver Springs had received tourists since the 1850s, but with the passing of the age of the stern-wheel steamers, business had dried to a trickle. In the 1920s, two Ocala businessmen, W. C. Ray and W. M. "Shorty" Davidson, leased the property and turned it into a modern attraction. Halting incoming traffic from the Silver River, they installed gas-powered glass-bottom boats in 1925. In the early 1930s, reptile shows and jungle cruises on the river added to the springs' appeal. One of the unexpected consequences of attempting to make the boat rides more exciting came when a tribe of rhesus monkeys was released onto an island. Their exhibitor had no idea they could swim. They soon overflowed the park, and continue to be a nonindigenous nuisance in Central Florida. Silver Springs became nationally famous as the backdrop for Tarzan movies and later for the TV series *Sea Hunt*. Reptile wrangler Ross Allen also publicized Silver Springs with his many appearances on television, including shows like *We the People* and *Ripley's Believe It or Not*.[54]

In 1962, the property was sold to the American Broadcasting Company (ABC), which continued the practice of adding on small attractions around the parking lot. By the late 1960s, a tourist at Silver Springs could fill up more than one day with the Springs, the Ross Allen show, the Deer Park, the Early America Museum, and the Prince of Peace Memorial, which housed hand-carved scenes from the life of Christ. Passing from local to corporate ownership guaranteed Silver Springs would receive even more national promotion, but did not ensure the owners would be concerned with much besides making money. Historian Rembert Patrick told an audience in 1962 that at "beautiful Silver Springs, Florida, unhappy looking Indians make beads, snakes are milked of their venom, and commercialism is rampant."[55]

Two other classic Florida springs saw changes and expanded facilities in the 1960s and early 1970s. Rainbow Springs, near Dunnellon, offered boat rides and postcards as early as 1938, but became a significant attraction in the 1950s when it was leased by Rock City Gardens, a leader in Southern tourism promotion. When that lease expired, the site passed to a corporation formed by Holiday Inn and S & H Green Stamps. What had once been a quiet retreat quickly became a gaudy show, complete with flashing neon signs and a "Forest Flite" monorail system with carts shaped like giant leaves. Homosassa Springs, in Citrus County, had been known for decades as "Florida's Fish Bowl" because of a special underwater viewing station for its astonishing habitat of both fresh- and salt-water fish. In the 1960s, it began to feature tame squirrels and an animal show starring Clarence the Crosseyed Lion from TV's *Daktari* and the titular bear of *Gentle Ben.* A miniskirt-clad Indian princess on Homosassa's sign pointed the way to the parking lot with a bow and arrow. In sharp contrast, Wakulla Springs, just south of Tallahassee, avoided Rainbow and Homosassa springs' fate thanks to its ownership by Ed Ball, a legendary Florida business tycoon. Ball opened a lodge on the site in 1937, and steadily improved the glass-bottom boats and jungle cruises, but stoutly refused to "turn Wakulla into a honky tonk" on the level of Cypress Gardens. By remaining in a single owner's hands, it reflected his conservative ideals about tourism and was largely unknown outside of the Panhandle.[56]

By the early 1970s, the days of Florida's small, often family-run attractions were numbered. The greatest threat on the horizon was the opening of Walt Disney World. Yet many promoters were happy to have a new neighbor. Dick Pope, Cypress Garden's maestro, loudly proclaimed that Disney would be good for Cypress Gardens' business. Anything that would attract more tourists to the relatively sleepy environs of Central Florida did, on the surface, sound like a good thing. Ultimately, however, Disney World sounded a death knell for smaller parks, which simply could not compete with its technology and national reputation.

By the mid-1970s, a vast majority of the small attractions were dead. Amusement parks and western towns were especially hard hit. Most closed their doors or limped along for a few seasons, looking ever more rusted and ragged and second-class when compared to the polished, high-tech world of the mouse. Today the western towns have vanished, their bones swallowed by shopping centers and parking lots, just as the TV shows that inspired them are relegated to cut-rate DVDs.[57] Jungle Land, Panama City's artificial volcano populated by bikini-clad women, belched its last smoke and became Alvin's Island Magic Mountain Mall.[58] However, the coming of Mickey Mouse—while instrumental in bringing the age of imagination to a close—was not the only factor in shuttering the small attractions. Super highways drew travelers away from the small towns and off the local roads. Travel patterns changed; people were no longer willing to ramble in search of oddball amusements. The growing impact of television cannot be underestimated. Major corporations like ABC and Disney could advertise their attractions, to the point that tourists once more had goals in travel, and those goals were to see Silver Springs or Disney World.[59]

But despite their brief lifespan, the glitzy attractions of the years between the war and the mouse made an indelible mark on Florida's national reputation. Greed often overrode true artistry; one observer opined that the open palm, rather than the sable palm, should be the state emblem. The state was becoming incidental; it was warm and open year-round, but its natural environment often took a backseat to attractions that could be installed anywhere. Exotic animals and western gunfights could be staged without any reference to the scenery or history unique to the state.[60] *Florida: Polluted Paradise*, a 1964 manifesto on the state's many failings, contained a rant against the growing impact of thoughtless tourism attractions, arguing "there is plenty wrong and ugly about this over-glamorized state." Describing the scene along the "hurdy-gurdy midways," the authors warned that Florida publicity was nothing but "dope" and that anyone who looked too deeply at the state's attractions would be cruelly disillusioned.[61]

Perhaps the best reflection of this "dope" and the trend to pack in novelty without context, purely in hopes of making a quick buck, was the most mercenary of all Florida attractions, Floridaland. An aggressively advertised amusement park situated on fifty acres between Sarasota and Venice, Floridaland was billed as "Everything you came to Florida to see!" That meant porpoise shows, a ghost town, a deer park, an Indian village, tropical gardens, a whiskey still, sea lions, and tour trams vaguely disguised as locomotives. The result was a baffling and unattractive mishmash of amusements, a "theme park in search of a theme." Like so many others, it failed to survive the 1970s.[62]

While the state encouraged its citizens to be "Friendly Floridians" and welcome guests, many natives and long-term residents were disgusted by what their state was becoming. A *Miami Herald* columnist noted that during this era, Floridians traded "natural treasures for material ones" and "might have made a better bargain." As the state dumped its Old South heritage, it failed to develop a more substantial image beyond "the great national sandbox."[63] Yet the period also provokes strong nostalgia, especially among aging baby boomers. As Tim Hollis, the author of numerous books on Florida tourism, states, the attractions like Floridaland were relics of an age when "getting there and seeing odd stuff along the way was fun." People liked to ramble and were delighted by novelties found along the road.[64] Another aspect of Florida's roadside attractions' appeal was their cheapness. A family could visit multiple sites for a few dollars. The era could also be seen as a more innocent time, when Americans were easily entertained and not so jaded, or wedded to fast food, corporate logos, and the safety of name brands when they vacationed. They could be fascinated—as was John Rothchild, the author of *Up for Grabs*, as a small boy in 1953—with coconuts carved into pirate heads, stuffed alligators, and pelicans made from seashells. When Walt Disney World and the other theme parks took over, much of the whimsy disappeared from Florida's highways.[65]

Florida travelers of the 1950s and 1960s firmly established the modern reputation of the "tacky tourist." Essentially passive travelers, they had little interest in recreation that involved anything more strenuous than tossing around a beach ball. Their reputation for being rude and obnoxious matched their tendency to carry cameras, dress in outlandish attire, and gullibly swallow any amount of hokum they were fed. Anyone with a headdress could be a Seminole, and every alligator was the world's largest. With twice as much leisure time, and wads more money than their grandparents had possessed in the 1890s, the new legions of Florida tourists could gawk at curios and bake in the sun without any sense of their own shallowness.[66]

It should also be noted that Florida's gaudy age of tourism laid the foundation for Disney's success. People perceived Florida as a land of fantasy and imagination in the decades before the mouse arrived. The Florida family vacation already existed; Disney did not have to invent it. Disney and the other major corporate theme parks that followed were building on an image of Florida that was already richly embedded in the national consciousness. Some attractions, like Silver Springs, Cypress Gardens, and Weeki Wachee, played on myths and images that seemed natural for Florida. Architectural critic Margot Ammidon holds that the many gardens, jungles, and springs of the postwar period form a collection of "Edens, underworlds, and shrines" that drew, perhaps often unconsciously, on shared folklore and biblical allusions. It is worth noting that the attractions that survived the period still convey a "surprising charm and beauty" in harnessing ancient tales of a lost paradise or enchanted creatures, such as mermaids, that can only be found in the most fantastic of places. Certainly this creativity, no matter how kitschy at times, shaped the perception of Florida as a land outside of the norm, where fantasies could be glimpsed for the paltry price of an admission ticket. As such, this age and its attractions laid the groundwork for the modern image of Florida, including the stereotype of its tourists, and also for the creation of the larger fantasy-lands that would drive most of Florida's original attractions out of business.[67]

Most important, the two decades following World War II confirmed what the 1920s and 1930s had suggested: tourism was Florida's premiere industry. A Florida vacation had previously been a status symbol; now it was realistic goal for millions of Americans. With segregation finally defeated, Florida's tourist attractions could be promoted both nationally and internationally; everyone would be welcome in this imaginary Eden. A giddy 1930 *National Geographic* article had suggested that Florida was growing out of its troubling dependence upon tourism, but by 1962 a practical businessman conceded that "tourists are of transcendent importance to the state despite all the bright words about 'Florida's achievement of a truly balanced economy' or 'a coming of age industrially.'"[68]

That dependence would deepen when a mouse moved into Orlando.

SEVEN

Magic Kingdoms

On November 22, 1963, a private plane took off from an airfield in Tampa, carrying a party of businessmen traveling under assumed identities. The flight took the group over Orlando. They gazed down on the new road construction of Interstate 4 (I-4), and saw where it intersected with the Florida Turnpike, forming a natural conduit of roads from the eastern coast. They also saw vast acres of swampy, undeveloped land. The entrepreneurs landed and boarded another plane for New Orleans, where they learned the news of the assassination of President John F. Kennedy. The national tragedy naturally overshadowed their brief flight, but the significance of that aerial journey over Orlando can never be overestimated, as one of the passengers was in the process of making the most important decision in the history of Florida tourism. His name was Walter Elias ("Walt") Disney.[1]

Walt Disney's life story could easily have been conjured in his own dream factory. The son of poor parents and one of five children, he grew up in Marceline, Missouri, and with his brother Roy launched an animation studio in the 1920s. Though never a great artist, Disney excelled because he "created memorable characters, placed them in engaging storylines that retained the innocence of a bygone era, and employed the latest technological advancements." Disney's entertainment empire and his influence on popular culture made him one of the most influential Americans of the twentieth century. Always on the lookout for new challenges, by the 1950s

Disney was determined to open a theme park based on his own characters. He saw it as a way for people to engage in three-dimensional interactions with familiar stories. It also gave him a chance to experiment with new ideas and attractions, to constantly modify and improve his work. Disneyland opened in Anaheim, California, in 1955.[2]

Disneyland proved to be a remarkable success, and a much more reliable generator of funds than Disney's movies. Disney recognized the elemental changes in American culture in the 1950s and tapped into the middle-class desire to avoid chaos, crime, and squalor. The very things that had made amusement parks of the past appealing—their grittiness and seediness, their flirtation with fringe elements—were characteristics that post–World War II parents with young children rejected as undesirable.[3] Amusement parks had to be cheap to get customers, but families of the 1950s could afford better quality entertainment. Disposable per capita personal income increased by nearly 500 percent in the years between 1940 and 1970. Together, the baby boom and the bustling economy guaranteed a market for wholesome family fun. Disney capitalized on his empire of homogenized fairy tales and romanticized Americana to provide the newly mobile bourgeoisie with just what they and their children wanted: safe, clean, instantly recognizable fantasies.[4]

Initially, Disney resisted calls from other cities to replicate his world inside their borders. Part of Disneyland's appeal was its uniqueness, which it would hardly possess if every major metropolis had a similar park. But Disney also recognized that most of his visitors were from California. Less that 10 percent of guests had crossed the Mississippi to see Mickey Mouse. Studies for new sites began in 1958, and after Disneyland was praised in a 1963 speech as the best piece of urban design in America, Disney became much more interested in building not just a second park, but a futuristic city.[5]

Disney had learned valuable lessons in California and was determined to apply them to his future park/town. Already confined by an urban border, Disneyland was unable to expand beyond well-defined limits. Imaginative designs within the park were hindered by building codes and regulations. Hemmed into the approximately 160-acre lot, Disney could not control the types of businesses that quickly grew up around his kingdom. Tourists ran a gauntlet of dingy restaurants, hotels, and souvenir stands before entering Disneyland. To avoid these unpleasant aspects, Disney and his legions of researchers sought a place where a park could be operational year-round, in a region not overly developed yet threaded by an adequate highway system, so that visitors could reach the new park by car.[6] For his "Project X," as the venture was initially called, Disney needed somewhere easily accessible to East Coast residents, a place with land so cheap his company could scoop up a major chunk of real estate, ensuring future expansion. Disney coveted a spot where civic boosters would embrace him and lawmakers would bow to his will. Various sites were considered and rejected—Niagara Falls, St. Louis, Washington, D.C.—before Disney narrowed his search to Florida and took his secretive flight.[7]

The ultimate selection of Orlando came on the advice of Bill Lund, a real estate consultant and financial analyst Disney commissioned to study and compare the Ocala and Orlando areas. Lund was charged with assessing the local economy, land prices, highways, topography, and climate of both cities, reporting back in just sixty days. Lund's work was a covert operation. Disney liked Lund's report and after the plane ride made the final decision for Orlando, sending Bob Foster, his general counsel, to Central Florida to begin acquiring options on massive amounts of acreage. Dummy corporations started collecting land along the Orange-Osceola county lines with a stealth that would have made James Bond proud.[8]

Orlando had long been hoping for something profitable to come along. Though the city did not actively court Disney, town boosters were searching for some type of "gimmick" to stop people from bypassing their burg en route to Miami and other more popular South Florida destinations. In 1969, a mere 3.5 million tourists visited Orlando. It was a disappointing figure, considering the high hopes that had arisen with the spate of highway and turnpike construction in the previous decade. Orlando had lobbied for the Florida Turnpike, succeeding in getting the route drawn from Wildwood to Ft. Pierce rather than straight down the east coast. I-4 had been developed primarily with manufacturing and industrial uses in mind; the opening of Cape Canaveral and the U.S. Missile Test Center in 1956 promised much for the entire region. The interstate was not without its detractors, however, especially Orlando residents who predicted a major highway running through their city would generate slums and congestion.[9]

While Orlando benefited from better highways, most Floridians were in no mood to support further construction. In 1965, Florida voters defeated a $300 million state road bond issue. Accusations of corruption in the administration of Governor Haydon Burns soured many voters on supporting highway improvements. Floridians also feared that the state would be saddled with debt and that valuable funds would be diverted from education; as usual, Floridians longed for economic development and growth but were unwilling to pay for it, and lacked faith that tourism would eventually return dividends on such a hefty investment. Disney officials were not pleased, but the die had already been cast. Few highway advocates could have imagined how important these major roads were to Walt Disney's decision to locate his eastern kingdom on the outskirts of the "City Beautiful."[10]

As five corporations began gobbling up Central Florida property in the summer of 1965, speculation began to mount over the real force behind the secretive purchases. Most rumors cast the mysterious land grab as the work of various industrial giants angling to bring large manufacturing plants to the region. McDonald Aircraft, Ford Motor Company, Hughes Tool, and Hercules Powder were likely suspects, though the Disney name was timidly floated as well.[11] By June, Disney had purchased or optioned 27,258 acres in Orange and Osceola counties. The forty-two-square-mile tract was twice the size of Manhattan and approximately the same girth as San Francisco. Something more than just an industrial complex was afoot. *Orlando Sentinel* reporter Emily Bavar put the question directly to Walt Disney while on a press junket to Disneyland in October 1965, and his awkward denial/nondenial seemed to confirm what many had begun to openly speculate. The *Sentinel* ran the story, and Governor Burns's October 15 address to the Florida League of Municipalities, in which he said that Disney would soon bring in "the greatest attraction yet known in the history of Florida," made the official announcement, on November 15, 1965, anticlimatic. The governor and Walt Disney were suitably vague about what the "greatest attraction" would consist of, revealing only that it would cost $100 million, employ some 4,000 people, and include a "City of Tomorrow" that would be self-contained within the park.[12] Floridians vested in tourism were astounded and hopeful. Dick Pope, the entrepreneur and showman behind Cypress Gardens, drove the welcome wagon for Disney, announcing, "Anyone who is going to spend $100 million near me is good, and a good thing."[13]

Walt Disney did not survive to see his dream of a futuristic city and amusement park rise from the Florida swamps. He succumbed to lung cancer on December 15, 1966, only days after his sixty-fifth birthday. Though Disney had worked on his beloved city project up to the hours before his death, his corporation was far from enthusiastic about an experiment in urban planning. Certain that it would be less entertaining, and therefore much less profitable, than a theme park, Roy Disney decided the company should stick with what it did best. "Disneyland East," however, was sold to the state as a reflection of Disney's original vision. With great canniness, the Disney Corporation asked for startling powers for its Florida enclave.[14]

Walt Disney's last movie, a short called the Epcot film, was shown to a legion of state officials and reporters on February 2, 1967. Speaking from the grave, Disney outlined his dream of a futuristic town. Afterward, Roy Disney essentially threatened to pull the project unless the state made a series of astonishing concessions. By claiming that the company was focused on constructing a model city for some 20,000 residents, Disney sought almost sovereign status within Florida, along with numerous perks, including the widening of I-4 at the park entrance and the construction of three highway interchanges. The company also asked for special legislation to protect its trademark and trade names. Newly inaugurated governor Claude Kirk, a probusiness Republican, eagerly supported the package, in which Disney made no demands for tax money while pledging the creation of 50,000 new jobs and a revenue stream of an estimated $6.6 billion over the next decade. The Florida legislature eagerly and obediently passed the 481 pages of proposals. As Carl Hiaasen, legendary Florida novelist and newspaper columnist, notes, "Never before or since has such outlandish dominion been given to a private corporation."[15]

The Reedy Creek Improvement District, as the property was officially titled, became an autonomous political district, empowered to issue tax-exempt bonds. Two towns, Lake Buena Vista and Bay Lake, were also incorporated. The state approved these measures on the false premise that Disney was building a company town, not merely looking for protection of its own interests and enough land mass to respond to any outside challenge to its profits. In return, Disney promised jobs, money, and a never-ending stream of tourists. The company also pledged to pay for its own fire protection, sewage system, and internal roadways, and to establish a wildlife conservation program. Naively believing that the new jobs and revenues generated by Disney and its inevitable tourism would counter any fudging of county regulations or future problems, Florida lawmakers essentially allowed Disney World to become a "Vatican with mouse ears," an independent entity in the heart of the Sunshine State.[16]

Disney still had to sell itself to the people of Florida. In the late 1960s, relatively few Americans had ever been to Disneyland in Anaheim. Most Floridians had no concept of the type of entertainment complex that was being planned; at best, they assumed it was a zoo or an amusement park on the lines of those in Jacksonville and Panama City. Sandy Quinn, the first Disney director of marketing, went on a speaking tour of Florida businesses and chambers of commerce, urging people to brainstorm ways to surf the coming wave of tourism. He was often patronized, his message met with skepticism. A group of Miami Beach hotel managers informed him that people came to Florida for beaches and hotels, not for amusement parks. Some citizens remembered the irresponsible promises of the land boom and assumed this was just another scam.[17] While most Floridians had difficulty imagining Disney World as more than a roadside attraction, a few soothsayers warned that a wave of Tinkerbell's wand might not be magical. Shortly after the official announcement, Martin Anderson reminded readers in an *Orlando Sentinel* editorial, "You cannot dump 50,000 tourists a day into this community along with 50,000 new jobs and build 40,000 new homes without putting somebody out of joint."[18]

The Disney Preview Center was more successful in spreading the message of the upcoming Magic Kingdom. Opened in Lake Buena Vista on January 10, 1970, and staffed by a bevy of attractive young women, the center featured a huge model of the park, conceptual art drawings, and a film revealing plans for the resort. Tickets, hotel reservations, and souvenirs were also available. Employees recorded the license plates of the center's visitors, giving planners an idea of from where their future guests would come. During nearly two years of operation, the Preview Center hosted over a million visitors and presold some $11 million in tickets.[19]

Walt Disney World opened on October 1, 1971, at a final cost of $400 million. While not an exact replica of Disneyland, there were many familiar touches. Visitors entered down an idealized 1890s American Main Street that led to Cinderella's castle, the visual focus point of the park. It served as a hub with pathways leading off to Adventureland, Frontierland, Fantasyland, and Tomorrowland. Many attractions were not working, and vital landscaping had been completed only hours before the gates were unlocked. The crowd was disappointing, a mere 10,400 guests. Some naysayers wondered if the mouse had laid an egg. While opening day was a "brutal disappointment" in terms of numbers, it was probably a blessing in disguise for the company, as it gave park managers time to work out the bugs in malfunctioning rides and complete the construction of the Contemporary Hotel. By the holiday season, the turnstiles began to clack more rapidly. The day after Thanksgiving saw traffic backed up for ten miles and some 56,000 guests stampeding into the Magic Kingdom, forcing it to shutter its ticket windows early in the afternoon. Visitors were advised to budget $33 a day for a family of four to cover attraction tickets and food. At the end of its first year Disney World could brag that it had logged 10,712,991 visitors and banked total gross revenues of $139 million. Perhaps more important, the shift toward Central Florida tourism was already visible. The month Disney World opened, an estimated 10.8 percent of Florida visitors were headed to the Orlando area, up from 3.7 percent the previous year. Tourists traveling to Dade County dropped from 10 percent to 7.7 percent.[20]

Disney World's first year was a golden one for its neighbors. The wealth of visitors was shared, both in terms of hotel rooms booked and outside attraction tickets sold. Orlando had approximately 6,000 hotel rooms in 1971, forcing potential Disney World guests to bunk as far away as Daytona and Tampa. Virtually all the major attractions saw a sharp boost in attendance from the previous year: Cypress Gardens, 38 percent; the Kennedy Space Center, 27 percent; Silver Springs, 28 percent; and St. Augustine's Castillo de San Marcos, 29 percent. Dick Pope's prophecy, that Disney millions would be good for everyone, seemed to be coming true.[21]

As Disney World proved its ability to lure mass quantities of tourists, Orlando and Kissimmee exploded. The entire area became a "paradise for builders." Land values shot up, so that farmers and grove owners saw their plots more than triple in value. Many were unable to resist selling out and relocating with their small fortunes as developers gambled like Las Vegas high rollers. Approximately 20,000 new hotel and motel units were being hammered into place in early 1972, and some developers speculated that restaurants would have to grow by 650 percent over the next four years to adequately feed the influx of hungry tourists. Unemployment dropped while sales skyrocketed. A 1972 *U.S. News and World Report* article chronicled the astonishing growth of what had previously been a sleepy agricultural town. "Employment is climbing, construction is hitting record peaks, retail sales are soaring, and the population is growing at an eye-popping rate."[22]

Another reason for the growth was the arrival of a second major theme park. Ten miles north of Disney, Sea World of Florida was the third of the Sea World franchises, after Sea World of California, in San Diego, and Sea World of Ohio, in Cleveland. It broke ground shortly after the opening of Disney World, and welcomed its first guests in 1973. The popular aquatic park followed a long tradition of porpoise shows and aquariums, though its inland location made it unique in Florida. In 1976, it was purchased by Harcourt Brace Jovanovich, which assured its expansion into an even larger theme park. Disney was not initially concerned about the competition, as it had no rival water-oriented attraction. Instead, Disney executives viewed the construction as helpful, a sign that Central Florida would become the ultimate destination for Sunshine State tourists. Bob Mathieson, head of operations for Disney, welcomed Shamu and friends with a "more the merrier attitude," and executives for Sea World were often invited, along with Cypress Gardens's Dick Pope, to preview Disney's expansions.[23]

Such phenomenal growth inevitably generated a backlash from area residents. Highways snarled, lakes fouled, and property taxes shot into the stratosphere.[24] One Kissimmee retiree saw the taxes levied on his tiny home jump from $109 to $600, far more than he could afford on his fixed income. He promptly sold out, moving away from both staggering property values and the growing traffic just beyond his door. Agricultural production dropped when citrus growers and cattle ranchers sold out to developers. The transient population rose precipitously, with the Orlando Salvation Army reporting that it provided assistance to a record 67,000 indigents in 1971. Many residents blamed Disney World for attracting disreputable types, con men and criminals, and even hippies. There was a rise in crime, especially prostitution and drug use. Speaking to a *National Geographic* reporter in 1973, the chairman of the Orange County Board of Commissioners unleashed a tirade against the rapid development. "Unless he is a land speculator, owns a bank, or sells insurance . . . the average taxpayer around here has not only had zero profit from this tremendous growth, he is paying for it. . . . No hard feelings, but I wish the mouse had stayed in California."[25]

What Central Florida gained in terms of overall revenue and development, it lost in cohesion and ideals. Orlando was no longer a calm place to enjoy the quiet style of Florida living. All the worst aspects of tourism hit the city at once. Neighboring communities such as Altamonte Springs, which had virtually shut their doors in the summer, were dragged into the ever-widening circle of development, losing their identities, as they became nothing more than bedroom communities for Orlando. As one community spokesman confessed, "Disney World would be great if it were in Miami."[26]

Disney World faced its first major challenge in the national energy crisis that began in October 1973. An Organization of Petroleum Exporting Countries (OPEC) oil embargo raised the specter of rationing, causing a 15 percent drop in Florida tourism during the crucial Christmas holidays. Though forced to lay off workers, Disney World saw no real threat of closing, even when tourism across Florida dropped by 22 percent in the first quarter of 1974 and some attractions lost almost half of their normal number of guests. By April, the embargo had ended, and in May Disney executives made the decision to begin expansion at the Florida park.[27] The Southern Governors' Conference, held September 15–17, 1975, at the Walt Disney World Contemporary Hotel, was the stage for the announcement of the expansion plan. Walt Disney's final dream, the "experimental prototype community of tomorrow," would be constructed in Florida. Officially designated the Epcot Center, it was a major undertaking and promised to be something very different to the Magic Kingdom.[28]

The development of Epcot reflected the evolution of American amusement parks from the 1960s to the 1990s. Parks responded to the aging of their visitors, shedding the image of being entertainment geared to young children. Disney officials also recognized that in order to survive, their resort had to grow and change, and offer something more pleasing to adults. Older tourists frequently responded to the park as a 1974 visitor from Connecticut did, deeming the Magic Kingdom "just one big whirl of nothing. . . . I'm glad I saw it, but I sure wouldn't come all the way to Florida to see it again." Rides and attractions would age, but if the resort offered fresh entertainment that was visually and intellectually satisfying, the lure of seeing something new from the world-famous Disney brand would be too much to resist. Epcot would, in theory, be a "thinking man's theme park."[29]

Walt Disney's dream of a futuristic community had very little in common with the glorified World's Fair that opened on October 1, 1982. Consisting of a "Future World" dominated by the iconic geodesic sphere Spaceship Earth, where cutting-edge technologies were displayed, and a "World Showcase" around an artificial lake, with pavilions featuring cuisine, products, and a few films about foreign countries, the Epcot Center cost an estimated $900 million.[30] One hundred and fifty press organizations and all three major television networks covered the official ceremonies, and soon more people were visiting the fake monuments in the World Showcase than their real counterparts in Paris and Mexico. Attendance at Walt Disney World soared by 81 percent in Epcot's first year of operation. It was a welcome change; park attendance had been in decline the four years that preceded Epcot's opening. The swelling numbers of tourists spent more time at the resort, extending their vacations to take in the extra attractions. Epcot also benefited from demographic changes. By 1988, the average age of an amusement park visitor was thirty-five, and while Disney's focus remained on families with young children, Epcot could be sold as educational entertainment directed to older juveniles and their chaperons.[31]

While Governor Reubin Askew had previously predicted that Epcot would help bring about world peace, critics were quick to point out how little the theme park resembled Walt Disney's ideal. Despite the quirky, scaled minivillages around the artificial lake, the primary focus of the park was the futuristic pavilions sponsored by major corporations. Visitors were inundated with ads for General Motors, Kodak, Exxon, Kraft, Coca-Cola, General Electric, United Technologies, and American Express.[32] The high-tech gizmos came with a price; even the most determined tourist could be subliminally saturated by the logos and cheerful theme songs blasting from the exhibits. Critics charged that the Disney vision of the future was too optimistic, while the Disney version of the past was whitewashed and sanitized. The park experienced horrendous failures in its rides and attractions, which seemed to break down more often than they operated. On opening day, the robotic Benjamin Franklin in the American Adventure could not decide whether he wanted to walk up the stairs or sit in his chair. The park seemed grim and humorless, with little to do in the World Showcase except shop and eat. "Where's Mickey?" was the sad plea of many children, for Mickey and company had been banned from the park as too frivolous for such a serious undertaking. Older children griped that if they had wanted all this "educational junk," they would have gone to school. Throughout the opening month, record numbers of refunds were given to disappointed guests, but despite the complaints, by 1982 some 22.7 million people were arriving at the Walt Disney World resort.[33]

Desperate to survive, many smaller parks in Florida sold out to large corporations, which could afford expansion and national advertising. But a prime example of how not to compete with Disney was the rise and very rapid fall of Circus World, aka Boardwalk and Baseball. In 1974, the owners of Ringling Brothers Circus opened a preview center for a new Orlando theme park that would feature circus-based rides and shows. The next year new displays were added to the preview center, along with a carousel and audience participation games. Meanwhile, Ringling Brothers sold everything to Mattel, which expanded the quasi-park in 1982, so that it offered a traditional wooden roller coaster, a Wild West show, and more carnival rides. A private developer bought the struggling attraction in 1984. In 1986, Harcourt Brace Janovich purchased the park and renamed it Boardwalk and Baseball. Opening anew on Veterans Day of 1987, the park displayed historic baseball relics from Cooperstown. The idea quickly floundered. Anheuser-Busch purchased Boardwalk and Baseball in 1989, but quickly found it to be a proverbial money pit, unable to compete with the larger attractions surrounding it. On January 17, 1990, with a small crowd of customers in the park, the plug was pulled for the last time, and a decade later the site was converted into condominiums and shopping malls.[34]

Epcot was bad news for smaller attractions, but good news for the surrounding Central Florida counties, at least in terms of construction and jobs. By 1984, Epcot was credited with generating $500 million in new hotel construction with an 83 percent occupancy rate. Around Central Florida, successful parks like Busch Gardens and Sea World increased their attractions, keeping people in the area longer. Orange County wisely added a 700,000-square-foot convention center on International Drive, and the center's opening in 1983 put Orlando on a par with New Orleans and Atlanta as a host city. Specialized attractions blossomed, including a number of dinner shows on International Drive that catered to the hungry and footsore who sought amusement when the parks closed early.[35] But Disney soon countered Orlando's bid for convention dollars with its own convention center, which opened in 1989 as part of the Dolphin and Swan hotels. The same year also saw the debut of Pleasure Island (a center for nightlife) and Typhoon Lagoon (a water park). Disney seemed determined to compete with International Drive, to suck all visitors into its sphere, furthering the perception among locals that Disney was greedy and unconcerned about the wider Central Florida community.[36]

In 1989, a third major park was added to the Disney complex. Disney-MGM Studios was an attempt to bring old Hollywood to modern Florida. The park featured memorabilia, mock-ups of familiar movie sets, stunt shows, and a ride through a collection of film scenes brought to life with animatronics. Better known for its animation than its live-action features, in 1985 Disney partnered with MGM/UA in order to gain the rights to some 250 classic films, plus the use of the famous roaring lion logo.[37] The following year, the Disney resort's most notable rival opened just a few miles away on I-4. Universal Studios had a major advantage in the movie theme park business. It was already world famous for its Hollywood studio tour, which it promised to duplicate in Florida, and it invested in far more thrill rides and audience-participation attractions. From the start, Universal billed itself as the place to take older children and teenagers who did not need to be babied by Disney's cartoon creatures. At the same time, it made no pretense of being educational. At a cost of $600 million, Universal Studios was all about Hollywood glamour and high-tech fun, designed to appeal to an older, thrill-seeking public.[38]

Before the curtains rose, the two parks waged a backstage war, accusing each other of stealing ideas and investors. Disney-MGM seemed to have the advantage; it opened first and was already connected as a "third gate" to the other thriving theme parks. But Universal had more modern film properties and thrills. Both Disney-MGM and Universal experienced problems in their initial years of operation, with rides that constantly malfunctioned and stunt shows that racked up injuries to cast members. Guests at both attractions complained about not getting their money's worth. Yet the parks eventually overcame these perceptions, especially by adding ever more daring thrill rides, including the thirteen-story free fall in Disney's Tower of Terror and the motion simulator experience of Universal's Back to the Future. By the mid-1990s, Universal Studios hosted seven million guests per year, and Disney World welcomed approximately thirty million.[39]

In 1999, Universal expanded, adding a second gate, the Islands of Adventure. No particular theme was clear, as the park included attractions based on Dr. Suess stories, comic book superheroes, popular movies, and ancient myths and legends. The adventures in the Islands included two high-tech roller coasters, two log flumes, white-water rapids, and a 3-D dark ride that sent its victims hurdling off a skyscraper, with Spiderman swinging to the rescue. Three luxury hotels opened to serve both properties, and an area for nightlife was wedged between the parks. The expansion of Universal Studios raised the likelihood that Orlando-area visitors would graft extra days to their stay to sample competing entertainment wares. The major growth in two resort areas generated the need for even more hotels and restaurants.[40]

With such growth in the theme parks came repetition of familiar problems. Outside the gates was ugly sprawl; fragmented land ownership and weak government oversight led to land being sold in uneven parcels with little in the way of use restrictions. Today, the area around the theme parks is a gawky mess, a collection of hotels, tacky souvenir stores, water parks, and failed attractions. But a repulsive tourist district was just the tip of Orlando's grubby social/economic problems iceberg.[41]

The rapid growth of Disney, Sea World, and Universal Studios and the service industries that complement them never factored in the needs of real people, that is, the nontourists. Orlando's population more than doubled from 1971 to 1999. By the mid-1980s, Orlando was the second fastest growing urban area in the Sunbelt, and by 1994 it was the nation's fastest growing region, with a metropolitan population exceeding one million. The excessive growth contributed negatively to the quality of life for most residents. Service workers dominated the Orlando area economy;

jobs might be plentiful, but they were generally low status, low skill, and low pay, making workers virtually invisible to the outside world. These invisible workers were ignored in the decades of frenetic growth, and their ramshackle communities, plagued by poor roads and inadequate housing, made them look like bad neighbors. Traffic congestion, public facility deficits, affordable housing shortages, and a low-wage economy continue to be by-products of the unprecedented growth of the tourist industry in Central Florida. Tourism revenues, no matter how vast, fail to offset expenditures for law enforcement, highways, education, and public welfare.[42]

In 1995, Disney executives announced the creation of a fourth major theme park in the Disney resort. Originally named Disney's Wild Animal Kingdom, it was described as an eco-friendly, thrilling yet educational venue where guests could have "close encounters with exotic creatures." Disney planned to invest $750 million in the new park. It was, perhaps, bad timing, as awareness of environmental issues and animal rights was reaching a new height. Despite Disney's pledges that Animal Kingdom would not be a zoo—and its enlistment of some of the world's most famous names in animal preservation, including chimp expert Dr. Jane Goodall—many activists were appalled. The deaths of a number of animals purchased from other zoos, including a black rhinoceros, cheetahs, Asian otters, and a hippopotamus, shortly before the park's grand opening led to more suspicions. Twenty protestors waved signs reading "Dead Animal Kingdom" and "Disney: A Tragic Kingdom for Animals" at the flood of guests as the park opened on April 22, 1998, Earth Day.[43]

As with the other parks, Animal Kingdom did not immediately live up to expectations. It had only one thrill ride, Countdown to Extinction, which constantly broke down and was deemed insufficiently scary. Visitors touring on the safari ride complained that not enough animals were in view, and that the dead mother elephant (a fake one, supposedly shot by poachers) traumatized their children. When the Discovery River Boat turned out not to be the fun-loving, pun-loving Jungle Cruise—and skippers showed off real snakes and spiders to skittish guests—refunds were demanded. The park was hot and muggy; few visitors understood that they were supposed to slow down and look for the birds and animals hiding amid the dense foliage. The park's heavy-handed, rather ironic message of eco-friendliness and antidevelopment was lost on most visitors, who soon headed off to other parks in the complex. But despite initial disappointments, Animal Kingdom adapted, and with the addition of new thrill rides, including the epic roller coaster Expedition Everest that sends riders hurdling backward, chased by a ferocious Yeti, the park has prospered.[44]

Walt Disney World, the largest tourist attraction in the world, will never finish reshaping itself and the Orlando area. The massive land grant and extraordinary powers granted to the corporation in the 1960s continued into the 1990s and beyond. Disney possesses such vast acreage that the potential for expansion remains nearly unlimited. Even in periods of park attendance decline, the resort has grown.[45] Earlier managers had purposefully underbuilt hotels and avoided such tourist traps as miniature golf and water parks, in order to keep the Disney standard high and allow other businesses to flourish in Disney's wake. With a major shakeup in corporate leadership in the 1990s, Disney World changed its policies and began the "Disney Decade," a major expansion project that littered its Florida property with budget hotels, water parks, and miniature golf courses. A fleet of buses operates almost around the clock to transport guests from hotels to attractions, free of charge. Once a visitor turns off I-4 and enters the Disney enclave, the sense of the real world disappears in a "sanitized sensory bombardment."[46] Competitors are frustrated when tourists echo New Hampshire visitor Wayne Bachard: "We went to the parks, we played golf, we rented boats, we went swimming, we did anything we could have wanted to do and we never left Disney World. It's unbelievable."[47]

Disney's expansion has generated criticism, from more than just its competitors. Carl Hiaasen spared no punches in his 1998 book, *Team Rodent: How Disney Devours the World,* fanaticizing about filling Bay Lake with "hungry bull gators" before conceding that the Magic Kingdom is "not a safe place for a reptile." By the early twenty-first century, it had become trendy to mock Disney as a cultural paradigm. In 2001, the *Washington Post* noted that critiquing and criticizing Disney was "one of the faster-growing branches of academia." Yet more people have sung along with the rowdy, animatronic Pirates of the Caribbean than live in the United States. Undoubtedly future attractions will be planned in response to the nature of tourists, especially the growing number of international and older guests.[48]

Six of America's largest theme parks are in Central Florida. Fodor's guidebooks count more than eighty fun zones in the Orlando area. With such diversity of entertainment, nightlife, shopping, and convention space, Orlando now dominates the Florida tourist industry, a remarkable feat for a town that was known only for oranges less than fifty years ago. While the mechanics and technology involved in theme park operations still seem advanced to the casual visitor, the ideas behind them are as old as Flagler's hotels or the 1960s roadside attractions. Florida as a "fantasyland" is in no way new. What changed was the way this area of Florida developed. The Central Florida parks were born full grown; the region did not go through the period of discovery, change, and revitalization that older tourist cities, like St. Augustine and St. Petersburg, experienced. Both the "promises and problems" were mature at the beginning. For millions of people, especially foreign tourists, the Orlando area is Florida, especially as every imaginable form of recreation is available, from golf courses to thrill rides to beaches—though admittedly the beaches are contained in water parks. In an ironic Florida twist, artificial shorelines are often more popular than the real things. But for residents of Central Florida, forced to endure traffic jams and low wages, "living with the mouse"—not to mention Shamu and Spiderman—will never be easy.[49]

Dealing with the new worlds of the theme parks, and finding ways to spread the financial benefits of tourism without acquiring its social problems, would require the greatest leap of the state's collective imagination as a new century for tourism approached.

EIGHT

Which Way to Paradise?

"Disney World spoiled us by giving us twelve good months," a Jacksonville motel owner sighed. It was January 1974, the country was deep in an energy crisis, and the fears of either rationing or exorbitantly priced (99 cents a gallon) gasoline had caused a sharp and bitter plummeting of tourist revenues. To the chagrin of Florida businessmen and women, the fears were greater than the actual emergency. Gasoline was available, but few tourists were willing to take the risk to travel far from home, especially for a winter season.[1] The new reality of Florida tourism was that despite having pulled Florida out of a five-year tourism slump, the monolith in Orlando could not save everyone. Instead, Disney World would soon be the bully charged with putting smaller operations out of business.[2] The story of the post-Disney era is one of constant struggle against economic downturns and natural disasters, and of constant reinvention and searching for niche markets. From the final decades of the twentieth century to the present day, Florida's tourism industry has remained adaptive and expansive, ready to sell the next version of the sunshine paradise.

The energy crisis of 1973–1974 gave the Florida tourism industry a fright it had not experienced since the days of restricted travel during World War II.[3] Tourism dropped by an estimated 22–25 percent in the crucial first quarter of 1974, prompting Florida governor Reubin Askew to go to Washington to directly lobby Federal Energy Director William E. Simon for more gasoline allotments for the state, arguing that "curtailment of travel" would critically endanger Florida's economy and tax base. He also asked President Nixon to endorse vacation travel. Whatever affected tourism affected the rest of the state's industries, and though the Arab oil embargo was lifted in the spring of 1974, it was well into the summer before tourism numbers returned to normal. Some attractions suffered substantial losses. A dramatic recession kept the American economy in the doldrums throughout 1974–1975, but once the energy crunch passed, Florida tourism recovered at a remarkable rate.[4]

The decade of the 1970s eventually proved to be a good one, pointing to a bright future for Florida tourism. Walt Disney World, as expected, flourished and expanded. Tourism rose overall by 11 percent. By 1978, one out of every eight jobs in Florida was generated by tourism, making Florida second only to California in the number of tourist industry employees. The strength of tourism helped raise the average income of Floridians almost to the national standard, an astonishing achievement for the South. Seen as a "clean" nonsmokestack industry that was still somewhat seasonal, but much less than it had been in the previous decades, tourism made Florida unique and prosperous. "It is clear that tourism is of considerably greater importance for Florida than for almost all other states," a government study reported.[5]

Looking for ways to compete against theme parks, more Florida cities revitalized their historic downtowns in the 1960s–1980s. In Key West, the Old Island Restoration Foundation worked to preserve what was left of the port city's nineteenth-century buildings, beginning with an 1840 frame home dubbed the Audubon House. In 1972, the Key West Historic District was placed on the National Register of Historic Places. Over two decades, the center of Key West became, in the words of one author, "a multi-million dollar tourist trap that brought jobs to the city and nurtured one of the island's most beloved modern traditions, the nightly lemminglike march to Mallory Square to watch, and applaud, the setting sun."[6] After a clumsy attempt to establish a living history village on the beach, Pensacola finally understood the importance of tourism as a third pillar of its economy and established a historic district around Seville Square in 1967. While recognizing that Pensacola would never be "a Williamsburg," residents hoped that by creating a revitalized downtown and promoting Ft. Pickens, Pensacola would garner a larger share of the tourist market. By the early 1980s, it was estimated that Pensacola received approximately 1.8 million visitors a year.[7]

But new and worrisome trends were also clear; tourists were increasingly being funneled to the theme parks and away from the beaches and historic sites, despite many cities' best efforts. St. Augustine, for example, struggled with consistently declining numbers of visitors even as the overall figure for the state was rising. Vast investment in restoration of the city's historic district failed to impress, as tourists were opting to cut their stay in the Oldest City short or avoid it all together. A 1979 letter to the editor of the *St. Augustine Record* put the problem plainly: history did not draw the crowds that thrill rides and cartoon characters did, and even mature guests were bored with St. Augustine's nonexistent nightlife. "Dictums" that banned modern businesses from the town center were lethal. Let tourist-oriented businesses come, the writer urged, build "good restaurants, beer joints, and other diversions." History alone would not keep the town competitive. "Conclusion: Don't get hung up on history, the glorification of the Spanish heritage, the oldest this and the oldest that."[8] The warning was prophetic. By 1985, the *Jacksonville Times-Union* noted that St. Augustine tourism had peaked in 1976 and that a number of historic houses, including the old Spanish military hospital, had been closed for lack of interest. "People won't buy history alone, year after year." Yet as another St. Augustine resident observed in 1989, no matter what route the city chose, it could never match Disney and the other corporations in national advertising and promotion—"There's no way on God's green earth we will ever be able to compete with that."[9]

The 1970s–1990s saw consistent expansion not only of Disney World but also of the other Central Florida theme parks and area attractions. To the west, Busch Gardens grew with new attractions added almost yearly, all based on African themes such as a Moroccan village, the Congo River, and a preserve for gorillas and chimpanzees. Steel roller coasters and other thrill rides wiped away the park's rather humble beginnings as an eclectic zoo and brewery tour.[10] Sea World added a ski show, honing in on Cypress Gardens' trademark, in 1976. The Nautilus Theater was added in 1983 and

Shamu Stadium in 1984. The park's largest growth came in the early 1990s, when exhibits including Terrors of the Deep (a collection of oceanic predators), the Wild Arctic, and Key West were added, along with thrill rides. Sea World of Florida has grown into the most popular marine life park in the world, promoted as a center of both entertainment and education. Though labeled an "abusement park" by People for the Ethical Treatment of Animals (PETA), it counters its use of captive creatures for amusement by publicizing its research, rehabilitation, and breeding programs. Universal Studios welcomed its 1999 expansion, Islands of Adventure, which made the park a full competitor with Disney. Church Street Station, a downtown Orlando complex of bars and restaurants, all loosely typed together with a turn-of-the-century theme, was destined to be the loser in the 1980s expansion. Collectively, pubs like Rosie O'Grady's Goodtime Emporium, Phineas Fogg's Dance Club, and the Cheyenne Saloon and Opera House offered novelty amusements and drinks in the hours after the parks closed, though the creation of discos and themed restaurants (such as the Hard Rock Café at Universal Studios and Pleasure Island at Disney World) made it less likely that tourists would make the drive into town to sample what were essentially just more of the same stylized novelties.[11]

Most of the attractions of Florida's age of imagination were history themselves by the 1980s. In a 1976 interview, Arthur McKee Latta, the manager of McKee Jungle Gardens and the grandson of the attraction's founder, voiced his thoughts on the family business's recent closing. "I'm somewhat disgusted with humanity, I guess. People no longer want to feel like Thoreau. They want things thrown at them. They want to be mind-boggled." Less than a quarter of Florida's small tourist attractions survived their encounter with Mickey Mouse, Shamu, and Spiderman.[12]

Cypress Gardens, which had been both the leading Florida attraction of the 1960s and a proud family business, sold out to corporate ownership in 1985. A few floundering attractions were rescued by the state, which turned them into state parks. In 1986, Wakulla Springs was put up for sale by Ed Ball's heir, the Nemours Foundation, and purchased for $7.15 million, to eventually become the Ed Ball Wakulla Springs State Park. Rainbow Springs closed as a tourist attraction in 1973 after a series of corporate owners failed to find a way to keep it relevant to modern tourists. The state added Rainbow Springs to its property collection in 1990, and opened it as a park in 1995. Homosassa Springs was also gathered into the state park system. These springs function with a great deal of assistance and volunteer work by locals who love these old-style attractions.[13]

The 1980s saw theme park expansion, more service industry jobs, cheap gasoline, and record numbers of foreign visitors fleeing from threats of terrorism at home. But the decade also saw publicity problems for the state. In April 1980, the Mariel boatlift brought over 125,000 Cuban refugees to Miami, which had already absorbed approximately 60,000 people fleeing Haiti since 1977. Simultaneously, Miami's black citizens awaited the verdict in the trial of four police officers accused of killing a black man for a minor traffic offense. On May 17, the officers were acquitted, and within a few hours a seismic riot erupted, centered in the Liberty City section of Miami. Four days later eighteen people were dead, and property damage was assessed at $80 million. Combined with the rumors that most Mariel refugees were criminals and outcasts, and national news reports that depicted Miami as the drug capital of America, the Magic City lost its reputation as a tourist mecca.[14]

But the 1990s was an even more pivotal and problematic decade for Florida tourism. During 1992 and 1993, Florida experienced a thirteen-month crime wave that saw the murders of ten foreign visitors, including British bus driver Gary Colley, who was shot at a rest station near Tallahassee. The killings, though random and unconnected, cast a pall over the $30-billion-a-year tourist business. Tourists, often easily identifiable by accents, clothing, and rental cars, had always been prone to victimization, but the savagery of the attacks was unprecedented.[15] European newspapers depicted Florida as a strange mix of urban ghetto and Wild West. By 1995, the number of European visitors, especially from Germany and Great Britain, was off by 20 percent, and the number of Canadians—always stalwarts of the trade—had plummeted by 16 percent, due to the cruel combination of the well-publicized killings and a weak Canadian dollar. The negative effect on tourism led to state efforts to increase safety for all tourists, including removing distinctive license plates from rental cars and installing nighttime security in rest areas.[16]

Florida was also less desirable to African American visitors in the last decades of the twentieth century. Miami gained an especially unappealing reputation after the 1980 riots revealed the festering problems of race relations in what should have been a "melting pot." In 1990, the Miami city commission snubbed the visiting Nelson Mandela. Miami attorney H. T. Smith and other black community leaders demanded an apology and called for African Americans to boycott the city. The boycott lasted until 1993, costing the city an estimated $54 million in lost revenues from pulled conventions. Miami Visitors Bureau president Merrett Stierheim argued that the boycott actually hurt African Americans, who made up some 25 percent of all hotel employees in Dade County. The fallout led to studies that found disgracefully small numbers of black citizens working in higher-paying tourism jobs, despite being more than one-fifth of all tourism employees in Miami.[17] Following the boycott, Florida made a point to court black visitors in the mid-1990s, introducing a first for tourism promotion, a commercial starring an African American couple discussing the pleasures of a Florida vacation. Previously, Disney World was the only Florida attraction to even advertise in black media.[18]

By mid-decade, a sense of urgency permeated tourism promoters and the state government. A 1994 survey of focus groups, sponsored by the Florida Commission on Tourism, found Americans' perceptions of Florida were changing, but not for the better. Florida was no longer a land of sunshine and relaxation, an unspoiled paradise, but a dirty, crowded, overpriced piece of junk. Florida was "too tacky," appropriate only for families with young children who were willing to be fleeced in order to meet Mickey Mouse. More mature and sophisticated travelers planned to go elsewhere, making Florida at best a "backup" destination. The groups expressed a sense of "been there, done that, and bought the t-shirt."[19]

A 1995 study found certain validity to the focus groups' perceptions. The average out-of-state tourist was a member of an affluent young family. He or she spent an average of $141 per day on a roughly two-week vacation. However, the study also noted the importance of a long neglected group, in-state tourists. These travelers were more often older and blue-collar. While they spent roughly the same amount of time visiting Florida attractions, their journeys were usually split up into long weekends and holidays. They were savvier, prone to demand in-state discounts and save money by bunking with friends and family. But the in-state guest unloaded an average of $98 a day, meaning that the thrifty resident tourist still spent more than the average American tourist elsewhere, who only released $77 a day. Somehow, the state needed to attract more of both types of guests, and demonstrate that Florida was not the gaudy sideshow former visitors

recalled. Even the image of tourists as sweaty, ill-dressed, and overbear-
ing needed to be tweaked, just as Florida desperately required a facelift to
show off its variety and vitality.[20]

On May 30, 1996, Governor Lawton Chiles signed a bill to abolish the
Department of Commerce's Division of Tourism and turn tourism promotion over to the newly created Florida Tourism Industry Marketing Corporation, a public/private partnership. Matching funds from state coffers
and businesses were designated to help establish a new image for Florida.
Chiles held that private agencies understood tourism promotion much
better than the government did, as the Division of Tourism had been woe-
fully inadequate in promoting the state over the past decade. The corporation adopted the name Visit Florida, and created a new logo (FLA/USA),
a toll-free hotline for tourism information, and eventually a place on the
World Wide Web.[21]

Florida tourism promoters also sought to better understand and serve
their niche markets. Tourists would always flock to the theme parks, but
if specialized groups could be lured to the state parks and historic sites,
these places would have a greater hope of survival. Ecotourism had been
shamefully neglected, especially as Florida drew almost a million nature-
oriented tourists in 1996. In 1997, the state created an office of ecotourism
within the State Division of Recreation and Parks, a natural fit for a state so
blessed with wetlands and other wild areas.[22]

Along with nature lovers, the state concentrated on reestablishing con-
nections with foreign and minority guests. In 1996, just 612,000 Canadians
visited the Orlando area, a staggering reversal from 1990, when over one
million Canadians spent time in the theme parks. Special discounts were
offered, including a Disney plan to accept Canadian dollars on par with
American currency. Further efforts were made to attract tourists from
Central and South America, as well as appeals to the American Hispanic
population.[23] The African American travel market in the United States
was estimated at up to $30 billion a year, and Florida was eager to make
amends for past slights to travelers of color. Visit Florida emphasized cultural festivals and historic sites, especially Eatonville, the first incorporated
black community in America and the home of Zora Neale Hurston. African American tour groups were eagerly sought because they tended to go
farther and stay longer, though as one operator noted, there was no "one

size fits all" formula to attract black visitors.[24] Promoters rarely remind African Americans of the ghosts of segregation in tourism. While tour guides in St. Augustine now drive their trams through Lincolnville and point out a house Martin Luther King Jr. visited, no one mentions that the dock for the rehabilitation station at Silver Springs was once the launching point for Paradise Park boats, significantly downstream and hidden. Sites and attractions continue to emphasize noncontroversial topics for their minority guests, including historic firsts, churches, and homes associated with famous people.[25]

Another vitally important niche market caters to Florida's many gay/ lesbian travelers. Generally affluent and often childfree, usually unwilling to let any natural or political disaster cancel a trip, and incredibly loyal to favorite destinations, the gay/lesbian community has a special relationship to certain areas in Florida. Following its bohemian renaissance in the 1930s, Key West became famous for same-sex courtship and unrestrained nightlife in the 1950s. The city was one of the first in America to openly recruit gay and lesbian travelers, and its gay-oriented Fantasy Fest began in 1979 as a way to encourage autumn tourism. South Florida openly promoted its gay/lesbian-friendly beaches, resorts, and nightlife as American attitudes became more tolerant of sexual diversity. Miami Beach declared itself to be the "gay and lesbian destination of the nineties." In 1991, Gay Days was organized in Orlando. Initially a one-afternoon gathering in theme parks, it has grown into a weeklong celebration in early June that attracts over 100,000 travelers yearly.[26]

Celebrations and promotions of gay/lesbian tourism have not escaped controversy. Key West's festival drew criticism for its emphasis on flamboyance and intoxication. Conservative residents of Miami objected to the new neighbors and guests. "That's not the kind of society we want to see," Orthodox Rabbi Phineas Weberman told the *New York Times*. In 2007, Ft. Lauderdale mayor Jim Naugle caused outrage by blaming homosexual travelers for a "climate of permissiveness" in the city. Most famously, in 1997 the Southern Baptist Convention called for its members to boycott all Disney products, including the theme parks, because of Gay Days, supposed pornography hidden in animated movies, and other moral "offenses." Disney responded by pointing out that it did not sponsor but did recognize Gay Days, the same way it recognized special tourism events for other interest groups. The boycott had no direct measurable effect on the Disney company.[27] The recession of 2009, however, led to fears across South Florida that the gay/lesbian market would decline because economic hardship was widespread across even the formerly most prosperous members of its community.

One significant victory for Florida in the mid-1990s was its ability to retain its crown as the king of the family tourism business. In the early years of the decade, Las Vegas made a serious bid to lure away family vacationers, building amusement parks and thrill rides inside hotels. Floridians flirted with revenge in the form of a referendum on legalizing casino gambling, but the measure was defeated in 1994. While Florida received a record 43.5 million visitors in 1996, Las Vegas was soon shuttering its family-themed attractions and reembracing its image of sleaze and glitz. A number of factors contributed to the failure to make Las Vegas kid-friendly, but many observers noted that Las Vegas simply could not compete with Florida's reputation or its products. Disney and Universal Studios would easily spend on one ride what Las Vegas entrepreneurs spent on the entire entertainment complex—and it showed.[28]

By the dawn of the twenty-first century, Florida tourism was at an all-time high. Banner crowds swelled the theme parks in 1997. That year a total of almost forty-seven million visitors toured the state. The next year the numbers topped forty-eight million. Tourist-related employment rose by 4.8 percent, with the creation of 820,900 jobs. Florida's unemployment level was less than 5 percent. Tickets, hotel rooms, and souvenir sales pumped $41 billion into the state, accounting for $2 billion in tax monies. Tourism sales-tax collections accounted for 20 percent of Florida's total 1997 sales-tax collections. The tourist "season" was nearly obsolete, as theme parks hosted special events, including Halloween parties and Mardi Gras festivals, in the "shoulder months" of early spring and fall between travel peaks. Survey results proved Visit Florida campaigns were succeeding; 37 percent of Americans planning vacations for the 2000–2001 season listed Florida as their number one destination. Floridians had every reason to be confident that a strong economy would continue to bring tourists and greenbacks to the state.[29]

Then on September 11, 2001, four airplanes hijacked by terrorists brought an abrupt and violent end to Americans' sense of personal security. The planes crashed into the World Trade Center, the Pentagon, and a field in Pennsylvania, at the cost of thousands of lives. This event, which quickly became known as the 9/11 tragedy, shook America to its core. Disney World closed early, its cast members cautious not to create a panic in the fantasy kingdom by revealing the real reason for the abrupt shuttering of the park. Immediately after 9/11, more then 250 groups canceled their conventions in Orlando.[30] In the wake of the attacks, tourism was restricted and reshaped. The most obvious result was an unwillingness of many Americans and foreigners to travel, due to fear of attack and impending war. As flights resumed and parks reopened, security measures became ever more repressive, and travelers often complained of being treated like suspected criminals. Many people chose to vacation in their own homes.

Florida tourism faced an unprecedented challenge; could its fragile nature survive events that made Americans insecure and wary of large crowds and cultural icons? "Tourism is so fickle," one St. Augustine official sighed, "it won't take much to throw it off." Visit Florida countered with a concentrated effort to keep Florida tourism active in the wake of 9/11. Public service announcements by Governor Jeb Bush were matched to campaigns designed to encourage local residents to visit the theme parks. The Federal Bureau of Investigation (FBI) decisively debunked rumors that Disney World had been a terrorist target. The markets within easy driving distance of Florida were saturated with advertising and special promotions to counteract the airline cancellations.[31] A year after 9/11, many Central Florida hoteliers agreed that except for the loss of conventions and foreign travelers, tourism had not taken the hit they expected. The Florida tourism industry, admittedly, was fortunate in the event's timing; September is a traditionally slow month. Had the tragedy occurred in the summer, during the peak of family travel, it would have been much harder for Florida tourism to recover.[32]

Nature also seemed to be conspiring against Florida in the years surrounding the dawn of the new millennium. Hurricane Andrew, a Category 5 storm that many considered the "mother of all hurricanes," battered Homestead in 1992. It was just the beginning of a lengthy chain of environmental woes. Hurricane Opal smashed the western Panhandle in October 1995, its tidal surge ripping up key tourist facilities from Pensacola to Mexico Beach. The summer of 1998 brought nearly 2,200 wildfires that ravaged half a million acres, destroyed more than 300 homes, and caused the cancellation of tourist-oriented activities in many towns. But the worst punishment came in 2004, when an unprecedented four major hurricanes smacked Florida in six weeks: Charley, Frances, Ivan, and Jeanne. Polk County was a favorite target, as three of the storms crossed in it their travels. The Orlando theme parks closed for three days; frightened travelers huddled in their hotel rooms, short on food and water. Once the storms passed the loss of power made evacuation difficult.[33] By the time the nightmare year ended, vital tourism centers, including Sanibel Island, Orlando, Daytona, Stuart, Tampa, and Pensacola, had suffered severe damage. Insurance rates skyrocketed, and many properties were never rebuilt. After Opal, Florida tourism officials placed an advertisement in *USA Today* reminding the nation, "We're Still Open," and a similar message was broadcast after Charley, but by late 2005 a tourist would have good reason to doubt that claim.[34] Though Hurricane Katrina was mild-mannered when it crossed the southern tip of Florida in 2005, its growth into the monster storm of the new century and its devastation of New Orleans—a city precariously balanced on the economic tightrope of tourism—added a potent reminder of how vulnerable Florida was to such inescapable attacks.

A number of Florida attractions that had staggered through the lean years of the late twentieth century finally surrendered to the inevitable. In Orlando, the $100 million Florida Splendid China theme park, which had battled cultural criticism, protests, and sagging post-9/11 attendance, closed in 2003. It joined a long list of failed Central Florida attractions, becoming a haunted ruin where vandals painted graffiti on the miniature monuments and daredevil skateboarders filmed their feats for YouTube.[35] At Panama City Beach, an area "mugged and gagged" by 1950s and 1960s tourism development, declining revenues and natural disasters knocked out the few remaining gaudy-age landmarks. Though the beaches would always be popular, many Goofy Golf courses and amusement parks were blown away by hurricanes and economic winds of change. On Labor Day, 2004, the venerable Miracle Strip Amusement Park, a forty-one-year-old institution crammed with wooden roller coasters and haunted houses, locked its doors.[36]

The Gulf Coast region continues to struggle with tourism and its impact on the economy and its identity. It was the last major region of Florida to develop, as its tourism industry did not become significant until after the Great Depression. Despite the best efforts of developers to spin the strip as the Emerald Coast, most Floridians know it as the "Redneck Riviera" because it attracts primarily spring break and summer visitors from Alabama, Mississippi, Louisiana, Arkansas, and Texas. Excessive population growth in the 1950s and 1960s was linked to the enlargement of military facilities, and with the expansion came infrastructure helpful to the promotion of tourism. The new roads and airports of the mid-twentieth century led to a dramatic increase of tourism as a Panhandle industry. It seemed only natural for the Gulf to develop a strong tourism sector, as it was blessed with an ideal climate and pristine, plentiful beaches. Panama City stuck with the youth market, while Pensacola boosted its historical merits and Destin built high-priced condos. The result has been uneven development and growth over the last several decades, and a constant frustration that the winter snowbirds are tightfisted and pump only limited funds into the community coffers.[37]

Across Florida, one by-product of twenty-first-century tourism appears to be a quest for novelty and freedom. Tourists will try almost anything to experience Florida in a new way. While some visitors are content to take traditional tours, others want more exciting or independent ways to sightsee. St. Augustine, for example, offers almost every imaginable way to view the Oldest City, whether on the traditional trams, via horse-drawn carriage, or as part of a cycling posse. Tourists can rent MP3 players to listen to prerecorded messages about historic sites, or toddle around in minicars. Ghost tours, which originated as a way of amusing school groups, grew in the 1990s as a means of giving tourists something to do when the downtown shops closed. Traveling through St. Augustine in 2009, one would think the spirits had finally seized control of the Oldest City, based on the glaring eyes and blood oozing from the multiple ghost tour billboards.[38]

A second theme of the millennial age is the longing for authenticity, a search for an extreme counterpoint to the theme parks. While boating on the St. Johns, author Bill Belleville discovered the thriving airboat tour business, operating out of gentrified fish camps "with just enough raucous good-ole-boy feel left to make it seem authentic, especially to northern tourists looking for tastes of the real Florida after mind-numbing doses of virtual reality at nearby Disney World." The bumps on the river and the creatures sighted along its banks made for a "Mr. Toad's Wild Ride" that was more intellectually satisfying, even if it was taken in a "minibus version" of an airboat with padded, pewlike seats. Belleville recognized the cyclical nature of Florida tourism history, noting that "these buslike commercial airboats are the modern-day steamship, with working outdoorsmen and their cargo replaced by visitors yearning for a glimpse of a rare place, like the early tourists who visited the river in the mid and late nineteenth century."[39]

Heritage tourism, another aspect of the search for authentic Florida, holds promise for luring twenty-first-century travelers from the theme parks. Fifteen hundred Florida sites are listed on the National Register of Historic Places, and more than half of Florida's 340 museums are considered historical. In 2005, approximately 44 percent of Florida's visitors enjoyed some type of history-oriented experience, whether taking in a living history demonstration in St. Augustine or watching the Battle of Olustee reenactment near Lake City. Heritage tourism generates several billion dollars a year in tourist expenditures, and multiple agencies now work to stimulate interest in Florida's small towns, historic sites, and cultural events. But even the definition of Florida heritage can be baffling and ironic. Key West, for example, celebrates Ernest Hemingway, a nonnative resident who abandoned the city in disgust when it became a tourism center. The town also lauds John James Audubon, Harry Truman, and Jimmy Buffet as icons; none were or are natives. Meanwhile, vacationers rarely learn about the fishermen, wreckers, or cigar makers who actually built America's "Last Resort."[40]

One of the greatest challenges the tourist industry faces is meeting the desires and expectations of Gen X (born between 1963 and 1978) and Gen Y (born between 1978 and 1997) travelers. Increasingly affluent and mobile, younger guests are not sated with history lectures or astonished by mechanized theme parks. Many of them seek real-life thrills, often found in extreme sports or wilderness adventures. The younger generations rarely demonstrate loyalty to a particular attraction or community, and will not return once the thrill is gone. Accommodating these guests with packages, tours, and activities will be difficult for anyone over the age of fifty who considers a proper vacation to be a relaxing one. The younger tourists are bursting with energy, and—as marriage rates continue to drop and couples wed later in life—they are frequently unencumbered by children. Many are also brimming with a sense of responsibility and green-awareness. "Voluntourism," which combines sightseeing with charitable projects such as building homes, may well have a strong appeal to the new youth market.[41]

Tourism is generally considered a recession-proof business, though certainly any major crisis like the Arab oil embargo, or hurricanes, or 9/11—can deal a major, if usually short-lived blow to its profitability. The trip to Florida is an iconic bit of American culture; witness the sports figure who, after winning a big game, happily proclaims, "I'm going to Disney World." Aging baby boomers consider travel a necessity, not a luxury. A family trip, especially to the theme parks, has become the modern American equivalent of the medieval holy pilgrimage. For millions of American parents, taking their offspring to the Magic Kingdom "has come to represent an inelastic cultural demand, regardless of the cost."[42] With the ease and new sense of safety in international travel, more people from around the world can and will come to Florida. In 2006, 83.9 million people visited Florida. Travel for pleasure is now the third largest family expense in the developed world, after food and housing. The tourist industry represents more than 11 percent of the world's gross domestic product and employs 10 percent of the total global workforce. These numbers are predicted to grow rapidly, even to double in the early part of the twenty-first century. The World Tourist Organization predicts that a billion people will travel in 2010. Florida will expect its share of them.[43]

Unfortunately, this share may be limited if Florida cannot live up to the reputation it has nurtured as a sunshine paradise. Many of the classic attractions that created the fanciful image of Florida are now in serious decay. A June 2009 visit to Silver Springs found the crowds sparse and the famous glass-bottom boats dirty. No longer does a photographer snap a group shot before the party embarks; perhaps no one would want it. A sad mishmash of carnival rides, a performance stage shaped like a plantation facade, and an arcade where dingy dioramas from the 1960s lurk in the shadows sully the once beautiful spring basin. Despite the friendliness of the staff, the guest departs with a sense of sadness and loss. Cypress Gardens closed on September 23, 2009, its owners unable to find a combination of nostalgia and thrills strong enough to survive the 2009 recession.

Natural disasters and pollution threaten other once-gorgeous places. South of Tallahassee, Wakulla Springs rarely runs its own glass-bottom boats, because tannic acid from overbuilding in the capital city has disgracefully polluted the waters, turning the once magnificent view of the spring bowl, clear for 120 feet, into a murky brown stew. There are hopeful signs—Cypress Gardens is destined to become Legoland Florida, Disney and Universal remain strong, St. Augustine has recently updated and improved its Visitors' Center, in some South Florida areas the recessionary downturn was not as dire as predicted—but in 2010 the future seems uncertain.[44] Can Florida tourism endure the combined pressure of the crumbling environment, staggering population growth, and a shaky economy?

The impact of tourism will also continue to cause political and cultural conflict in Florida's towns. Many residents believe that emphasizing tourism guarantees that they will lose control over their communities. They sense that they will have to adopt masks, or be constantly aware of being on stage, judged by outsiders.[45] Quarrels over tourism have led to municipal divorces. Panama City Beach incorporated in 1970, largely as a result of debate over increased tourism, which beach developers wanted and Panama City residents did not. The results were garish. Even traditional tourist communities, such as those along Florida's beaches, increasingly say "not in my back yard" and reject tourism expansion. Graffiti on St. Augustine's public market shouts "Locals are number 1!"[46]

Conflicts can be found in Florida whether the community is experienced with tourism or has largely avoided it. In St. Johns County, home to St. Augustine, residents are divided along lines of residency, age, and social class in their reaction to tourists. Young, affluent families line the northern part of the county, which serves largely as a bedroom community for Jacksonville. In general, these residents embrace tourism. Southern St. Johns County is home to a large number of older residents, principally retirees, who live on fixed incomes and object to increased taxes, schools, and tourists. To aged immigrants looking to enjoy their golden years in a Crescent Beach condo, tourists are a noisy nuisance, a blight on the peace and quiet. To Yuppie families who are rarely bothered by flowered-shorts-wearing types in their gated communities, tourism profits finance the amenities they desire, including golf courses and upscale restaurants. Self-interest and exposure to the pitfalls of tourism drive all arguments. But as a writer for the *Jacksonville Times-Union* warns, "The person who is anti-tourist wouldn't have any of the things he enjoys in St. Johns. If he doesn't believe that, he can go to live in Starke."[47]

Even small, rural communities are beginning to feel the impact of tourism. In Madison County, a proposal to turn an old railroad bed into a biking trail, as a way of attracting visitors, met with resistance from families whose property fronted the path. Locals feared that "hoodlums" would take over the trail and that nearby residents would be aggravated by pleas to use phones and bathrooms. The most innocuous encouragement of tourism can raise hackles whenever locals perceive a threat to community traditions and standards. Towns not already dependent on tourism look at its inevitable sour fruits—fast food restaurants, souvenir shops, arcades, miniature golf courses, hotels, billboards, tour trams, traffic jams, cheesy entertainment—and shudder.[48]

Floridians must make peace with tourism. It is impossible to imagine Florida without it, especially as over 80 percent of employment in Florida consists of service-related jobs and Florida continues to depend on tourism for vital tax revenues. Nor would most Floridians really want their state to close its doors, even if many residents find tourists to be "ill-dressed, ill-mannered, road-congesting nuisances." There is a certain pride in being a Florida resident, in living in the fantasy land that so many Americans eagerly pay to see, for only two weeks or less, because they expect it to be better than the "real world" they left behind.[49] But Floridians must also find ways to make sure that tourism benefits the diverse regions of the state equally and that issues of pollution and land use are met with thoughtfulness rather than greed. If Florida wants to continue attracting tourists with its natural beauty, then the state must take special measures to preserve that beauty. Existing infrastructure needs attention; abandoned attractions and destitute hotels will hardly appeal to future visitors. Florida has a reputation for low business taxes and local governments friendly to tourism developers, but the state must not become so blindly committed to tourism that a future disaster, with its inevitable drop in travel, would cripple the state economically.[50]

Florida must also preserve its tourism history. The past is instructive; in 1907, residents of St. Augustine considered removing the old stone gates for something "more attractive." Older tourist attractions defined Florida for generations, and they should be considered as historical as city gates. In 2008, Weeki Wachee Springs, a classic Florida attraction since 1947, was added as the 160th state park. Florida Park Service Director Mike Bullock assured Floridians that the traditional mermaid show would be "preserved for generations," yet in 2009 critics questioned whether it was a tradition worth maintaining. One *St. Petersburg Times* columnist argued that tax-supported parks should have something "more natural than water slides and a slightly sexist entertainment." Nostalgia will continue to battle political correctness; Floridians will have to make difficult choices about what aspects of tourism history should be preserved.[51]

And while Florida will continue to profit from its many resources, the state should fight the trend to turn all cultural and natural wonders into "access zones" available only to those who have the money to pay. Native greed should not be the most vivid memory of a Florida vacation. Nor should reckless, thoughtless growth of tourism be tolerated. As tourism critic Larry Krotz writes, "blind growth is no longer the god it once was. People understand that growth has a price."[52]

Most important, Florida cannot be content to become a disposable state. As environmentalist Thomas Barbour writes, Florida "must cease to be purely a region to be exploited and flung aside, having been sucked dry, or a recreation area visited by people who come only for a good time, and feel no sense of responsibility, and have no desire to aid and improve the land of their temporary enjoyment." Floridians already suffer from a lack of common identity, and few issues unite them. A stronger stance on tourism, especially an insistence on more careful planning and management of it, might be a good start on building a cultural bridge.[53]

Florida has always been a land of imagination, constantly evolving into the most modern image of paradise. From the gasping invalids of the 1820s to the moneyed tourists of the Flagler era, to the tin can tourists, the family vacationers, and the Gen-X adventurers, every wave of tourists has applied its own fantasies to a land beautiful and flexible enough to accommodate them. Floridians must now seize control of these images and come to terms with tourism as a driving economic and social force. Floridians must realize, before it is too late, that their sunshine paradise will survive only with great love and care.

ACKNOWLEDGMENTS

Writing a book on tourism is like taking a long journey. No matter how well one plans ahead, there will be unexpected developments, bumps in the road, occasional bad weather, and both disappointment and exhilaration. I would like to thank all the people who provided directions and assistance, and who traveled with me along the way.

Thanks first of all to Wofford College, and especially Dean David S. Wood, for the research grant that allowed me to take the time and money to make the trip, and to my colleagues in the History Department, who tolerate my travels, both physical and mental. My home base in South Carolina has always been wonderfully supportive and encouraging. A special debt is owed to the librarians of Wofford, in particular Paul Jones, who helped me track down obscure books, and Phillip Stone, who provided essential editing and critiquing. Wofford English professor Deno Trakas and Wofford biology professors G. R. Davis and Ab Abercrombie must also be credited with promoting this project when I was ready to abandon it; their belief in it and me has made all the difference.

Thanks are also due to the wonderful people at the University Press of Florida for their hard work and beautiful design. I owe a debt of gratitude to my editor, Meredith Morris-Babb, who not only answered all my questions but also never let me get past her at a convention without asking when I was sending a book to her in Gainesville.

Many people throughout Florida have inspired me with their expertise and their willingness to share their knowledge. I salute a number of prominent Florida historians and writers, including William Warren Rogers, Gary Mormino, Raymond Arsenault, Joe Knetsch, Lu Vickers, and especially Brian Rucker, my friend and colleague from graduate school who knows absolutely everything there is to know about the Panhandle. Along with the great historians of the state are the great libraries and archives, and I am especially appreciative of the fine people of the State Library of Florida and the Florida State Archives for their dedicated assistance to this project. A special tip of the tourist hat goes to the staff of the State Photographic Archives for their role in finding distinctive images for the text.

As always, friends and family make a road trip memorable. Thanks are due to Richard A. Bartlett, Jean Rowe, Shari Rowe Kohli, Michele Lellouche, Dwain Pruitt, Jeff Mandel, James Alexander, Mary Alexander, and my many Livejournal Internet pals. My mother, LaNora Zipperer, has shown endless patience with this project, for which I thank her with all my heart.

Finally, the journey would not have been possible without my fellow tourist, Wofford biology professor John Moeller, whose love and support is always my GPS.

NOTES

Chapter 1. Salubrious Air

1. Frederic D. Lente, *Florida as a Health-Resort* (New York: D. Appleton, 1876), 7; Hampton Dunn, "Florida: Jewel of the Gilded Age," *Gulf Coast Historical Review* 10 (1994): 19; Michael Gannon, ed., *The New History of Florida* (Gainesville: University Press of Florida, 1996), 17.

2. Douglas T. Peck, "Reconstruction and Analysis of the 1513 Discovery Voyage of Juan Ponce de Leon," *Florida Historical Quarterly* 71 (October 1992): 135; Gannon, *New History of Florida*, 17–20.

3. Daniel J. Boorstin, *The Image: Or, What Happened to the American Dream* (New York: Athenaeum, 1962), 85.

4. Jeremy Rifkin, *The Age of Access: The New Culture of Hypercapitalism, Where All of Life Is a Paid-For Experience* (New York: Jeremy P. Tracher/Putnam, 2000), 147; Dona Brown, *Inventing New England: Regional Tourism in the Nineteenth Century* (Washington, D.C.: Smithsonian Institution Press, 1995), 16; Ronald R. Schultz and William B. Stronge, *The Social and Economic Effects of the Florida Tourist Industry* (Boca Raton: Florida Atlantic University, 1978), 5; Manning J. Dauer, *Florida Politics and Government* (Gainesville: University Presses of Florida, 1980), 34.

5. Cindy S. Aron, *Working at Play: A History of Vacations in the United States* (New York: Oxford University Press, 1999), 30–33.

6. Jonathan Dickinson, *Jonathan Dickinson's Journal, Or, God's Protecting Providence* (Port Salerno, Fla.: Florida Classics Library, 1985), 7, 10–11.

7. John Viele, *The Florida Keys: True Stories of the Perilous Straits* (Sarasota, Fla.: Pineapple Press), 2:19–51; Christopher R. Eck, "Beasts and Savages: Taming the Wilds of Florida in the Popular Imagination for Five Centuries," *South Florida History* 29 (2001): 14–15; Mary S. Mattfield, "Journey to the Wilderness: Two Travelers in Florida, 1696–1774," *Florida Historical Quarterly* 45 (April 1967): 339.

8. Charlotte M. Porter "Philadelphia Story: Florida Gives William Bartram a Second Chance," *Florida Historical Quarterly* 71 (January 1993): 317–318; Kathryn Hall Proby, *Audubon in Florida* (Miami: University of Miami Press, 1974), 26.

9. Gannon, *New History of Florida*, 156–164; Jerrell Shofner, *Florida Portrait: A Pictorial History of Florida* (Sarasota, Fla.: Pineapple Press, 1990), 49–63.

10. Jean Parker Waterbury, ed., *The Oldest City: St. Augustine Saga of Survival* (St. Augustine, Fla.: St. Augustine Historical Society, 1989), 171; Benjamin F. Rogers, "Florida Seen through the Eyes of Nineteenth Century Travelers," *Florida Historical Quarterly* 34 (October 1955): 178.

11. Gannon, *New History of Florida*, 207–228; Tracy J. Revels, *Grander in Her Daughters: Florida's Women during the Civil War* (Columbia: University of South Carolina Press, 2005), 1–9.

12. Richard Harrison Shyrock, ed., *Medicine in America: Historical Essays* (Baltimore: Johns Hopkins University Press, 1966), 142–143; John Duffy, *The Sanitarians: A History of American Public Health* (Urbana: University of Illinois Press, 1990), 197–198; James Laver, *Costume and Fashion: A Concise History* (New York: Thames & Hudson, 1995), 170.

13. Duffy, *Sanitarians*, 197–198; Shryock, *Medicine in America*, 143–144.

14. Aron, *Working at Play*, 16–20.

15. Waterbury, *Oldest City*, 140.

16. Waterbury, *Oldest City*, 154–155; Wayne Haynes Simmons, *Notices of East Florida* (facsimile of 1822 edition; Gainesville: University of Florida Press, 1973), xx–xxii.

17. Thomas Graham, *The Awakening of St. Augustine: The Anderson Family and the Oldest City 1821–1924* (St. Augustine, Fla.: St. Augustine Historical Society, 1978), 13, 57.

18. Graham, *Awakening of St. Augustine*, 34; Rogers, "Florida," 179.

19. Anya Jabour, "The Privations and Hardships of a New Country: Southern Women and Southern Hospitality on the Florida Frontier," *Florida Historical Quarterly* 75 (Winter 1997): 261–262, 265.

20. Graham, *Awakening of St. Augustine*, 57–59, 75; Proby, *Audubon in Florida*, 17; Waterbury, *Oldest City*, 151.

21. Waterbury, *Oldest City*, 171.

22. Floyd Rinhart and Marion Rinhart, *Victorian Florida: America's Last Frontier* (Atlanta: Peachtree, 1986), 15; Graham, *Awakening of St. Augustine*, 57–59.

23. Waterbury, *Oldest City*, 174.

24. Graham, *Awakening of St. Augustine*, 31; Rufus King Sewall, *Sketches of St. Augustine* (facsimile of the 1848 edition; Gainesville: University Presses of Florida, 1976), xv–xxv.

25. Earl R. Beck, "German Tourists in Florida: A Two-Century Record," *Florida Historical Quarterly* 61 (October 1982): 163–165; Gannon, *New History of Florida*, 215; Graham, *Awakening of St. Augustine*, 24: Waterbury, *Oldest City*, 174; Proby, *Audubon in Florida*, 15.

26. Ralph L. Rusk, *The Life of Ralph Waldo Emerson* (New York: C. Scribner's Sons, 1949), 120–121; Alan J. Downes, "The Legendary Visit of Emerson to Tallahas-

see," *Florida Historical Quarterly* 34 (April 1956): 334–336; Robert D. Richardson Jr., *Emerson: The Mind on Fire* (Berkeley: University of California Press, 1995), 73; Gay Wilson Allen, *Waldo Emerson* (New York: Penguin Books, 1981), 95–101; Graham, *Awakening of St. Augustine*, 24.

27. Howard R. Floan, *The South in Northern Eyes, 1831 to 1861* (Austin: University of Texas Press, 1958), 149–151; Charles Henry Brown, *William Cullen Bryant* (New York: Scribner, 1971), 286–287; Waterbury, *Oldest City*, 174.

28. "An Invalid," *A Winter in the West Indies and Florida* (New York: Wiley and Putnam, 1839), 152.

29. Charles A. Clinton, *A Winter from Home* (New York: John F. Trow, 1852), 9–10, 12.

30. James Stirling, *Letters from the Slave States* (London: John W. Parker and Son, 1867), 213.

31. Joseph Hutchins Colton, *Colton's Traveler and Tourist's Guide-Book through the United States of America and the Canadas* (New York: J. H. Colton, 1853), 102.

32. Clinton, *Winter from Home*, 9.

33. Proby, *Audubon in Florida*, 17; Graham, *Awakening of St. Augustine*, 59–64.

34. Thomas D. Clark, *The Emerging South* (New York: Oxford University Press, 1961), 25; Graham, *Awakening of St. Augustine*, 75.

35. John Pope, *A Tour through the Southern and Western Territories of the United States of North-America* (facsimile of the 1792 edition; Gainesville: University Presses of Florida, 1979), 44.

36. Brian Rucker, *Image and Reality: Tourism in Antebellum Pensacola* (Bagdad, Fla.: Patagonia Press, 2009), 2–48.

37. Maureen Ogle, *Key West: History of an Island of Dreams* (Gainesville: University Press of Florida, 2003), 40; "An Invalid," *Winter in the West Indies*, 119–122, 128, 130–131, 148.

38. Carlton Holmes Rogers, *Incidents of Travel in the Southern States and Cuba* (New York: R. Craighead, 1860), 195.

39. "Rambler," *Guide to Florida* (facsimile of the 1875 edition; Gainesville: University of Florida Press, 1964), xiii, Burke G. Vanderhill, "The Historic Spas of Florida," *West Georgia College Studies in the Social Sciences* 12 (June 1973): 59; Rembert W. Patrick, "The Mobile Frontier," *Journal of Southern History* 29 (February 1963): 5.

40. Vanderhill, "Historic Spas," 61–62.

41. Eric Musgrove, *Reflections of Suwannee County* (Live Oak, Fla.: Eric Musgrove Books, 2008), 35.

42. Vanderhill, "Historic Spas," 62–63.

43. Patricia Clark, "'A Tale to Tell from Paradise Itself': George Bancroft's Letters from Florida, March 1855," *Florida Historical Quarterly* 48 (January 1970): 272; Vanderhill, "Historic Spas," 63–65.

44. Ledyard Bill, *A Winter in Florida* (New York: Wood & Holbrook, 1869), 100.

45. Vanderhill, "Historic Spas," 65–66; Pennsylvania Railroad, *Florida: Winter*

Pleasure Tours under the Personally Conducted System of the Pennsylvania Railroad, Season of 1896 (Philadelphia: Allen, Lane & Scott, 1895), 24.

46. Vanderhill, "Historic Spas," 166–167.

47. Patrick, "Mobile Frontier," 7; Julian Ralph, *Dixie: Or, Southern Scenes and Sketches* (New York: Harper and Brothers, 1895), 169–170; John M. Spivak, "Paradise Awaits: A Sampling and Brief Analysis of Late 19th Century Promotional Pamphlets on Florida," *Southern Studies* 21 (1982): 436.

48. Vanderhill, "Historic Spas," 69–71.

49. Vanderhill, "Historic Spas," 67–69; "Safety Harbor Resort," www.safetyharborresort.com, accessed August 9, 2009.

50. Vanderhill, "Historic Spas," 71–72.

51. Tracy J. Revels, *Watery Eden: A History of Wakulla Springs* (Tallahassee, Fla.: Sentry Press, 2002), 24–29; Virginia Steele Wood, "Elijah Swift's Travel Journal from Massachusetts to Florida, 1857," *Florida Historical Quarterly* 55 (October 1976): 186.

52. Tim Hollis, *Dixie Before Disney: 100 Years of Roadside Fun* (Jackson: University Press of Mississippi, 1999), 145; Clark, "Tale to Tell," 271; Richard A. Martin, *Eternal Spring: Man's 10,000 Years of History at Florida's Silver Springs* (St. Petersburg, Fla.: Great Outdoors, 1966), 106–109.

53. Bill, *Winter in Florida*, 76.

54. Clark, "Tale to Tell," 271; Patrick, "Mobile Frontier," 7; Silvia Sunshine (pseud. Abbie M. Brooks), *Petals Plucked from Sunny Climes* (Nashville, Tenn.: Southern Methodist Publishing House, 1880), 27.

55. Bill, *Winter in Florida*, 169.

Chapter 2. Sportsman's Paradise

1. Martin, *Eternal Spring*, 121–122. Woolson was a niece of the famous author James Fenimore Cooper.

2. Rogers, "Florida," 184.

3. Aron, *Working at Play*, 34, 41–43, 128.

4. Rifkin, *Age of Access*, 147; Gary R. Mormino, "Florida's Gilded Year, 1886," *Gulf Coast Historical Review* 10 (1994): 39–40; Aron, *Working at Play*, 45, 47–51.

5. Gannon, *New History of Florida*, 232; Graham, *Awakening of St. Augustine*, 86; Revels, *Grander in Her Daughters*, 11, 34, 175.

6. Henry F. W. Little, *The Seventh Regiment New Hampshire Volunteers in the War of the Rebellion* (Concord, N.H.: Ira C. Evans, 1896), 75; James M. Nichols, *Perry's Saints: Or, The Fighting Parson's Regiment in the War of the Rebellion* (Boston: D. Lothrop, 1886), 179–180.

7. "Rambler," *Guide to Florida*, ix–x.

8. John R. Adams, *Harriet Beecher Stowe* (Boston: Twayne, 1989), 74–75; Joan D.

Hedrick, *Harriet Beecher Stowe: A Life* (New York: Oxford University Press, 1994), 330, 340; Forrest Wilson, *Crusader in Crinoline: The Life of Harriet Beecher Stowe* (Philadelphia: J. B. Lippincott, 1941), 576.

9. Adams, *Harriet Beecher Stowe*, 76; Patrick, "Mobile Frontier," 8; Jerrell Shofner, *Nor Is It Over Yet: Florida in the Era of Reconstruction 1863–1877* (Gainesville: University Presses of Florida, 1974), 26.

10. Adams, *Harriet Beecher Stowe*, 76; Lyman Beecher Stowe, *Saints, Sinners, and Beechers* (Indianapolis: Bobbs-Merrill, 1934), 225–226.

11. Mormino, "Florida's Gilded Year," 33; Gannon, *New History of Florida*, 259; Musgrove, *Reflections of Suwannee County*, 40.

12. William D. Kelley, *The Old South and the New: A Series of Letters* (New York: Knickerbocker Press, 1888), 15; Gannon, *New History of Florida*, 257–259.

13. Whitelaw Reid, *After the War: A Tour of the Southern States 1865–1866* (facsimile of the 1866 edition; New York: Harper and Row, 1965), 179.

14. Gannon, *New History of Florida*, 257–259; Shofner, *Nor Is It Over Yet*, 259.

15. "Rambler," *Guide to Florida*, xii.

16. Gannon, *New History of Florida*, 260; Edward N. Akin, *Flagler: Rockefeller Partner and Florida Baron* (Gainesville: University Press of Florida, 1992), 114–115; Samuel Curtis Upham, *Notes from Sunland* (Bradentown, Fla.: Samuel Curtis Upham, 1881), 8–10, 12.

17. Frank L. Snyder, "Nancy Hynes DuVal: Florida's First Lady, 1822–1834," *Florida Historical Quarterly* 72 (July 1993): 33.

18. James R. McGovern, *The Emergence of a City in the Modern South: Pensacola 1900–1945* (DeLeon Springs, Fla.: E. O. Painter Printing, 1976), 39; John Lee Williams, *A View of West Florida* (facsimile of the 1827 edition; Gainesville: University Presses of Florida, 1976), 10; Shofner, *Nor Is It Over Yet*, 269–270; Gannon, *New History of Florida*, 276; Simmons, *Notices of East Florida*, xxxi; David Nolan, *Fifty Feet in Paradise: The Booming of Florida* (New York: Harcourt Brace Jovanovich, 1984), 187; Lente, *Florida as a Health-Resort*, 16.

19. Jay Barnes, *Florida's Hurricane History*, 2nd ed. (Chapel Hill: University of North Carolina Press, 2007), 54–79; David L. Willing, "Florida's Overseas Railroad," *Florida Historical Quarterly* 35 (April 1957): 296.

20. Sidney Lanier, *Florida: Its Scenery, Climate and History* (Gainesville: University of Florida Press, 1973), xi; Reid, *After the War*, ix; "Rambler," *Guide to Florida*, xv.

21. "Rambler," *Guide to Florida*, 63, 65.

22. Lente, *Florida as a Health-Resort*, 18–19.

23. Spivak, "Paradise Awaits," 430–433.

24. Lanier, *Florida*, xii–xiii; Gene M. Burnett, *Florida's Past: People and Events That Shaped the State* (Sarasota, Fla.: Pineapple Press, 1986), 54–55.

25. Lanier, *Florida*, xii–xiii, xxxiv–xxxvi; Burnett, *Florida's Past*, 57.

26. Lente, *Florida as a Health-Resort*, 4.

27. Shofner, *Nor Is It Over Yet*, 258, 261, 263–264; John T. Foster Jr. and Sarah Whitmer Foster, *Beechers, Stowes, and Yankee Strangers: The Transformation of Florida* (Gainesville: University Press of Florida, 1999), 55, 93.

28. Larry Roberts, *Florida's Golden Age of Souvenirs, 1890–1930* (Gainesville: University Press of Florida, 2001), 16; James Robertson Ward, *Old Hickory's Town: An Illustrated History of Jacksonville* (Jacksonville: Florida Publishing, 1982), 158–159; Ralph, *Dixie*, 172.

29. James B. Crooks, "Changing Face of Jacksonville, Florida: 1900–1910," *Florida Historical Quarterly* 62 (April 1984): 451; C. W. Johnston, *The Sunny South and Its People* (Chicago: Rand McNally, 1918), 251; Rinhart and Rinhart, *Victorian Florida*, 46–54.

30. Upham, *Notes from Sunland*, 11.

31. Rinhart and Rinhart, *Victorian Florida*, 24–25; Graham, *Awakening of St. Augustine*, 155–156.

32. Christopher R. Eck, "Beasts and Savages: Taming the Wilds of Florida in the Popular Imagination for Five Centuries," *South Florida History* 29 (2001): 15; Pennsylvania Railroad, *Florida Excursion Routes for the Season of 1874–75* (Philadelphia: Allen, Lane & Scott, 1874), 4; Robert Barnwell Roosevelt, *Florida and the Game Water-Birds of the Atlantic Coast and the Lakes of the United States* (New York: Orange Judd, 1884), 9–10.

33. Upham, *Notes from Sunland*, 12.

34. Rinhart and Rinhart, *Victorian Florida*, 25–26, 37; "Rambler," *Guide to Florida*, 141–142.

35. Jim Robison and Mark Andrews, *Flashbacks: The Story of Central Florida's Past* (Orlando, Fla.: Orange County Historical Society, 1995), 178; Cheryl Atwell and Vincent Clarida, *Daytona Beach and the Halifax River Area* (Charleston, S.C.: Arcadia, 1998), 93.

36. Alfred Jackson Hanna and Kathryn Abbey Hanna, *Florida's Golden Sands* (Indianapolis: Bobbs-Merrill, 1950), 223; John Muir, *A Thousand Mile Walk to the Gulf* (Boston: Houghton Mifflin, 1916), 95.

37. Gannon, *New History of Florida*, 25; Rinhart and Rinhart, *Victorian Florida*, 29.

38. Foster and Foster, *Beechers, Stowes, and Yankee Strangers*, 95; "Rambler," *Guide to Florida*, 127; Rinhart and Rinhart, *Victorian Florida*, 34; Margaret Deland, *Florida Days* (Boston: Little, Brown, 1889), 59–60.

39. Stirling, *Letters from the Slave States*, 1867; Ralph, *Dixie*, 166–167; Muir, *Thousand Mile Walk*, 109.

40. Ralph, *Dixie*, 185; Rogers, "Florida," 184; Musgrove, *Reflections of Suwannee County*, 40; Bob Bass, *When Steamboats Reigned in Florida* (Gainesville: University Press of Florida, 2008), 92; E. A. Mueller, "Suwannee River Steamboating," *Florida Historical Quarterly* 45 (January 1967): 284.

41. Ralph, *Dixie*, 184–185.

42. "Rambler," *Guide to Florida*, 98, 132–136.

43. Shofner, *Nor Is It Over Yet*, 261; George Washington Olney, *A Guide to Florida "The Land of Flowers"* (New York: Catlin & Lydecker, 1874), n.p.

44. Bill, *Winter in Florida*, 143; Stirling, *Letters from the Slave States*, 216.

45. Mormino, "Florida's Gilded Year," 39; "Rambler," *Guide to Florida*, 138–140; Joe M. Richardson, "The Florida Excursion of President Chester A. Arthur," *Tequesta* 24 (1964): 44.

46. Ogle, *Key West*, 95, 116–117.

47. F. Trench Townshend, *Wild Life in Florida with a Visit to Cuba* (London: Hurst and Blackett, 1875), 10, 13–14.

48. Roosevelt, *Florida and the Game Water-Birds*, 11; Foster and Foster, *Beechers, Stowes, and Yankee Strangers*, 95, 106.

49. Musgrove, *Reflections of Suwannee County*, 16.

50. Shofner, *Nor Is It Over Yet*, 26, McGovern, *Emergence of a City*, 2–3; Johnston, *Sunny South*, 285, 311.

51. McGovern, *Emergence of a City*, 71–72; Crooks, "Changing Face of Jacksonville," 45; Johnston, *Sunny South*, 241, 251.

52. Johnston, *Sunny South*, 259–260, 285.

53. Ralph, *Dixie*, 162.

54. Aron, *Working at Play*, 111–113.

55. Nevin Otto Winter, *Florida: The Land of Enchantment* (Boston: Page, 1918), 153; Eliot Kleinberg, *Historical Traveler's Guide to Florida* (Sarasota, Fla.: Pineapple Press, 2006), 8; James J. Horgan and Lewis N. Wynne, eds., *Florida Decades: A Sesquicentennial History 1845–1995* (Saint Leo, Fla.: Saint Leo College Press, 1995), 75; John L. McKinnon, *History of Walton County* (Gainesville, Fla.: Palmetto Books, 1968), 358–362.

56. Mormino, "Florida's Gilded Year," 41; Aron, *Working at Play*, 113–114, 119; Horgan and Wynne, *Florida Decades*, 67–79.

57. Shofner, *Nor Is It Over Yet*, 265; "Rambler," *Guide to Florida*, 95.

58. Bass, *When Steamboats Reigned in Florida*, 92–93; Ralph, *Dixie*, 189; Hollis, *Dixie Before Disney*, 145; Margot Ammidon, "Edens, Underworlds, and Shrines: Florida's Small Tourist Attractions," *Journal of Decorative and Propaganda Arts* 23 (1998): 245, Martin, *Eternal Spring*, 152–156.

59. "Rambler," *Guide to Florida*, 128; Hollis, *Dixie Before Disney*, 146; Gannon, *New History of Florida*, 259.

60. Waterbury, *Oldest City*, 181–182; Reid, *After the War*, 171; "Rambler," *Guide to Florida*, 114.

61. Waterbury, *Oldest City*, 187; Graham, *Awakening of St. Augustine*, 153–154.

62. George H. Chapin, *Health Resorts of the South* (N.p.: George H. Chapin, 1893), 44–45.

63. Lanier, *Florida*, xxxvii–xxxviii; Graham, *Awakening of St. Augustine*, 159–163; "Rambler," *Guide to Florida*, 103; Waterbury, *Oldest City*, 189–191; Mormino, "Florida's Gilded Year," 37.

Chapter 3. A Winter Playground

1. Susan R. Braden, *The Architecture of Leisure: The Florida Resort Hotels of Henry Flagler and Henry Plant* (Gainesville: University Press of Florida, 2002), 20–23; Hap Hatton, *Tropical Splendor: An Architectural History of Florida* (New York: Alfred A. Knopf, 1987), 23; Sidney Walter Martin, *Florida's Flagler* (Athens: University of Georgia Press, 1949), 64.

2. Martin, *Florida's Flagler*, 90–91.

3. Bill, *Winter in Florida*, 19–20; Akin, *Flagler*, 117.

4. Graham, *Awakening of St. Augustine*, 168–169; Waterbury, *Oldest City*, 192; Martin, *Florida's Flagler*, 95, 106; Akin, *Flagler*, 116–117.

5. Akin, *Flagler*, 116; Martin, *Florida's Flagler*, 114–115; Braden, *Architecture of Leisure*, 23–24.

6. Jean Parker Waterbury, *Markland* (St. Augustine, Fla.: St. Augustine Historical Society, 1989), 52; Waterbury, *Oldest City*, 192–196; Martin, *Florida's Flagler*, 106–113.

7. Martin, *Florida's Flagler*, 117–121; Braden, *Architecture of Leisure*, 106.

8. Cleveland Amory, *The Last Resorts* (New York: Harper and Brothers, 1948), 336.

9. Charles Ledyard Norton, *A Handbook of Florida* (New York: Longmans, Green, 1894), 173; Martin, *Florida's Flagler*, 121–123; Waterbury, *Oldest City*, 194.

10. Dunn, "Florida," 21–22; Martin, *Florida's Flagler*, 123; Waterbury, *Oldest City*, 194; David Nolan, *The Houses of St. Augustine* (Sarasota, Fla.: Pineapple Press, 1995), 48.

11. Graham, *Awakening of St. Augustine*, 169–173.

12. Braden, *Architecture of Leisure*, 13–14; Ralph, *Dixie*, 173, 178.

13. Beck, "German Tourists," 168–169; Waterbury, *Oldest City*, 192; Martin, *Florida's Flagler*, 125–126.

14. Hatton, *Tropical Splendor*, vix.

15. Ralph, *Dixie*, 173–174; Braden, *Architecture of Leisure*, 13–14.

16. Ralph, *Dixie*, 169–170.

17. Pennsylvania Railroad, *Florida*, 7.

18. Beck, "German Tourists," 169–171.

19. Martin, *Florida's Flagler*, 128–129; Nolan, *Houses of St. Augustine*, 46–48.

20. Hanna and Hanna, *Florida's Golden Sands*, 313.

21. Martin, *Florida's Flagler*, 130–133.

22. Ralph, *Dixie*, 195; Martin, *Florida's Flagler*, 135–136; Stuart B. McIver, *Dreamers, Schemers, and Scalawags: The Florida Chronicles* (Sarasota, Fla.: Pineapple Press, 1994), 181–182.

23. Martin, *Florida's Flagler*, 136–137.

24. Martin, *Florida's Flagler*, 138–139.

25. Martin, *Florida's Flagler*, 141–143; Braden, *Architecture of Leisure*, 212.

26. Amory, *Last Resorts*, 338; Akin, *Flagler*, 146; Martin, *Florida's Flagler*, 145–147.

27. Amory, *Last Resorts*, 339–340; Martin, *Florida's Flagler*, 147–149.

28. Amory, *Last Resorts*, 339–340.

29. Braden, *Architecture of Leisure*, 15.

30. Braden, *Architecture of Leisure*, 222–229.

31. "Rambler," *Guide to Florida*, 140–141; Polly Redford, *Billion-Dollar Sandbar: A Biography of Miami Beach* (New York: E. P. Dutton, 1970), 20–26.

32. Martin, *Florida's Flagler*, 152–153; Redford, *Billion-Dollar Sandbar*, 27–28.

33. Paul S. George, "Passage to the New Eden: Tourism in Miami from Flagler through Everest G. Sewell," *Florida Historical Quarterly* 59 (April 1981): 443; Martin, *Florida's Flagler*, 153–155, 158; Redford, *Billion-Dollar Sandbar*, 28–29; Eric P. Nash and Randall C. Robinson Jr., *MiMo: Miami Modern Revealed* (San Francisco: Chronicle Books, 2004), 9.

34. Martin, *Florida's Flagler*, 162–163; Nicholas N. Patricios, *Building Marvelous Miami* (Gainesville: University Press of Florida, 1994), 111; Nathan D. Shappee, "Flagler's Undertakings in Miami in 1897," *Tequesta* 19 (1957): 8; Redford, *Billion-Dollar Sandbar*, 29–31.

35. John F. Eades, "City Planning in West Palm Beach during the 1920s," *Florida Historical Quarterly* 75 (Winter 1997): 278–279; George, "Passage to the New Eden," 445; Martin, *Florida's Flagler*, 163.

36. Martin, *Florida's Flagler*, 164–165.

37. Burnett, *Florida's Past*, 246–249; Amory, *Last Resorts*, 342; Martin, *Florida's Flagler*, 170–195.

38. Willing, "Florida's Overseas Railroad," 287–290; Martin, *Florida's Flagler*, 202–206.

39. Nolan, *Houses of St. Augustine*, 48; Willing, "Florida's Overseas Railroad," 295–298.

40. Willing, "Florida's Overseas Railroad," 300–301; Martin, *Florida's Flagler*, 209–225.

41. Braden, *Architecture of Leisure*, 27.

42. Martin, *Florida's Flagler*, 202, 226–227; Willing, "Florida's Overseas Railroad," 301; Baynard Hardwick Kendrick, *Florida Trails to Turnpikes 1914–1964* (Gainesville: University of Florida Press, 1964), 139.

43. Akin, *Flagler*, 208, 226–227; Martin, *Florida's Flagler*, 245–249.

44. Braden, *Architecture of Leisure*, 19; James W. Covington, *Plant's Palace: Henry B. Plant and the Tampa Bay Hotel* (Louisville, Ky.: Harmony House, 1991), 65; Dunn, "Florida," 23.

45. Braden, *Architecture of Leisure*, 32–36; Gary R. Mormino, "Roadsides and Broadsides: A History of Florida Tourism," *Forum: The Magazine of the Florida Humanities Council* 10 (Fall 1987): 9.

46. Hatton, *Tropical Splendor*, 25–26; Dunn, "Florida," 23.

47. Covington, *Plant's Palace*, 58, 64–65; Dunn, "Florida, 25.

48. Kelly Reynolds, *Henry Plant: Pioneer Empire Builder* (Cocoa: Florida Historical Society Press, 2003), 168; G. Hutchinson Smyth, *The Life of Henry Bradley Plant* (New York: G. P. Putnam's Sons, 1898), 79; Covington, *Plant's Palace*, 64.

49. Reynolds, *Henry Plant*, 168, 170–172; Covington, *Plant's Palace*, 66–67, 74–75; Burnett, *Florida's Past*, 188–189.

50. Covington, *Plant's Palace*, 69; Braden, *Architecture of Leisure*, 36–37; Michael Sanders, *Clearwater: A Pictorial History* (Norfolk, Va.: Donning, 1983), 27.

51. Covington, *Plant's Palace*, 69–71; Braden, *Architecture of Leisure*, 37–39.

52. Hatton, *Tropical Splendor*, 30; Dunn, "Florida," 23–25.

53. Braden, *Architecture of Leisure*, 1; Hatton, *Tropical Splendor*, vix.

54. Braden, *Architecture of Leisure*, 106, 124–129.

55. Waterbury, *Oldest City*, 200–202; Braden, *Architecture of Leisure*, 125–132.

56. Michael Reynolds, "Profit from Pretense," *Jacksonville Today* (June 1988): 42; James J. Miller, *An Environmental History of Northeast Florida* (Gainesville: University Press of Florida, 1998), 179; Patricia C. Griffin, "The Impact of Tourism and Development on Public Ritual and Festival, St. Augustine, Florida, 1821–1987" (Ph.D. diss., University of Florida, 1988), 123–124; Nolan, *Fifty Feet in Paradise*, 295; Stephen Birmingham, *The Right People: A Portrait of the American Social Establishment* (Boston: Little, Brown, 1968), 274; Nixon Smiley, *Florida: Land of Images* (Miami: E. A. Seeman, 1973), 53; Braden, *Architecture of Leisure*, 199.

57. Redford, *Billion-Dollar Sandbar*, 31.

58. Braden, *Architecture of Leisure*, 3; Hanna and Hanna, *Florida's Golden Sands*, 231.

59. Amory, *Last Resorts*, 329.

60. Eck, "Savages and Beasts," 16, 19; Beck, "German Tourists," 171; Aron, *Working at Play*, 154; Warren James Belasco, *Americans on the Road: From Auto Camps to Motel, 1910–1945* (Baltimore: Johns Hopkins University Press, 1979), 71.

61. Braden, *Architecture of Leisure*, 13.

Chapter 4. Tin Can Heaven

1. Johnston, *Sunny South*, 252–253.

2. Patrick, "Mobile Frontier," 10–11; Judith A. Adams, *The American Amusement Park Industry: A History of Technology and Thrills* (Boston: Twayne, 1991), 57–62.

3. Adams, *American Amusement Park Industry*, 57–62.

4. James B. Crooks, *Jacksonville After the Fire, 1901–1919: A New South City* (Jacksonville: University of North Florida Press, 1991), 105–106; James B. Crooks, "Changing Face of Jacksonville, Florida: 1900–1910," *Florida Historical Quarterly 62* (April 1984), 443, 449–450; Ann Hyman, *Jacksonville Greets the Twentieth Century: The Pictorial Legacy of Leah Mary Cox* (Gainesville: University Press of Florida, 2002), 95.

5. McGovern, *Emergence of a City*, 17–18; Raymond Arsenault, *St. Petersburg and the Florida Dream, 1888–1950* (Gainesville: University Press of Florida, 1996), 202.

6. Arsenault, *St. Petersburg and the Florida Dream*, 62–63, 81, 144–145.

7. Arsenault, *St. Petersburg and the Florida Dream*, 145–146; Gary R. Mormino, *Land of Sunshine, State of Dreams: A Social History of Modern Florida* (Gainesville: University Press of Florida, 2005), 79.

8. Arsenault, *St. Petersburg and the Florida Dream*, 143–144, 147–148, 205, 252.

9. Arsenault, *St. Petersburg and the Florida Dream*, 145–147, John T. Farris, *Seeing the Sunny South* (Philadelphia: J. B. Lippincott, 1921), 150–155; Gannon, *New History of Florida*, 430.

10. Canter Brown Jr., *In the Midst of All That Makes Life Worth Living: Polk County, Florida to 1940* (Tallahassee, Fla.: Sentry Press, 2001), 271; John A. Jakle, *Motoring: The Highway Experience in America* (Athens: University of Georgia Press, 2008), 107; John A. Jakle and Keith A. Sculle, *The Gas Station in America* (Baltimore: Johns Hopkins University Press, 1994), 3; Foster Rhea Dulles, *America Learns to Play: A History of Recreation*, 2nd ed. (New York: Appleton-Century-Crofts, 1965), 321; James J. Flink, *The Car Culture* (Cambridge, Mass.: MIT Press, 1975), 156; Patrick, "Mobile Frontier," 11; Hatton, *Tropical Splendor*, 175.

11. Clifton Johnson, *Highways and Byways of Florida* (New York: Macmillan, 1918), 200; George, "Passage to the New Eden," 451; Hollis, *Dixie Before Disney*, 5–7; Gannon, *New History of Florida*, 293, 430–431.

12. Frank Parker Stockbridge and John Holliday Perry, *Florida in the Making* (New York: DeBwer, 1926), 145.

13. Brown, *In the Midst of All*, 271; Johnson, *Highways and Byways*, 200–201.

14. Brown, *In the Midst of All*, 271.

15. Charlie Hailey, "Southern Camp(Sites): Florida's Vernacular Spaces from John Ruskin to the Tin Can Tourists of the World," *Southern Quarterly* 42 (2003): 80; Gannon, *New History of Florida*, 292–293.

16. Belasco, *Americans on the Road*, 71.

17. Beck, "German Tourists," 173–174.

18. Mary Crehore Bedell, *Modern Gypsies: The Story of a Twelve Thousand Mile Motor Camping Trip Encircling the United States* (New York: Brentano's, 1924), 28–33.

19. Hatton, *Tropical Splendor*, 177; Gannon, *New History of Florida*, 292–293.

20. William B. Stronge, *The Sunshine Economy: An Economic History of Florida since the Civil War* (Gainesville: University Press of Florida, 2008), 91.

21. Arsenault, *St. Petersburg and the Florida Dream*, 189.

22. Belasco, *Americans on the Road*, 121–122, 124.

23. Brown, *In the Midst of All*, 271.

24. McGovern, *Emergence of a City*, 91; Eades, "City Planning in West Palm Beach," 279.

25. Redford, *Billion-Dollar Sandbar*, 130–132.

26. Richard Alan Nelson, "Palm Trees, Public Relations, and Promoters: Boosting Florida as a Motion Picture Empire, 1910–1930," *Florida Historical Quarterly* 61 (April 1982): 384–385; George, "Passage to the New Eden," 452–453.

27. Arsenault, *St. Petersburg and the Florida Dream*, 143, 186–204.

28. Nolan, *Fifty Feet in Paradise*, 188; Arsenault, *St. Petersburg and the Florida Dream*, 204; Patricios, *Building Marvelous Miami*, 72–73; Ogle, *Key West*, 137; Patricia Buchanan, "Miami's Bootleg Boom," *Tequesta* 30 (1970): 13–14.

29. George, "Passage to the New Eden," 456; Arsenault, *St. Petersburg and the Florida Dream*, 204; Redford, *Billion-Dollar Sandbar*, 197; Beck, "German Tourists," 173.

30. Amory, *Last Resorts*, 345; Redford, *Billion-Dollar Sandbar*, 195–196.

31. Redford, *Billion-Dollar Sandbar*, 196–197.

32. Redford, *Billion-Dollar Sandbar*, 96.

33. Mark S. Foster, "In the Face of 'Jim Crow': Prosperous Blacks on Vacations, Travel and Outdoor Leisure, 1890–1945," *Journal of Negro History* 84 (Spring 1999): 141–142.

34. John A. Jakle, Keith A. Sculle, and Jefferson S. Rogers, *The Motel in America* (Baltimore: Johns Hopkins University Press, 1996), 72–73; Foster, "In the Face of 'Jim Crow,'" 141–142.

35. Mormino, *Land of Sunshine*, 97.

36. Marsha Dean Phelts, *An American Beach for African Americans* (Gainesville: University Press of Florida, 1997), 1–10.

37. Russ Rymer, *American Beach: A Saga of Race, Wealth, and Memory* (New York: Harper Collins, 1998), 161; Phelts, *American Beach*, 11, 56–59, 62, 66–67.

38. Arsenault, *St. Petersburg and the Florida Dream*, 208; McGovern, *Emergence of a City*, 55–56.

39. Gannon, *New History of Florida*, 19–27.

40. Ammidon, "Edens, Underworlds, and Shrines," 257.

41. Patsy West, "Indian Tourism," *South Florida History* 27 (Winter 1998–1999): 23.

42. West, "Indian Tourism," 26–27; Dorothy Downs, *Art of the Florida Seminole and Miccosukee Indians* (Gainesville: University Press of Florida, 1995), 85; Brent Richards Weisman, *Unconquered People: Florida's Seminole and Miccosukee Indians* (Gainesville: University Press of Florida, 1999), 125.

43. Ken Breslauer, *Roadside Paradise: The Golden Age of Florida's Tourist Attractions 1929–1971* (St. Petersburg, Fla.: RetroFlorida, 2000), 12; West, "Indian Tourism," 24–25.

44. Breslauer, *Roadside Paradise*, 6–8; Hollis, *Dixie Before Disney*, 132; Hatton, *Tropical Splendor*, 160–163.

45. Howard Lawrence Preston, *Dirt Roads to Dixie: Accessibility and Modernization in the South, 1885–1935* (Knoxville: University of Tennessee Press, 1991), 116–118.

46. Redford, *Billion-Dollar Sandbar*, 135, 146, 149.

47. John M. Williams and Iver W. Duedall, *Florida Hurricanes and Tropical Storms* (Gainesville: University Press of Florida, 1997), 14–15; Barnes, *Florida's Hurricane History*, 112–113, 116, 126.

48. Barnes, *Florida's Hurricane History*, 127–129, 130, 137; George, "Passage to the New Eden," 457; Williams and Duedall, *Florida Hurricanes and Tropical Storms*, 15; Lawrence E. Will, *Okeechobee Hurricane and the Hoover Dike* (St. Petersburg, Fla.: Great Outdoors, 1961), 85–88.

49. Patrick, "Mobile Frontier," 13; Robert J. Huckshorn, *Government and Politics in Florida* (Gainesville: University Press of Florida, 1991), 36.

Chapter 5. Blitzkrieg of Joy

1. Ruthmary Bauer, "Sarasota: Hardship and Tourism in the 1930s," *Florida Historical Quarterly* 76 (Fall 1997): 138.

2. Arsenault, *St. Petersburg and the Florida Dream*, 186–187, 255, 260–263; Aron, *Working at Play*, 242, 246; Breslauer, *Roadside Paradise*, 12–13.

3. George, "Passage to the New Eden," 12–13; Redford, *Billion-Dollar Sandbar*, 199.

4. George, "Passage to the New Eden," 455; Redford, *Billion-Dollar Sandbar*, 201–202.

5. Bauer, "Sarasota," 148–150.

6. Garry Boulard, "'State of Emergency': Key West in the Great Depression," *Florida Historical Quarterly* 67 (October 1988): 166, 172; Dunwood Long, "Key West and the New Deal, 1934–1936," *Florida Historical Quarterly* 46 (January 1968): 209–213.

7. Boulard, "'State of Emergency,'" 172–175; Long, "Key West and the New Deal," 213–215; Ogle, *Key West*, 176.

8. George W. Seaton, *Cue's Guide to What to See and Do in Florida* (New York: Prentice-Hall, 1940), 45–46; Long, "Key West and the New Deal," 217–218.

9. Boulard, "'State of Emergency,'" 174; Ogle, *Key West*, 166, 170, 173, 184; William C. Barnett, "Inventing the Conch Republic: The Creation of Key West as an Escape from Modern America," *Florida Historical Quarterly* 88 (Fall 2009): 165.

10. Redford, *Billion-Dollar Sandbar*, 206; Cecil Roberts, *Gone Sunwards* (New York: Macmillan, 1936), 182.

11. Redford, *Billion-Dollar Sandbar*, 203.

12. Gannon, *New History of Florida*, 319–320.

13. Frederick W. Dau, *Florida Old and New* (New York: G. P. Putnam's Sons, 1934), 321.

14. Seaton, *Cue's Guide*, vi, 6, 8.

15. Lorenz More, ed., *Florida Hotel and Travel Guide, 1941 Edition* (New York: Florida Guide, 1941), 23–24.

16. Seaton, *Cue's Guide*, 379; Nash and Robinson, *MiMo*, 16.

17. Reinhold P. Wolff, *Tourist Days and Tourist Spending in Southeastern Florida, 1953–54* (University of Miami: Bureau of Spending and Economic Research, 1955), 3–4; Frank Parker Stockbridge and John Holliday Perry, *So This Is Florida* (New York: R. M. McBride, 1938), 10, 25–28.

18. Redford, *Billion-Dollar Sandbar*, 218–219; Stephen E. Branch, "The Salesman and His Swamp: Dick Pope's Cypress Gardens," *Florida Historical Quarterly* 80 (Spring 2002): 491; Gary R. Mormino, "Midas Returns: Miami Goes to War, 1941–1945," *Tequesta* 57 (1997): 5.

19. Nixon Smiley, *Yesterday's Miami* (Miami: E. A. Seeman, 1973), 108; Helen Muir, *Miami, U.S.A.* (Miami: Pickering Press, 1953), 201–202; Benjamin F. Rogers, "Florida in World War II: Tourists and Citrus," *Florida Historical Quarterly* 39 (July 1960): 40; *Life*, March 23, 1942, 92–97.

20. Charlton W. Tebeau, *A History of Florida* (Coral Gables, Fla.: University of Miami Press, 197), 419; Donald W. Curl, *Palm Beach County: An Illustrated History* (Northridge, Fla.: Windsor, 1986), 109; Redford, *Billion-Dollar Sandbar*, 218–219.

21. Breslauer, *Roadside Paradise*, 14.

22. Muir, *Miami, U.S.A.*, 204.

23. Tebeau, *History of Florida*, 416–417; David Ramsey, "Military Installations in Florida during World War II" (unpublished research paper; Tallahassee: Florida State University, 1957), 1–2.

24. Burnett, *Florida's Past*, 188–189; *Life*, March 23, 1942, 92–97; Mormino, "Midas Returns," 12–13.

25. Mormino, "Midas Returns," 13; Redford, *Billion-Dollar Sandbar*, 219.

26. Redford, *Billion-Dollar Sandbar*, 219; Charlton W. Tebeau and Ruby Leach Carson, *Florida from Indian Trail to Space Age* (Delray Beach, Fla.: Southern Publishing, 1965), 2:84; Nash and Robinson, *MiMo*, 31.

27. Smiley, *Yesterday's Miami*, 108; Muir, *Miami, U.S.A.*, 208–209; Mormino, "Midas Returns," 7.

28. Stuart B. McIver, *Glimpses of South Florida History* (Miami: Florida Flair Books, 1988), 97; Muir, *Miami U.S.A.*, 209; Ward, *Old Hickory's Town*, 217; Waterbury, *Oldest City*, 234; Ianthe Bond Hebel, ed., *Centennial History of Volusia County, Florida: 1854–1954* (Daytona Beach, Fla.: College Publishing, 1955), 6–7.

29. Hampton Dunn, *Yesterday's St. Petersburg* (Miami: E. A. Seeman, 1973), 33; Hampton Dunn, *Yesterday's Clearwater* (Miami: E. A. Seeman, 1973), 31; Karl H. Grismer, *Tampa: A History of the City of Tampa and the Tampa Bay Region of Florida* (St. Petersburg, Fla.: St. Petersburg Publishing, 1950), 282; Arch Frederic Blakely, *Parade of Memories: A History of Clay County, Florida* (Jacksonville, Fla.: Drummond Press, 1973), 230–231; Charles H. Hildreth and Merlin G. Cox, *History of Gainesville, Florida, 1854–1979* (Gainesville, Fla.: Alachua County Historical Society, 1981), 152; Revels, *Watery Eden*, 45–46.

30. Virginia Elliot Teneich, *History of Hollywood* (Port Salerno, Fla.: Florida

Classics Library, 1989), 359; Nash and Robinson, *MiMo*, 31; Rogers, "Florida in World War II," 35; McGovern, *Emergence of a City*, 154–159.

31. Breslauer, *Roadside Paradise*, 14.

32. Lewis N. Wynne, ed., *Florida at War* (Saint Leo, Fla.: Saint Leo College Press, 1993), 16–17; Mark I. Greenberg, William Warren Rogers, and Canter Brown Jr., eds., *Florida Heritage of Diversity: Essays in Honor of Samuel Proctor* (Tallahassee, Fla.: Sentry Press, 1997).

33. Wynne, *Florida at War*, 23; Mark Derr, *Some Kind of Paradise: A Chronicle of Man and the Land in Florida* (New York: William Morrow, 1989), 336.

34. *Florida Highways*, June 9, 1942; *New York Times*, January 20, 1942.

35. *Florida Highways*, June 9, 1942; *Florida Highways*, April 21, 1942.

36. *Florida Highways*, November 9, 1942; *New York Times*, November 15, 1942.

37. *Florida Highways*, June 9, 1942.

38. *New York Times*, June 20, 1943; Rogers, "Florida in World War II," 36; *Florida Highways*, July 1943, 25.

39. *New York Times*, June 20, 1943; *Florida Highways*, July 1943, 25.

40. Rogers, "Florida in World War II," 37; Philip Wylie, "War and Peace in Miami," *New Republic*, February 21, 1944, 238; *Time*, January 10, 1944, 23.

41. *Time*, January 10, 1944, 23; *Time*, March 13, 1944, 13; Mormino, "Midas Returns," 29–30.

42. Wylie, "War and Peace in Miami," 239.

43. Muir, *Miami, U.S.A.*, 211.

44. Wylie, "War and Peace in Miami," 239.

45. *Newsweek*, March 13, 1944, 84; *Time*, March 13, 1944, 13; Mormino, "Midas Returns," 27.

46. *Time*, March 6, 1944, 84; *Time*, March 13, 1944, 13; *Florida Times-Union*, March 4, 1944.

47. *New York Times*, December 3, 1944.

48. *Florida Highways*, July 1943, 25; *Florida Highways*, January 1945, 61–62.

49. Philip J. Weilding and August Burghard, *Checkered Sunrise: The Story of Fort Lauderdale, 1793–1955* (Gainesville: University of Florida Press, 1966), 232; Edward F. Keuchel, *Florida: Enterprise Under the Sun* (Chatsworth, Fla.: Windsor, 1990), 104.

50. Keuchel, *Florida*, 104–105; James J. Carney, "Population Growth in Miami and Dade County, Florida," *Tequesta* 6 (1946): 50; Huckshorn, *Government and Politics in Florida*, 41; Nash and Robinson, *MiMo*, 31.

Chapter 6. State of Imagination

1. Patrick, "Mobile Frontier," 18.

2. David Colburn and Richard K. Scher, *Florida's Gubernatorial Politics in the Twentieth Century* (Tallahassee: University Presses of Florida, 1980), 73, 204–207;

John E. Evans, *Time for Florida: Report on the Administration of Farris Bryant, Governor, 1961–1965* (N.p.: John E. Evans, 1965), n.p.

3. Preston, *Dirt Roads to Dixie*, 116–118; John L. Jakle, *The Tourist: Travel in Twentieth-Century North America* (Lincoln: University of Nebraska Press, 1985), 218; Mormino, *Land of Sunshine*, 77.

4. Jakle, *Tourist*, 185; Patrick, "Mobile Frontier," 14; Redford, *Billion-Dollar Sandbar*, 220; Clark, *Emerging South*, 140, 148.

5. Patricia Moiney-Melvin, "Harnessing the Romance of the Past: Preservation, Tourism, and History," *Public Historian* 13 (Spring 1991): 37.

6. David Colburn and Lance deHaven-Smith, *Government in the Sunshine State* (Gainesville: University Press of Florida, 1999), 35; Kendrick, *Florida Trails to Turnpike*, 174; Huckshorn, *Government and Politics in Florida*, 41; Gannon, *New History of Florida*, 436; Tim Hollis, *Selling the Sunshine State: A Celebration of Florida Advertising* (Gainesville: University Press of Florida, 2008), 1–7; Nash and Robinson, *MiMo*, 15, 18, 32.

7. Raymond Arsenault, "The End of the Long Hot Summer: The Air Conditioner and Southern Culture," *Journal of Southern History* 50 (November 1984): 597–628; James L. Bossemeyer, "Travel: American Mobility," *Annals of the American Academy of Political and Social Sciences* 313 (September 1957): 114.

8. Muir, *Miami, U.S.A.*, 233–234.

9. Stephen J. Flynn, *Florida: Land of Fortune* (Washington, D.C.: Van Rees Press, 1962), 16–17.

10. Muir, *Miami, U.S.A.*, 233–234; Flynn, *Florida*, 17.

11. Jakle, *Tourist*, 4.

12. John F. Sears, *Sacred Places: American Tourist Attractions in the Nineteenth Century* (New York: Oxford University Press, 1989), 3; Florida Development Commission, *Tourist Studies in Florida* (Tallahassee: Florida Development Commission, 1959), 1.

13. Charles Hofmann, "Florida Folklore, Summer 1945," *Journal of American Folklore* 59 (January–March 1946): 69; Lamar York, "Post-bellum Florida: Southerly, but Not Southern," *Southern Studies* 9 (Spring 1998): 75.

14. Milton R. Konvitz, "The Extent and Character of Legally Enforced Segregation," *Journal of Negro Education* 20 (Summer 1951): 431.

15. Breslauer, *Roadside Paradise*, 15–16; "Paradise Park," http://www.lostparks.com/paradisepark.html/, accessed September 5, 2004; Hollis, *Selling the Sunshine State*, 179.

16. Chanelle Rose, "The 'Jewel' of the South? Miami, Florida and the NAACP's Struggle for Civil Rights in America's Vacation Paradise," *Florida Historical Quarterly* 86 (Summer 2007): 44–45; Marvin Dunn, *Black Miami in the Twentieth Century* (Gainesville: University Press of Florida, 1997), 160.

17. Revels, *Watery Eden*, 43–33.

18. Mormino, *Land of Sunshine*, 97; Tim Hollis, *Glass Bottom Boats and Mermaid Tails: Florida's Tourist Springs* (Mechanicsburg, Pa.: Stackpole Books, 2006), 12–13; Revels, *Watery Eden*, 44, 126–127.

19. William G. Crawford Jr., "The Long Hard Fight for Equal Rights: A History of Broward County's Colored Beach and the Fort Lauderdale Beach 'Wade-ins' of the Summer of 1961," *Tequesta* 67 (2007): 30–32; David Colburn, *Racial Change and Community Crisis: St. Augustine, Florida, 1877–1980* (New York: Columbia University Press, 1985), 143–146; Colburn and deHaven, *Government in the Sunshine State*, 41; David J. Garrow, ed., *St Augustine, Florida, 1963–1964: Mass Protest and Racial Violence* (Brooklyn, N.Y.: Carlson Publishing, 1989), 66–67.

20. Colburn and deHaven, *Government in the Sunshine State*, 41; Dunn, *Black Miami*, 216; Colburn, *Racial Change and Community Crisis*, 151.

21. Gary S. Cross, ed., *Encyclopedia of Recreation and Leisure in America* (Detroit: Charles Scribner's Sons, 2004), 88; Stuart B. McIver, *Fort Lauderdale and Broward County* (Woodlands Hills, Fla.: Windsor, 1983), 151–152.

22. James P. Gross, *Pop Culture Florida* (Sarasota, Fla.: Pineapple Press, 2000), 115–116; Stephen J. Whitefield, "Florida's Fudged Identity," *Florida Historical Quarterly* 71 (April 1994): 425.

23. Hollis, *Dixie Before Disney*, 65.

24. Boorstin, *Image*, 103.

25. Ammidon, "Edens, Underworlds, and Shrines," 240; Hatton, *Tropical Splendor*, 183.

26. Florida Development Commission advertisement, June 8, 1962, tourism clippings file, St. Augustine Historical Society Library.

27. Breslauer, *Roadside Paradise*, 15; Hatton, *Tropical Splendor*, 183; Hollis, *Dixie Before Disney*, 12–13.

28. Breslauer, *Roadside Paradise*, 9–10, 14.

29. Stockbridge and Perry, *Florida in the Making*, 147.

30. Hollis, *Dixie Before Disney*, 155–156; John Margolies, *Fun along the Road: American Tourist Attractions* (Boston: Bulfinch Press, 1998), 70–71.

31. Ammidon, "Edens, Underworlds, and Shrines," 252; Douglas Waitley, *Roadside History of Florida* (Missoula, Mont.: Mountain Press, 1997), 319–322; Hollis, *Dixie Before Disney*, 133–134; Branch, "Salesman and His Swamp," 484, 488.

32. Loren G. "Totch" Brown, *Totch: A Life in the Everglades* (Gainesville: University Press of Florida, 1993), 239–240.

33. Margolies, *Fun along the Road*, 70; Hollis, *Dixie Before Disney*, 158–160.

34. Hollis, *Dixie Before Disney*, 157–158; Ammidon, "Edens, Underworlds, and Shrines," 253–254.

35. "Birds of Prey," http://www.lostparks.com/bop.html/, accessed September 15, 2004; "Miami Rare Bird Farm," http://www.lostparks.com/mrbf.html/, accessed September 15, 2004.

36. Margolies, *Fun along the Road*, 54; Hollis, *Disney Before Dixie*, 45–48; Tim Hollis, *Florida's Miracle Strip: From Redneck Riviera to Emerald Coast* (Jackson: University Press of Mississippi, 2004), 72.

37. Vaughn L. Glasbow, *A Social History of the American Alligator: The Earth Trembles with His Thunder* (New York: St. Martin's Press, 1991), 188; Margolies, *Fun along the Road*, 80; Doug Kirby, Ken Smith, and Mike Wilkins, *The New Roadside America: The Modern Traveler's Guide to the Wild and Wonderful World of America's Tourist Attractions* (New York: Fireside Books, 1986), 13–14, Ammidon, "Edens, Underworlds, and Shrines," 258.

38. Hollis, *Florida's Miracle Strip*, 76–69; Peter Genovese, *Roadside Florida: The Definitive Guide to the Kingdom of Kitsch* (Mechanicsburg, Pa.: Stackpole Books, 2006), 45–46; "Florida's Reptile Land," http://www.lostparks.com/frland.html/, accessed September 10, 2004.

39. Breslauer, *Roadside Paradise*, 15–16; "Tommy Bartlett's Deer Ranch," http://www.lostparkscom/deer.html/, accessed September 15, 2004.

40. Ammidon, "Edens, Underworlds, and Shrines," 249; Jane Stern and Michael Stern, *The Encyclopedia of Bad Taste* (New York: Harper Perennial, 1990), 320–321; Hollis, *Dixie Before Disney*, 150–152, Hollis, *Glass Bottom Boats and Mermaid Tails*, 92–93. For the best comprehensive work on Weeki Wachee, see Lu Vickers and Sara Dionne, *Weeki Wachee: City of Mermaids* (Gainesville: University Press of Florida, 2007).

41. "Ancient America," http://www.lostparks.com/ancientamerica.html/, accessed September 5, 2004; "Melton's Autorama," http://www.lostparks.com/melton.html/, accessed September 2004; "Gresh Wood Parade," http://www.lostparks.com/gresh .thml/, accessed September 10, 2004.

42. Hatton, *Tropical Splendor*, 184; "Tom Gaskins' Cypress Knee Museum," http://www.lostparks.com/knees.html, accessed January 5, 2009.

43. Hollis, *Dixie Before Disney*, 53–54; "Treasureland," http://www.lostparks.com /tresland.html/, accessed September 5, 2004.

44. "Cross and Sword," http://www.lostparks.com/crossandsword.html, accessed September 5, 2004.

45. Kirby et al., *New Roadside America*, 125, 130; Peter Genovese, *The Great American Road Trip: US 1, Maine to Florida* (New Brunswick, N.J.: Rutgers University Press, 1999), 152–153.

46. Farris, *Seeing the Sunny South*, 125–126; Ammidon, "Edens, Underworlds, and Shrines," 246.

47. Hollis, *Dixie Before Disney*, 96; Genovese, *Roadside Florida*, 32–36.

48. *Tallahassee Democrat*, July 19, 2009; Hollis, *Dixie Before Disney*, 16–17, 54–55; Breslauer, *Roadside Paradise*, 16–17.

49. Waitley, *Roadside History of Florida*, 77–78.

50. Breslauer, *Roadside Paradise*, 16–17; "Pioneer City," http://www.lostparks .com/picity.html/, accessed September 5, 2004.

51. Hollis, *Dixie Before Disney*, 168.

52. Genovese, *Roadside Florida*, 36; Hollis, *Dixie Before Disney*, 168; Hollis, *Florida's Miracle Strip*, 115–143.

53. Adams, *American Amusement Park Industry*, 46; http://www.lostparks.com/piratesw.html/, accessed June 5, 2004.

54. Martin, *Eternal Spring*, 147; Breslauer, *Roadside Paradise*, 11; Ammidon, "Edens, Underworlds, and Shrines," 245; Hollis, *Disney Before Dixie*, 146–147.

55. Hollis, *Disney Before Dixie*, 123–124, 147–149; "Prince of Peace Memorial," http://www.lostparks.com/popm.html/, September 5, 2004; Patrick, "Mobile Frontier," 18.

56. Rainbow Springs, http://www.lostparks.com/rainbow.html/, September 5, 2004; Hollis, *Dixie Before Disney*, 152–153; Hollis, *Selling the Sunshine State*, 194; Revels, *Watery Eden*, 70.

57. Donald D. Spencer, *Early Florida Attractions on Old Postcards* (Ormond Beach, Fla.: Camelot, 2001), 76.

58. Hollis, *Florida's Miracle Strip*, 158–161, 169.

59. Hollis, *Disney Before Dixie*, 14–15; Breslauer, *Roadside Paradise*, 16–17.

60. Dean MacCannell, *The Tourist: A New Theory of the Leisure Class* (New York: Schocken Books, 1976,) 103; Patrick, "Mobile Frontier," 18; Richard D. Starnes, *Southern Journeys: Tourism, History, and Cultures in the Modern South* (Tuscaloosa: University of Alabama Press, 2003), 66.

61. June Cleo and Hank Mesouf, *Florida: Polluted Paradise* (Philadelphia: Chilton Books, 1964), ix, 2–3, 6.

62. Hollis, *Dixie Before Disney*, 170–171; "Floridaland," http://www.lostparks.com/fland.html/, accessed June 5, 2004.

63. Al Burt, *Al Burt's Florida* (Gainesville: University Press of Florida, 1997), 27; York, "Post-bellum Florida," 75.

64. Hollis, *Dixie Before Disney*, 174–175.

65. John Rothchild, *Up for Grabs: A Trip through Time and Space in the Sunshine State* (New York: Penguin Books, 1990), 2–5; Spencer, *Early Florida Attractions on Old Postcards*, 8; Breslauer, *Roadside Paradise*, 9–10.

66. Jakle, *Tourist*, 3.

67. Ammidon, "Edens, Underworlds, and Shrines," 239–246, 258–259.

68. John Oliver La Gorce, "Florida: The Fountain of Youth," *National Geographic*, January 1930, 87; Flynn, *Florida*, 6.

Chapter 7. Magic Kingdoms

1. Neal Gabler, *Walt Disney: The Triumph of the American Imagination* (New York: Vintage, 2007), 603, 605; Steven Watts, *The Magic Kingdom: Walt Disney and the American Way of Life* (New York: Houghton Mifflin, 1997), 423; David Koenig, *Realityland: True-Life Adventures at Walt Disney World* (Irvine, Calif.: Bonaventure

Press, 2007), 25; Richard E. Foglesong, *Married to the Mouse: Walt Disney World and Orlando* (New Haven, Conn.: Yale University Press, 2001), 14–15.

2. Steven Watts, "Walt Disney: Art and Politics in the American Century," *Journal of American History* 82 (June 1995): 84; Koenig, *Realityland*, 17–18.

3. Warren Leon and Roy Rosenzweig, eds., *History Museums in the United States: A Critical Assessment* (Chicago: University of Illinois Press, 1989), 159; Richard Corliss, "If Heaven Ain't A Lot Like Disney," *Time*, June 16, 1989, 80; Foglesong, *Married to the Mouse*, 3, 6; Adams, *American Amusement Park Industry*, 163.

4. Adams, *American Amusement Park Industry*, 102.

5. Stephen M. Fjellman, *Vinyl Leaves: Walt Disney World and America* (Boulder, Colo.: Westview Press, 1992), 110; Koenig, *Realityland*, 19–22; Foglesong, *Married to the Mouse*, 37; Watts, "Walt Disney," 108; Adams, *American Amusement Park Industry*, 141; Gabler, *Walt Disney*, 603.

6. Adams, *American Amusement Park Industry*, 137–138; Watts, *Magic Kingdom*, 422–423; Koenig, *Realityland*, 19–20.

7. Koenig, *Realityland*, 22–23; Fjellman, *Vinyl Leaves*, 110–111.

8. Foglesong, *Married to the Mouse*, 35; Fjellman, *Vinyl Leaves*, 111.

9. Foglesong, *Married to the Mouse*, 3, 22–32.

10. Foglesong, *Married to the Mouse*, 56–57; Colburn and Scher, *Florida's Gubernatorial Politics*, 207–209; Fjellman, *Vinyl Leaves*, 117.

11. Foglesong, *Married to the Mouse*, 40–41, 44–45; Watts, *Magic Kingdom*, 423.

12. Foglesong, *Married to the Mouse*, 49–51; Koenig, *Realityland*, 28–29.

13. Hollis, *Dixie Before Disney*, 18; Foglesong, *Married to the Mouse*, 55.

14. Fogleson, *Married to the Mouse*, 64, 66–70; Michael Barrier, *The Animated Man: A Life of Walt Disney* (Berkeley: University of California Press, 2008), 317–320.

15. *Tallahassee Democrat*, February 3, 1967; Foglesong, *Married to the Mouse*, 64, 66–70; Koenig, *Realityland*, 38–40; Watts, *Magic Kingdom*, 443–445; Fjellman, *Vinyl Leaves*, 121; Carl Hiaasen, *Team Rodent: How Disney Devours the World* (New York: Ballantine, 1998), 27.

16. Koenig, *Realityland*, 40–41; Fjellman, *Vinyl Leaves*, 118; Foglesong, *Married to the Mouse*, 5, 175–176; Hatton, *Tropical Splendor*, 189.

17. Koenig, *Realityland*, 51–53.

18. Fjellman, *Vinyl Leaves*, 120–121.

19. Keonig, *Realityland*, 54–56.

20. Fjellman, *Vinyl Leaves*, 126–129; Koenig, *Realityland*, 85–89, 96–97; Adams, *American Amusement Park Industry*, 141; Horgan and Wynne, *Florida Decades*, 196; Leonard E. Zehnder, *Florida's Disney World: Promises and Problems* (Tallahassee, Fla.: Peninsular Publishing, 1975), 242–244, 270; *Miami Herald*, August 8, 1971. The author was a visitor to Disney World in November 1971 and recalls the limited number of attractions and the unfinished look of the park.

21. Zehnder, *Florida's Disney World*, 244, 254–255.

22. Zehnder, *Florida's Disney World*, 243, 253, 271; Luther J. Carter, *The Florida Experience: Land and Water Policy in a Growth State* (Baltimore: Johns Hopkins University Press, 1974), 5, 35; Fjellman, *Vinyl Leaves*, 129.

23. Koenig, *Realityland*, 259.

24. Carter, *Florida Experience*, 5, 35.

25. Zehnder, *Florida's Disney World*, 245–247, 269, 278; Fjellman, *Vinyl Leaves*, 129–130; Joseph Judge, "Florida's Booming—and Beleaguered—Heartland," *National Geographic*, November 1973, 596.

26. Fjellman, *Vinyl Leaves*, 130; Jerrell Shofner, *A History of Altamonte Springs, Florida* (Altamonte Springs, Fla.: City of Altamonte Springs, 1995), 201–202; Zehnder, *Florida's Disney World*, 291.

27. Fjellman, *Vinyl Leaves*, 135; Zehnder, *Florida's Disney World*, 334–335.

28. Foglesong, *Married to the Mouse*, 100.

29. Adams, *American Amusement Park Industry*, 149; Alex Shoumatoff, *Florida Ramble* (New York: Harper and Row, 1974), 98; Anetta Miller, "Tourism 1981: Still a Growth Industry," *Florida Trend*, June 1981, 60.

30. Gabler, *Walt Disney*, 631; Adams, *American Amusement Park Industry*, 148; Koenig, *Realityland*, 170–171.

31. Adams, *American Amusement Park Industry*, 176; Foglesong, *Married to the Mouse*, 104.

32. Hatton, *Tropical Splendor*, 191; Foglesong, *Married to the Mouse*, 103–104.

33. Horgan and Wynne, *Florida Decades*, 203; Leon and Rosenzweig, *History Museums in the United States*, 174–177; Koenig, *Realityland*, 196–197, 233, 237, 240–241.

34. Adams, *American Amusement Park Industry*, 122–123; Foglesong, *Married to the Mouse*, 104–105; "Circus World," http://www.lostparks.com/cwld.html/, accessed September 5, 2005; "Boardwalk and Baseball," http://www.lostparks.com/bandb.html/, accessed September 5, 2004; "Boardwalk and Baseball Closes," *Florida Tourism Industry Report*, January 29, 1990, 1–2.

35. Foglesong, *Married to the Mouse*, 104–105.

36. Adams, *American Amusement Park Industry*, 159; Fjellman, *Vinyl Leaves*, 135, 144.

37. Jeff Kurtti, *Since the World Began: Walt Disney World, the First 25 Years* (New York: Hyperion, 1996), 124.

38. Adams, *American Amusement Park Industry*, 123.

39. Fjellman, *Vinyl Leaves*, 144; Waitley, *Roadside History of Florida*, 78–79; John Koenig, "The Invasion Continues," *Florida Trend*, March 1993, 74.

40. Jim Wilson, "Outdoing Disney," *Popular Mechanics*, July 1999, 78; Foglesong, *Married to the Mouse*, 3.

41. Foglesong, *Married to the Mouse*, 93–96.

42. Foglesong, *Married to the Mouse*, 4, 98–99; Fjellman, *Vinyl Leaves*, 138–139.

43. Koenig, *Realityland*, 292–294, 299–300; *Tallahassee Democrat*, June 21, 1995; *Orlando Sentinel*, April 23, 1998.

44. Koenig, *Realityland*, 301–302; *Orlando Sentinel*, April 22, 1999.

45. Adams, *American Amusement Park Industry*, 154, 156–157.

46. Horgan and Wynne, *Florida Decades*, 198; Corliss, "If Heaven Ain't a Lot Like Disney," 80.

47. Fjellman, *Vinyl Leaves*, 149.

48. Hiaasen, *Team Rodent*, 19; *Washington Post*, December 5, 2001; Gary R. Mormino, "Trouble in Tourist Heaven," *Forum: The Magazine of the Florida Humanities Council* 17 (Summer 1994): 13; Gannon, *New History of Florida*, 437.

49. Foglesong, *Married to the Mouse*, 3, 5; Fjellman, *Vinyl Leaves*, 147–148.

Chapter 8. Which Way to Paradise?

1. *Florida Times-Union*, January 30, 1974.

2. Griffin, "Impact of Tourism and Development," 14.

3. Fjellman, *Vinyl Leaves*, 133.

4. Fjellman, *Vinyl Leaves*, 134; Zehnder, *Florida's Disney World*, 319, 321, 324, 328, 330.

5. *St. Augustine Record*, February 28, 1980; *St. Augustine Record*, April 27, 2008; Schultz and Stronge, *Social and Economic Effects of the Florida Tourist Industry*, 20, 25.

6. Hatton, *Tropical Splendor*, 196; Ogle, *Key West*, 221–222.

7. Lucius Ellsworth and Linda Ellsworth, *Pensacola: The Deep Water City* (Tulsa, Okla.: Continental Heritage Press, 1982), 132–135.

8. *St. Augustine Record*, March 1, 1974.

9. *Florida Times-Union*, March 10, 1985; *St. Augustine Record*, August 23, 1989.

10. Waitley, *Roadside History of Florida*, 78–79.

11. Glenda E. Hood and Bill Bachmann, *Orlando: The City Beautiful* (Memphis, Tenn.: Towery, 1997), 308–309; Wenxian Zhang, "A Splendid Idea in China Turned Sour in Florida: The Rise and Fall of Florida's Splendid China," *Florida Historical Quarterly* 84 (Winter 2006): 431.

12. Breslauer, *Roadside Paradise*, 6–7.

13. Hollis, *Dixie Before Disney*, 135–136, 150; Revels, *Watery Eden*, 71–72.

14. *St. Petersburg Times*, December 22, 1986; Fjellman, *Vinyl Leaves*, 146; Alejandro Portes and Alex Stepick, *City of the Edge: The Transformation of Miami* (Berkeley: University of California Press, 1993), 18, 20–21, 47–51; Joan Didion, *Miami* (New York: Simon and Schuster, 1987), 42, 44–45; Miller, "Tourism 1981," 58; Raymond A. Mohl, "Changing Economic Patterns in the Miami Metropolitan Area, 1940–1980," *Tequesta* 42 (1982): 63.

15. *Tallahassee Democrat*, October 26, 1997; *Orlando Sentinel*, January 13, 1995;

Huckshorn, *Government and Politics in Florida*, 208; Mormino, "Trouble in Tourist Heaven," 12.

16. Colburn and deHaven, *Government in the Sunshine State*, 75; *Advertising Age*, April 12, 1993.

17. David R. Colburn and Jane L. Landers, eds., *The African American Heritage of Florida* (Gainesville: University Press of Florida, 1995), 355; *USA Today*, September 19, 1995; Dunn, *Black Miami*, 347–348.

18. *USA Today*, September 19, 1995; *Florida Times-Union*, June 7, 1993.

19. *Orlando Sentinel*, January 16, 1995.

20. *Orlando Sentinel*, August 17, 1995.

21. *Tampa Tribune-Times*, January 5, 1986; *Tampa Tribune*, June 20, 1996; *Miami Herald*, August 12, 1997; Monica Rowland "Menendez versus Mickey: A Study of Heritage Tourism in Florida" (master's thesis, University of South Florida, 2006), 40–41.

22. *Tallahassee Democrat*, January 2, 1997.

23. *Orlando Sentinel*, October 25, 1998; *St. Augustine Record*, April 27, 2008.

24. *Orlando Sentinel*, October 25, 1995.

25. Starnes, *Southern Journeys*, 245.

26. Ogle, *Key West*, 211–215, 237; Tammerlin Drummond, "Not in Kansas Anymore," *Time*, September 25, 1995, 54; *New York Times*, November 18, 2005; "History of Gay Days," http://www.gaydays.com/about/history.html, accessed January 6, 2010.

27. Mark I. Pinsky, *The Gospel According to Disney: Faith, Trust and Pixie Dust* (Louisville, Ky.: Westminster John Knox Press, 2004), 252–259; Drummond, "Not in Kansas Anymore," 54; *New York Times*, November 18, 2005; *New York Times*, August 16, 2007; *Washington Post*, December 5, 2001.

28. *Wall Street Journal*, November 5, 1997.

29. Rowland, "Menendez versus Mickey," 43; *Orlando Sentinel*, March 7, 1998; Colburn and deHaven, *Government in the Sunshine State*, 76; *Tallahassee Democrat*, October 26, 1997; Del Marth and Martha J. Marth, *Florida Almanac 2000–2001* (Gretna, Fla.: Pelican, 2000), 239.

30. *Variety*, November 19, 2001.

31. *St. Augustine Record*, November 6, 2001; *Variety*, November 19, 2001.

32. *South Florida Sun-Sentinel*, September 4, 2002.

33. *Miami Herald*, September 6, 2004.

34. *Miami Herald*, September 6, 2004; "Florida Tourism Grinds to a Halt," http://www.cnn.com/2004/TRAVEL/09/03/frances.tourism.ap/index.html, accessed September 4, 1004.

35. Zhang, "Splendid Idea in China," 411–439; *Orlando Sentinel*, July 16, 2009.

36. Hollis, *Florida's Miracle Strip*, 147–153, Hollis, *Dixie Before Disney*, 59–60; *Miami Herald*, April 14, 2004.

37. Hollis, *Dixie Before Disney*, 55–57, 60–61; *Tallahassee Democrat*, October 26,

1997; Patrick Moore, "'Redneck Riviera' or 'Emerald Coast'? Using Public History to Identify and Interpret Community Growth Choices on Florida's Panhandle," *Gulf Coast Historical Review* 18 (2003): 65, 69–81.

38. *St. Augustine Record*, August 5, 2001; *St. Augustine Record*, September 20, 2003; *St. Augustine Record*, May 1, 2005; author's visit to St. Augustine, June 24, 2009.

39. Bill Belleville, *River of Lakes: A Journey on Florida's St. Johns River* (Athens: University of Georgia Press, 2000), 27–28.

40. Rowland, "Menendez versus Mickey," 38–40; Barnett, "Inventing the Conch Republic," 139–141.

41. *St. Augustine Record*, April 22, 2007.

42. Linda Nazareth, *The Leisure Economy: How Changing Demographics, Economics and Generational Attitudes Will Reshape Our Lives and Our Industries* (Mississauga, Ont.: John Wiley & Sons Canada, 2007), 66; Pinsky, *Gospel According to Disney*, 233.

43. *St. Augustine Record*, April 27, 2008; Rifkin, *Age of Access*, 146; Larry Krotz, *Tourists: How Our Fastest Growing Industry Is Changing the World* (Boston: Faber and Faber, 1996), 205.

44. Author's visits to Silver Springs, June 28, 2009, Wakulla Springs, June 29, 2009, and St. Augustine, June 24, 2009; "Florida's Cypress Gardens to Become Legoland," http://www.msnbc.msn.com/id/35015761, accessed June 4, 2010; *Orlando Sentinel*, September 23, 2009; *Miami Herald*, November 17, 2009.

45. Brown, *Inventing New England*, 2–3, 217; Burt, *Al Burt's Florida*, 27.

46. Hollis, *Dixie Before Disney*, 61–62; John B. Boles, *The South through Time: A History of an American Region* (Englewood Cliffs, N.J.: Prentice Hall, 1995), 456; Moore, "Redneck Riviera," 69, 72; Brown, *Inventing New England*, 217; Griffin, "Impact of Tourism and Development," 67.

47. Moore, "Redneck Riviera," 73; Carter, *Florida Experience*, 320–321; *Florida Times-Union* clipping, n.d. (circa 1990s), St. Augustine Historical Society Library collection.

48. Barbara Jean Greiner, Madison County resident, interview by author, August 9, 2009; LaNora Zipperer, Madison County resident, interview by author, July 15, 2009.

49. Raymond Arsenault, "Is There a Florida Dream?" *Forum: The Magazine of the Florida Humanities Council* 17 (Summer 1994): 26; *Orlando Sentinel*, August 17, 1995; Shofner, *Florida Portrait*, 246–247.

50. Shofner, *Florida Portrait*, 246–247.

51. Burt, *Al Burt's Florida*, 94; Jerome Stern, "At Home in the Snake A-Torium," *Forum: The Magazine of the Florida Humanities Council* 17 (Summer 1994): 18, 21; Press release, "Florida's State Parks Welcome Weeki Wachee Springs," October 31, 2008, http://www.dep.state.fl.us/secretary/news/2008/10/1031_01.htm, accessed

May 18, 2010; Dan DeWitt, "What Should Weeki Wachee Springs State Park Become?" *St. Petersburg Times*, December 19, 2009.

52. Rifkin, *Age of Access*, 150–151; Krotz, *Tourists*, 204–205.

53. Mormino, "Trouble in Tourist Heaven," 14; Thomas Barbour, *That Vanishing Eden: A Naturalist's Florida* (Boston: Little, Brown, 1945), 237; David Colburn and Lance deHaven-Smith, *Florida Megatrends: Critical Issues in Florida* (Gainesville: University Press of Florida, 2002), 7.

SELECTED READINGS

Adams, John R. *Harriet Beecher Stowe*. Boston: Twayne, 1989.

Adams, Judith A. *The American Amusement Park Industry: A History of Technology and Thrills*. Boston: Twayne, 1991.

Akin, Edward N. *Flagler: Rockefeller Partner and Florida Baron*. Gainesville: University Press of Florida, 1992.

Ammidon, Margot. "Edens, Underworlds and Shrines: Florida's Small Tourist Attractions." *Journal of Decorative and Propaganda Arts* 23 (1998): 238–259.

Amory, Cleveland. *The Last Resorts*. New York: Harper and Brothers, 1948.

"An Invalid." *A Winter in the West Indies and Florida*. New York: Wiley and Putnam, 1839.

Aron, Cindy S. *Working at Play: A History of Vacations in the United States*. New York: Oxford University Press, 1999.

Arsenault, Raymond. "The End of the Long Hot Summer: The Air Conditioner and Southern Culture." *Journal of Southern History* 50 (November 1984): 597–628.

———. *St. Petersburg and the Florida Dream, 1888–1950*. Gainesville: University Press of Florida, 1996.

Barbour, Thomas. *That Vanishing Eden: A Naturalist's Florida*. Boston: Little, Brown, 1945.

Barnes, Jay. *Florida's Hurricane History*. 2nd ed. Chapel Hill: University of North Carolina Press, 2007.

Barrier, Michael. *The Animated Man: A Life of Walt Disney*. Berkeley: University of California Press, 2008.

Bass, Bob. *When Steamboats Reigned in Florida*. Gainesville: University Press of Florida, 2008.

Bauer, Ruthmary. "Sarasota: Hardship and Tourism in the 1930s." *Florida Historical Quarterly* 76 (Fall 1997): 135–151.

Belasco, Warren James. *Americans on the Road: From Auto Camps to Motel, 1910–1945*. Baltimore: Johns Hopkins University Press, 1979.

Belleville, Bill. *River of Lakes: A Journey on Florida's St. Johns River*. Athens: University of Georgia Press, 2000.

Bill, Ledyard. *A Winter in Florida*. New York: Wood & Holbrook, 1869.

Boorstin, Daniel J. *The Image: Or, What Happened to the American Dream*. New York: Athenaeum, 1962.

Boulard, Garry. "'State of Emergency': Key West in the Great Depression." *Florida Historical Quarterly* 67 (October 1988): 166–183.

Braden, Susan R. *The Architecture of Leisure: The Florida Resort Hotels of Henry Flagler and Henry Plant*. Gainesville: University Press of Florida, 2002.

Branch, Stephen E. "The Salesman and His Swamp: Dick Pope's Cypress Gardens." *Florida Historical Quarterly* 80 (Spring 2002): 483–503.

Breslauer, Ken. *Roadside Paradise: The Golden Age of Florida's Tourist Attractions 1929–1971*. St. Petersburg, Fla.: RetroFlorida, 2000.

Carter, Luther J. *The Florida Experience: Land and Water Policy in a Growth State*. Baltimore: Johns Hopkins University Press, 1974.

Clinton, Charles A. *A Winter from Home*. New York: John F. Trow, 1852.

Colburn, David. *Racial Change and Community Crisis: St. Augustine, Florida, 1877–1980*. New York: Columbia University Press, 1985.

Covington, James W. *Plant's Palace: Henry B. Plant and the Tampa Bay Hotel*. Louisville, Ky.: Harmony House, 1991.

———. *The Seminoles of Florida*. Gainesville: University Press of Florida, 1993.

Derr, Mark. *Some Kind of Paradise: A Chronicle of Man and the Land in Florida*. New York: William Morrow, 1989.

Dulles, Foster Rhea. *America Learns to Play: A History of Recreation*. 2nd ed. New York: Appleton-Century-Crofts, 1965.

Dunn, Hampton. "Florida: Jewel of the Gilded Age." *Gulf Coast Historical Review* 10 (1994): 19–28.

Dunn, Marvin. *Black Miami in the Twentieth Century*. Gainesville: University Press of Florida, 1997.

Eck, Christopher R. "Beasts and Savages: Taming the Wilds of Florida in the Popular Imagination for Five Centuries." *South Florida History* 29 (2001): 12–19.

Fairbanks, George R. *The History and Antiquities of the City of St. Augustine, Florida*. Facsimile reproduction of the 1858 edition. Introduction and index by Michael V. Gannon. Gainesville: University of Florida Press, 1975.

Farris, John T. *Seeing the Sunny South*. Philadelphia: J. B. Lippincott, 1921.

Fjellman, Stephen M. *Vinyl Leaves: Walt Disney World and America*. Boulder, Colo.: Westview Press, 1992.

Floan, Howard R. *The South in Northern Eyes, 1831 to 1861*. Austin: University of Texas Press, 1958.

Foglesong, Richard E. *Married to the Mouse: Walt Disney World and Orlando*. New Haven, Conn.: Yale University Press, 2001.

Foster, John T., Jr., and Sarah Whitmer Foster. *Beechers, Stowes and Yankee Strangers: The Transformation of Florida*. Gainesville: University Press of Florida, 1999.

Foster, Mark S. "In the Face of 'Jim Crow': Prosperous Blacks on Vacations, Travel and Outdoor Leisure, 1890–1945." *Journal of Negro History* 84 (Spring 1999): 130–149.

Gabler, Neal. *Walt Disney: The Triumph of the American Imagination*. New York: Vintage, 2007.

Gannon, Michael, ed. *The New History of Florida*. Gainesville: University Press of Florida, 1996.

Garrow, David J., ed. *St Augustine, Florida, 1963–1964: Mass Protest and Racial Violence*. Brooklyn, N.Y.: Carlson Publishing, 1989.

Hatton, Hap. *Tropical Splendor: An Architectural History of Florida*. New York: Alfred A. Knopf, 1987.

Hebel, Ianthe Bond, ed. *Centennial History of Volusia County, Florida: 1854–1954*. Daytona Beach, Fla.: College Publishing, 1955.

Hedrick, Joan D. *Harriet Beecher Stowe: A Life*. New York: Oxford University Press, 1994.

Hiaasen, Carl. *Team Rodent: How Disney Devours the World*. New York: Ballantine, 1998.

Hollis, Tim. *Dixie Before Disney: 100 Years of Roadside Fun*. Jackson: University Press of Mississippi, 1999.

———. *Florida's Miracle Strip: From Redneck Riviera to Emerald Coast*. Jackson: University Press of Mississippi, 2004.

———. *Glass Bottom Boats and Mermaid's Tails: Florida's Tourist Springs*. Mechanicsburg, Pa.: Stackpole Books, 2006.

———. *Selling the Sunshine State: A Celebration of Florida Advertising*. Gainesville: University Press of Florida, 2008.

Jackle, John L. *The Tourist: Travel in Twentieth-Century North America*. Lincoln: University of Nebraska Press, 1985.

Kirby, Doug, Ken Smith, and Mike Wilkins. *The New Roadside America: The Modern Traveler's Guide to the Wild and Wonderful World of America's Tourist Attractions*. New York: Fireside Books, 1986.

Koenig, David. *Realityland: True-Life Adventures at Walt Disney World*. Irvine, Calif.: Bonaventure Press, 2007.

Krotz, Larry. *Tourists: How Our Fastest Growing Industry Is Changing the World*. Boston: Faber and Faber, 1996.

Kurtti, Jeff. *Since the World Began: Walt Disney World, the First 25 Years*. New York: Hyperion, 1996.

Lanier, Sidney. *Florida: Its Scenery, Climate, and History*. Gainesville: University of Florida Press, 1973.

Lee, Henry. *The Tourist's Guide of Florida*. New York: Leve & Alden Printing, 1885.

Lente, Frederic D. *Florida as a Health-Resort*. New York: D. Appleton, 1876.

MacCannell, Dean. *The Tourist: A New Theory of the Leisure Class*. New York: Schocken Books, 1976.

Margolies, John. *Fun along the Road: American Tourist Attractions*. Boston: Bulfinch Press, 1998.

Martin, Richard A. *Eternal Spring: Man's 10,000 Years of History at Florida's Silver Springs*. St. Petersburg, Fla.: Great Outdoors, 1966.

Martin, Sidney Walter. *Florida's Flagler*. Athens: University of Georgia Press, 1949.

Mehling, Harold. *The Most of Everything: The Story of Miami Beach*. New York: Harcourt Brace, 1960.

Moiney-Melvin, Patricia. "Harnessing the Romance of the Past: Preservation, Tourism, and History." *Public Historian* 13 (Spring 1991): 35–48.

Mormino, Gary R. *Land of Sunshine, State of Dreams: A Social History of Modern Florida*. Gainesville: University Press of Florida, 2005.

———. "Roadsides and Broadsides: A History of Florida Tourism." *Forum: The Magazine of the Florida Humanities Council* 10 (Fall 1987): 9–12.

———. "Trouble in Tourist Heaven." *Forum: The Magazine of the Florida Humanities Council* 17 (Summer 1994): 11–13.

Mueller, E. A. "Suwannee River Steamboating." *Florida Historical Quarterly* 45 (January 1967): 271–288.

Muir, Helen. *Miami, U.S.A.* Miami: Pickering Press, 1953.

Muir, John. *A Thousand Mile Walk to the Gulf*. Boston: Houghton Mifflin, 1916.

Nash, Eric P., and Randall C. Robinson Jr. *MiMo: Miami Modern Revealed*. San Francisco: Chronicle Books, 2004.

Nolan, David. *Fifty Feet in Paradise: The Booming of Florida*. New York: Harcourt Brace Jovanovich, 1984.

Ogle, Maureen. *Key West: History of an Island of Dreams*. Gainesville: University Press of Florida, 2003.

Patrick, Rembert W. "The Mobile Frontier." *Journal of Southern History* 29 (February 1963): 3–18.

Phelts, Marsha Dean. *An American Beach for African Americans*. Gainesville: University Press of Florida, 1997.

Portes, Alejandro, and Alex Stepick. *City of the Edge: The Transformation of Miami*. Berkeley: University of California Press, 1993.

Preston, Howard Lawrence. *Dirt Roads to Dixie: Accessibility and Modernization in the South, 1885–1935*. Knoxville: University of Tennessee Press, 1991.

Ralph, Julian. *Dixie: Or, Southern Scenes and Sketches*. New York: Harper and Brothers, 1895.

"Rambler." *Guide to Florida*. Facsimile of the 1875 edition. Gainesville: University of Florida Press, 1964.

Redford, Polly. *Billion-Dollar Sandbar: A Biography of Miami Beach*. New York: E. P. Dutton, 1970.

Reid, Whitelaw. *After the War: A Tour of the Southern States 1865–1866*. Facsimile of the 1866 edition. New York: Harper and Row, 1965.

Revels, Tracy J. *Watery Eden: A History of Wakulla Springs*. Tallahassee, Fla.: Sentry Press, 2002.

Reynolds, Kelly. *Henry Plant: Pioneer Empire Builder*. Cocoa: Florida Historical Society Press, 2003.

Rieff, David. *Going to Miami: Exiles, Tourists, and Refugees in the New America*. Gainesville: University Press of Florida, 1987.

Roberts, Larry. *Florida's Golden Age of Souvenirs, 1890–1930*. Gainesville: University Press of Florida, 2001.

Rothchild, John. *Up for Grabs: A Trip through Time and Space in the Sunshine State*. New York: Penguin Books, 1990.

Rucker, Brian. *Image and Reality: Tourism in Antebellum Pensacola*. Bagdad, Fla: Patagonia Press, 2009.

Schultz, Ronald R., and William B. Stronge. *The Social and Economic Effects of the Florida Tourist Industry*. Boca Raton: Florida Atlantic University, 1978.

Sears, John F. *Sacred Places: American Tourist Attractions in the Nineteenth Century*. New York: Oxford University Press, 1989.

Sewall, Rufus King. *Sketches of St. Augustine*. Facsimile of the 1848 edition. Gainesville: University of Florida Press, 1976.

Smyth, G. Hutchinson. *The Life of Henry Bradley Plant*. New York: G. P. Putnam's Sons, 1898.

Spivak, John M. "Paradise Awaits: A Sampling and Brief Analysis of Late 19th Century Promotional Pamphlets on Florida." *Southern Studies* 21 (1982): 429–438.

Starnes, Richard D. *Southern Journeys: Tourism, History, and Cultures in the Modern South*. Tuscaloosa: University of Alabama Press, 2003.

Stronge, William B. *The Sunshine Economy: An Economic History of Florida since the Civil War*. Gainesville: University Press of Florida, 2008.

Vanderhill, Burke G. "The Historic Spas of Florida." *West Georgia College Studies in the Social Sciences* 12 (June 1973): 59–77.

Watts, Steven. *The Magic Kingdom: Walt Disney and the American Way of Life*. New York: Houghton Mifflin, 1997.

———. "Walt Disney: Art and Politics in the American Century." *Journal of American History* 82 (June 1995): 84–110.

Works Progress Administration. *Florida: Guide to the Southernmost State*. New York: Oxford University Press, 1939.

Wylie, Philip. "War and Peace in Miami." *New Republic*, February 21, 1944, 238–239.

INDEX

Tracy J. Revels is professor of history at Wofford College, Spartanburg, South Carolina. She is the author of the award-winning *Grander in Her Daughters: Florida's Women during the Clvil War* and *Watery Eden: A History of Wakulla Springs*.

The Wide Brim: Early Poems and Ponderings of Marjory Stoneman Douglas, edited by Jack E. Davis (2002)

The Architecture of Leisure: The Florida Resort Hotels of Henry Flagler and Henry Plant, by Susan R. Braden (2002)

Florida's Space Coast: The Impact of NASA on the Sunshine State, by William Barnaby Faherty, S.J. (2002)

In the Eye of Hurricane Andrew, by Eugene F. Provenzo Jr. and Asteric Baker Provenzo (2002)

Florida's Farmworkers in the Twenty-first Century, text by Nano Riley and photographs by Davida Johns (2003)

Making Waves: Female Activists in Twentieth-Century Florida, edited by Jack E. Davis and Kari Frederickson (2003)

Orange Journalism: Voices from Florida Newspapers, by Julian M. Pleasants (2003)

The Stranahans of Ft. Lauderdale: A Pioneer Family of New River, by Harry A. Kersey Jr. (2003)

Death in the Everglades: The Murder of Guy Bradley, America's First Martyr to Environmentalism, by Stuart B. McIver (2003)

Jacksonville: The Consolidation Story, from Civil Rights to the Jaguars, by James B. Crooks (2004)

The Seminole Wars: The Nation's Longest Indian Conflict, by John and Mary Lou Missall (2004)

The Mosquito Wars: A History of Mosquito Control in Florida, by Gordon Patterson (2004)

Seasons of Real Florida, by Jeff Klinkenberg (2004; first paperback edition, 2009)

Land of Sunshine, State of Dreams: A Social History of Modern Florida, by Gary Mormino (2005; first paperback edition, 2008)

Paradise Lost? The Environmental History of Florida, edited by Jack E. Davis and Raymond Arsenault (2005)

Frolicking Bears, Wet Vultures, and Other Oddities: A New York City Journalist in Nineteenth-Century Florida, edited by Jerald T. Milanich (2005)

Waters Less Traveled: Exploring Florida's Big Bend Coast, by Doug Alderson (2005)

Saving South Beach, by M. Barron Stofik (2005)

Losing It All to Sprawl: How Progress Ate My Cracker Landscape, by Bill Belleville (2006; first paperback edition, 2010)

Voices of the Apalachicola, compiled and edited by Faith Eidse (2006)

Floridian of His Century: The Courage of Governor LeRoy Collins, by Martin A. Dyckman (2006)

America's Fortress: A History of Fort Jefferson, Dry Tortugas, Florida, by Thomas Reid (2006)

Weeki Wachee, City of Mermaids: A History of One of Florida's Oldest Roadside Attractions, by Lu Vickers (2007)

City of Intrigue, Nest of Revolution: A Documentary History of Key West in the Nineteenth Century, by Consuelo E. Stebbins (2007)

The New Deal in South Florida: Design, Policy, and Community Building, 1933–1940, edited by John A. Stuart and John F. Stack Jr. (2008)

Pilgrim in the Land of Alligators: More Stories about Real Florida, by Jeff Klinkenberg (2008)

A Most Disorderly Court: Scandal and Reform in the Florida Judiciary, by Martin A. Dyckman (2008)

A Journey into Florida Railroad History, by Gregg M. Turner (2008)

Sandspurs: Notes from a Coastal Columnist, by Mark Lane (2008)

Paving Paradise: Florida's Vanishing Wetlands and the Failure of No Net Loss, by Craig Pittman and Matthew Waite (2009; first paperback edition, 2010)

Embry-Riddle at War: Aviation Training during World War II, by Stephen G. Craft (2009)

The Columbia Restaurant: Celebrating a Century of History, Culture, and Cuisine, by Andrew T. Huse, with recipes and memories from Richard Gonzmart and the Columbia restaurant family (2009)

Ditch of Dreams: The Cross Florida Barge Canal and the Struggle for Florida's Future, by Steven Noll and David Tegeder (2009)

Manatee Insanity: Inside the War over Florida's Most Famous Endangered Species, by Craig Pittman (2010)

Frank Lloyd Wright's Florida Southern College, by Dale Allen Gyure (2010)

Sunshine Paradise: A History of Florida Tourism, by Tracy J. Revels (2011)